TEACHING IN A
MULTICULTURAL SOCIETY

TEACHING IN A MULTICULTURAL SOCIETY

Perspectives and Professional Strategies

Edited by
Dolores E. Cross
Gwendolyn C. Baker
Lindley J. Stiles

THE FREE PRESS
A Division of Macmillan Publishing Co., Inc.
NEW YORK

Collier Macmillan Publishers
LONDON

The Free Press
A Division of Macmillan Publishing Co., Inc.
866 Third Avenue, New York, N.Y. 10022

Collier Macmillan Canada, Ltd.

Library of Congress Catalog Card Number: 76-14291

Chapter 2, ''A Historical Framework for Multicultural Education,'' by Meyer Weinberg. Copyright 1974 by Meyer Weinberg. Reprinted by permission of the author.

Quotations from Carl Sandburg, ''Prologue,'' in *The Family of Man*, comp. Edward Steichen (New York: Museum of Modern Art, 1955), pp. 2, 3. Copyright © 1955 by The Museum of Modern Art. Reprinted by permission of the publisher.

''Five Ways to Kill a Man,'' by Edwin Brock. Copyright © 1966 by Edwin Brock. From *Invisibility Is the Art of Survival* (New York: New Directions, 1972). Reprinted by permission of the author.

''Hard Times in the Mill.'' From John Anthony Scott, ed., *Living Documents in American History*, vol. 2 (New York: Washington Square Press, 1969), pp. 215–16. Copyright © 1963 by John Anthony Scott. Reprinted by permission of Simon & Schuster, Inc., Washington Square Press division.

''The Girl I Left Behind Me,'' collected, adapted, and arranged by John A. Lomax and Alan Lomax. TRO—© Copyright 1938 and renewed 1966 Ludlow Music, Inc., New York, N.Y. From John A. Lomax and Alan Lomax, *Cowboy Songs and Other Frontier Ballads,* rev. ed. (New York: Macmillan, 1938), pp. 58–59. Used by permission of Ludlow Music, Inc.

Printed in the United States of America

printing number

   3   4   5   6   7   8   9   10

Library of Congress Cataloging in Publication Data

Main entry under title:

Teaching in a multicultural society.

   Includes bibliographical references and index.
   1. Minorities--Education--United States.
2. Acculturation. I. Cross, Dolores E. II. Baker,
Gwendolyn C. III. Stiles, Lindley Joseph
LC3731.T4   371.9'7   76-14291
ISBN 0-02-906710-3

For those with hands extended

Contents

Part 3 PROGRAMS AND TEACHING STRATEGIES

Contributors

Gwendolyn C. Baker, Associate Professor, School of Education, University of Michigan

Clarence Beecher, Lecturer, African American Studies and Education, Northwestern University

Marshall Browdy, Assistant Professor of Medical Education, Center for Educational Development, University of Illinois at the Medical Center

J. Paul Bohannan, Professor of Anthropology, University of California, Santa Barbara

Dolores E. Cross, Assistant Professor and Director of Teacher Education, Claremont Graduate School

Harvey Daniels, Assistant Professor of Education, Rosary College

James Deslonde, Assistant Professor, School of Education, Stanford University

Robert Dixon, Professor, School of Education, University of Michigan

Glenn A. Doston, Assistant Professor, School of Education, University of Wisconsin–Parkside

Ann D. Gordon, Associate Editor, Jane Adams Papers Project

Ella Griffin, Education Program Specialist, Bureau of School Systems, U.S. Office of Education

Robert Gundlach, Instructor, School of Education, Northwestern University

Ralph Hansen, Chairperson, Department of Secondary and Postsecondary Education, San Francisco State University

Marvin Happel, Assistant Professor, School of Education, University of Wisconsin–Parkside

Asa Hilliard, Dean, School of Education, San Francisco State University

Robert P. Ho, Director of Teacher Education, State Department of Public Instruction, Maine

ERNECE B. KELLY, Teacher Trainer, Equal Educational Opportunity
  Project
GARVEY LAURENT, Liaison Office for Food and Agriculture Organization
  of the United Nations
YEMI LIGADU, Deputy Director, UNESCO Liaison Office with the
  United Nations
RAE MOSES, Assistant Professor of Linguistics, College of Arts and Sci-
  ences, Northwestern University
JAMES R. NEAL, Dean, School of Education, California State University–
  Sacramento
RUDOLF B. SCHMERL, Assistant Dean and Associate Professor, School
  of Education, University of Michigan
LINDLEY J. STILES, Professor of Education for Interdisciplinary Studies,
  Sociology, and Political Science, Northwestern University
CAROL H. TICE, Ann Arbor, Michigan, Public Schools
TERRENCE N. TICE, Associate Professor, School of Education, Univer-
  sity of Michigan
DOUGLAS S. WARD, Professor of Education, Northwestern University
MEYER WEINBERG, Editor, *Integrated Education;* Lecturer, School of
  Education, Northwestern University; Associate Professor, City Col-
  lege of Chicago
BENNIE WHITEN, JR., Director, New York Mission Society

Preface

Many men push through the darkness,
Carrying candles burning bright;
Each claims that his is the only,
Yet all use the same source of light.[1]

Learning to respect other cultures is a priority for all children, youths, and adults in schools. This mandate is particularly imperative today, when social and scientific forces make people of contrasting cultural commitments constantly aware of—and dependent upon—each other. It is a challenge that cannot be ignored. Contrary to some historical assumptions, cultural differences do not simply disappear as people associate with others. Despite outward signs of common culture that may develop, the closer people come together, the more they may try to preserve their cultural traditions. As a consequence, the dream of one culture, one people—one way—often espoused by social idealists, is more illusion than reality. Inescapably, and increasingly, people of the world live in multicultural societies. The challenge to all is to learn to respond honestly and positively to the differences that prevail.

CULTURE IS A WAY OF LIFE

The authors in this book use the term *culture* in an anthropological sense: that is, a culture is "the total of ways of living built up by a group of human beings and transmitted from one generation to the next."[2] Thus, culture is considered in the broadest sense as influences on life style that reach beyond biological heredity to include environmental forces. Our perception of culture is congruent with that expressed by Michel Leiris on behalf of UNESCO:

Culture in the true sense should be regarded as comprising the whole more or less coherent structure of concepts, sentiments, mechanisms, institutions, and objects which explicitly or implicitly condition the conduct of members of a group. . . .

Culture provides each new generation with a starting point (a system of rules and models of behavior, values, concepts, techniques, instruments, etc.) round which it will plan its way of life and on which the individual will draw to some extent and which he will apply in his own way and according to his own means in the specific situation confronting him. Thus it is something which can never be regarded as fixed forever but is constantly undergoing changes. . . .[3]

The diverse and changing nature of culture is influenced by what the individual discovers about self and society as well as by borrowings (spontaneous and under constraint) from outside. Additionally, individual inclinations and environmental conditions generate adaptations and reactions to cultures that are different from the individual's starting point. Nevertheless, the roots of cultural responses are remarkably virile; as a consequence, some cultural characteristics and commitments survive geographic transplantations, political oppression, and educational imposition of "established traditions." Thus, a multicultural concept is an inevitable reality in any society where there are people of various cultural backgrounds who are changing, moving about, and learning. The multicultural concept implies a view of life in which we recognize and cherish the differences among groups of people and search for ways to help such traits to be positive influences on both the individuals who possess them and all others with whom they associate in our society.

Like the term *culture,* the authors tend to define *society* in its broadest sense. While our focus is on the political unit—a city, state, or nation—where cultural patterns tend to be politically spotlighted, our concern ranges to the behavior of people wherever they live in companionship, as they do in schools and neighborhoods, rather than isolation. In a definition we favor particularly, society is an organized "body of individuals living as members of a community: a society pledging equal rights for all."[4] The ideal of the multicultural society, then, is the recognition of cultural equality.

THE PROFESSIONAL MANDATE

Teachers traditionally have been called "carriers of culture." They are seen as the primary *professional* social agents responsible for passing culture from adults to the next generation. If the United States, or any community, represented a pure unicultural society, this clear-cut assignment to imbue children with the values and perspectives of a single tradition could be readily understood and carried out. Where diverse cultural patterns prevail, as they do in the schools in the United States, such a simplistic approach cannot be justified. As a consequence, controversy has begun to generate over whose culture should be perpetuated.

We, the authors and consultants of this book, propose that teachers and other educational personnel must assume the professional mandate to *initiate and maintain a multicultural approach in their professional practice.* Implicit in such an approach is the responsibility to transmit the traditions of all cultures—equally and respectfully. Students must be taught not only to cherish their own ways of life but also to respect those of others. Thus, teachers must take the responsibility of creating and maintaining learning situations that nurture and preserve the cultural traditions of all.

To follow the multicultural mandate, teachers and other educators must maintain truly professional relationships with students and parents. All must be treated, or served educationally in this case, with respect and equality. Like the medical doctor who must supply health services to all kinds of clients, educational professionals must provide instruction and counsel to children of many cultures without favor, prejudice, or distinction. Ideally, teachers should feel brotherhood for people of all cultures; realistically, such a genuine response cannot always be expected. Nevertheless, professionally, the teacher and educator have the obligation to maintain a posture that is respectful and supportive as well as educationally beneficial for all.

PURPOSE OF THIS BOOK

The basic purpose of this book is to advance the multicultural society by helping teachers and their students to learn to respond with intellectual honesty to the multicultural conditions that prevail. Such an objective stems from the authors' common conviction that the school is the forum from which perceptions of movement toward the multicultural society will emerge. Our specific aim is to help teachers and administrators, as well as the students and parents they serve, to see each other not as abstractions (or stereotypes) but as real, discrete beings, with personal hopes, joys, sufferings, abilities, and life styles, and to discern a common humanity among the various groups—national and international. We admit some professional bias in the belief that ability to live in a multicultural society must be learned in schools. Most of the authors and consultants, in one way or another, are involved in preparing teachers and other educational personnel as well as in making policies for educational programs. We hold no illusions, however, that, given deeply entrenched racism, our schools and teachers can bring about a healthy response to multicultural conditions by their efforts alone. Nor do we believe that the ideal multicultural society will spring up one day fully formed and functioning like a shiny new toy. As Griffin points out in chapter 3, we must deal with the school's role in teaching values and developing controls (including self-controls) in the people who work in such institutions. We must also suggest new directions and teach people to assess their potential.

The contributors to this book are sensitive to the gains for implementing the multicultural concept that have come—and must continue to come—from legal judgments, political action, and economic policy, as well as from the varieties of human decisions and interactions that take place in groups and communities across the nation. However, we believe it is imperative for participants (teachers and students) in learning situations to respond to cultural diversity in ways that are wholesome for the individual and beneficial to the society. Our message is directed specifically to those who teach because we are convinced that such positive responses to multicultural traditions *must and can be learned*.

WHAT BROUGHT US TOGETHER

The contributors to this book, including both professors and graduate students, represent a variety of disciplines and are primarily from the faculties of two midwestern universities—Northwestern University in Evanston, Illinois, and the University of Michigan in Ann Arbor, Michigan. The project grew out of the activities of the Center for the Teaching Professions at Northwestern University, which encourages and supports research and experimentation to improve teaching in all its aspects. Dolores E. Cross, then of the faculty of the School of Education, Northwestern University, brought us together. It was she who had the inspiration for the project. Deeply committed to developing teaching and learning processes that are responsive to the reality and integrity of cultural diversity, she organized the Northwestern University group and developed the link with the contributing scholars of the University of Michigan. Her dedicated and inspired leadership throughout has been the moving force behind the book. She chaired faculty-student seminars and worked closely with individual contributors as well as coeditors. Gwendolyn C. Baker organized and chaired the University of Michigan group. Lindley J. Stiles took responsibility for putting the book together.

Contributors of the book joined in the project because of a common awareness that we in the United States, particularly, are foundering in our efforts to understand, accept, and make the most of the multicultural conditions that exist. The possibility of developing redefinitions of perspectives and relationships, compatible to our multicultural milieu, appealed to us. Then, too, we believe the time is ripe for a rejuvenation of faith and confidence in what can be accomplished if all respond honestly and positively to cultural diversity. Our overall motivation focused on the help we could provide to teachers by supplying fresh and creative insights about how succeeding generations of students can be guided to confront realistically the multicultural reality.

HOW THE BOOK WAS DEVELOPED

The process by which this book was developed basically was one of self- and reeducation. Members of the team, operating separately and in joint sessions, analyzed where the United States is with respect to our national response to cultural diversity. In this process, the authors consulted experts—both within and outside the universities. In addition, we found it beneficial to study typical incidents from elementary and secondary schools that reveal various kinds of responses by teachers to the cultural differences of students. Open comparisons of the perceptions, attitudes, alternative ideas, and experiences of members of the teams proved worthwhile also. Throughout, subgroups and individuals were carrying on research, the results of which were analyzed.

The writing was done by the subteams or individual authors after each had submitted a preliminary overview to a campus group for review and criticism. As the format for the book developed, additional authors—Ella Griffin, Asa Hilliard, James Deslonde, Ernece B. Kelly, and Robert P. Ho—were invited to contribute chapters and specialized help on topics considered vital to the book's message. Other consultants—Bennie Whiten, Jr., J. Paul Bohannan, Douglas S. Ward, James R. Neal, Garvey Laurent, and Yemi Ligadu—contributed valuable suggestions. After the chapters were written, with a few exceptions, they were again given the benefit of the assessments of all involved in the project. Subsequently, criticisms and suggestions were sought from outside reviewers and the final editing was done.

Thus, this is not the usual type of multiple authorship in which each contributor independently prepares an assigned chapter and an editor puts the whole together. Rather, the publication is a product of interdisciplinary scholarship developed through sharing and discussing the diverse cultural and academic perspectives of individual contributors. Yet it must be emphasized that this cooperative approach made room for differences of opinion and for the advancement of alternative concepts and strategies. Each author and/or writing team was free to make a case for particular points of view or instructional strategies; but each did so against a background of criticism from colleagues who sometimes held contrasting views.

SPONSORED BY THE CENTER FOR THE TEACHING PROFESSIONS

The sponsorship of The Center for the Teaching Professions at Northwestern University has been a vital factor in the development of this publication. The center itself, the first of its kind in the world, was created with support of The W. K. Kellogg Foundation and Northwestern University. Its central mission is to improve teaching, particularly in collegiate, graduate, and professional schools, as well as in adult education programs. The impact of the center's research and demonstration reaches into elementary and secondary schools as well, because the theories and strategies for teaching that are studied tend to have broad applications wherever teaching and learning are taking place. Thus, the center is concerned with teaching behavior in relationship to cultural diversities that may be present among students and within the larger society. As a consequence, the center undertook the sponsorship of this project and has provided various kinds of assistance (including financial) to the work throughout. In return, royalties from the sale of this book will go to the center to support other kinds of research and development activities to improve teaching.

ORGANIZATION OF THE BOOK

The contents of this book are organized to provide both perspectives on the multicultural society and strategies for teaching them. Part 1 includes three chapters dealing with the nature and extent of cultural diversity in the United States and the world. Dolores E. Cross, Marvin Happel, Glenn A. Doston, and Lindley J. Stiles, in chapter 1, discuss the multicultural concept and illustrate ways in which teachers respond to it. Meyer Weinberg, in chapter 2, presents an analysis of how minorities in the United States are treated when a unicultural condition is the goal. In chapter 3, Ella Griffin considers the complex problems of moral education in a multicultural world and shows that it is possible to promote moral behavior while maintaining respect for diverse traditions.

The myths and realities of multicultural societies are the focus of part 2. The idea that all can be Americanized, or homogenized into a common culture, is debunked in chapter 4 by Rudolf B. Schmerl; his personal experience convinces us that we are all immigrants. James Deslonde, in chapter 5, exposes another myth by showing that desegregation efforts fail when teachers are not sensitive to cultural differences. The complex problems of language learning—which are deeply embedded in cultural traditions—are considered in chapter 6 by Rae Moses, Harvey Daniels, and Robert Gundlach. The highly controversial myths about human intelligence are exposed by Asa Hilliard in chapter 7. Terrence N. Tice concludes this part, in chapter 8, with a critical analysis of the objectives appropriate in a multicultural society.

Part 3 includes chapters that deal with various practical aspects of educational programs and teaching strategies. It aims to help teachers and educational leaders who are committed to the multicultural approach to select specific strategies for achieving their goals. The techniques of modifying curriculums to make them compatible with multicultural objectives are discussed by Gwendolyn C. Baker, Marshall Browdy, Clarence Beecher, and Robert P. Ho in chapter 9. How to adapt learning and teaching to carry out the curricular objectives is the concern of chapter 10, by Dolores E. Cross, Gwendolyn C. Baker, Robert Dixon, Ralph Hansen, and Robert P. Ho. Ernece B. Kelly, in chapter 11, shows how language arts can be taught in light of the reality of diverse cultures without infringing on the traditions of any. Ann D. Gordon, in chapter 12, discusses how U.S. history can be taught to advance the multicultural traditions that prevail. As will be noted, the chapters in part 3 are focused on specific, key aspects of teaching in our multicultural society and are illustrated by examples drawn from the authors' specialties. The general principles illustrated, however, are applicable to teaching any subject.

ACKNOWLEDGMENTS

In addition to those named in the list of contributors, which includes researchers and consultants as well as authors, appreciation is expressed to others who helped in one way or another to make this book a reality. B. Claude Mathis, Director of The Center for the Teaching Professions, Northwestern University, has provided both financial and professional support throughout. B. J. Chandler, Dean, School of Education, Northwestern University, has encouraged staff members to participate in the project and has made it possible for them to do so. William Hazard, Associate Dean, School of Education, Northwestern University, contributed valuable advice. Wilbur Cohen, Dean, and Frederick Bertolaet, Associate Dean, School of Education, University of Michigan, have supported the Michigan team's efforts. Besides writing chapter 3, Ella Griffin gave helpful advice. Appreciation is also due to Glenn A. Doston, who helped with the editing; to Margaret King and Peggy Sheriffe, who typed several drafts of the chapters; to Kay McCormick and Cheryl Gay, who prepared the final manuscript; and to Colleen McDonald, Sally Goodman, Jean Bratton, and Cynthia Garrels, who helped with proofreading.

Part 1

THE MULTICULTURAL CONDITION

1. Responding to Cultural Diversity

Dolores E. Cross, Marvin Happel, Glenn A. Doston, and Lindley J. Stiles

For each child to feel that it is somebody requires that children be allowed to move in every direction within the social system and within the world, "without prejudice." [1]

Individuals of both minority and majority cultures have been leaders for educational change throughout the history of the United States. Today, the efforts of such leaders are focused largely on increasing accountability and achieving humaneness under the aegis of pluralism—which is identified by a variety of terms, including *multicultural, cultural pluralism, cross-cultural, bilingual, multiethnic*. In general, their approaches are concerned with legitimizing the differing cultural presences, as reflected in physical, emotional, intellectual, and spiritual attributes. Such legitimation is seen in the restating, rethinking, and reviewing of perspectives to accommodate diverse cultural experiences. While achieving the full promise of pluralism, or multiculturalism, is likely to be a slow and arduous process, the current proliferation of programs, strategies, and guidelines suggests significant local, state, and national confidence that we can move toward multiculturalism as established social policy. Such a goal, given our espoused commitments to equality, is deceptively simple.

For all who strive to understand the complexities of designing, implementing, and evaluating strategies in the name of multiculturalism, two considerations are paramount:

1. that we in the United States are socialized to ignore the close connection between racial myths, stereotypes, and racism—perpetuated in the past and present through nonproductive conflicts on local, national, and international levels; and

3

2. that we are socialized to ignore the fact that it is the *reaction* to cultural differences, not cultural differences in themselves, that creates social conflicts.

While we feel that these social indoctrinations are unavoidable, we are also aware that individuals and communities vary in their internalization of images that denigrate the humaneness of those who are culturally different. Additionally, individuals vary in their ability to react to cultural differences in ways that reflect humaneness. The intent, in this first chapter, is to articulate some perceptions, behaviors, and personal/professional resources of teachers that can act to constrain or facilitate the development of constructive responses to cultural diversity. It is hoped that readers will see the promise of pluralistic or multicultural approaches and become aware that we are just beginning to realize that promise.

CONSEQUENCES OF STEREOTYPES

Too black a hue marks the coward, as witness Egyptians and Ethiopians, and so does also too white a complexion, as you may see from women. So the hue that makes for courage must be intermediate between these extremes.[2]

Aristotle, the author of the foregoing bit of silliness, was not the first to make absurd generalizations on the bases of skin color, ethnicity, national origin, or sex—or any other natural or acquired characteristics. Stereotypes, akin to superstitions, have permeated our thinking and influenced our behavior throughout history. They tend to be transmitted from one generation to the next as "established truths"; thus, the sins of the fathers are visited upon the children as individuals and social groups delude themselves about their presumed superiority.

It does not take a historian to see the consequences of such delusion for multicultural societies such as our own, or to estimate its effect on international relationships. Wherever cultural superiority is presumed, by individuals or nations, tension and conflict ultimately predominate. On the community level, these commonly take the form of crime, deprivation, persecution, and injustice. On the international level, distrust, imperialism, and war between nations are the consequences. The cyclic effect of cultural denigration is well established: those who presume superiority and those they castigate ultimately become engulfed in conflict that brings suffering or destruction to all.

Conflict, Racial Myths, and Racism

Said and Simmons, quoting from Raymond Aron, state that ethnic conflict will replace class conflict in the latter third of the twentieth century.[3] This conflict, they predict, will be characterized by passion to separate, or secede, and the tendency of ethnic nations to destroy each other in terms of population, government, education and territory. Their prediction is based on observations of the international scene—Ireland, the bloody struggle of Biafra, the secession of Bangladesh, and the no-negotiating posture in the Middle East. But similar observations can be made in the United States as well—in the political wars over which group should be favored, and in our history of race riots and gang warfare. Ethnic conflict can lead to fragmentation, and destruction is a real threat. But it must be remembered that some degree of ethnic conflict is useful if it prompts us to rethink and restate our historical, psychological, sociological, and educational perspectives, as well as to review our habits of personal interaction. Ethnic conflict does not have to lead to dissociation, separation, and fragmenting political wars. The desire for secession, the need to separate experienced by many ethnic minorities in the United States, is influenced by negative reactions to the culture's racial myths and stereotypes, and their attending message of racism.

Racism as a socioeconomic and political exercise creates a climate of self-hate and self-doubt that makes coming together after separation (implied in some versions of pluralism) difficult, if not impossible. It has divided the majority into minority subgroups. While we often refer to racism and its fury (in our planning, writing, and researching), we are socialized to neutralize its crippling impact, in the United States particularly. Racism is neutralized by our concentration on the likes and dislikes of the racist, and by our failure to confront the nature of the racist's reasoning. Also, many hold attitudes that negatively define capacities as predetermined and intellectually limited because they are presumed to be dictated by genetic membership in a group identifiable as a race. Racism is further neutralized by romanticizing poverty to the point of absurdity; by teachers ignoring the differences in teaching styles needed when assessing the oppressed; by our viewing cultural styles as biologically self-perpetuating (e.g., a static structural concept); by our minimizing the impact of disdainful verbal and nonverbal reactions to the culture experienced by minorities and the resulting influences on language (e.g., black English, slang, and idiom) as well as behavior. Racism is neutralized when we praise as great works of art such experiences as D. W. Griffith's *Birth of a Nation,* a film that upholds racial myths and glorifies imperial ambition.

A constructive level of ethnic conflict, in praise of diversity, is deferred by failure to confront denigrating racial images that prevail in the literature, deceptive research, and ethnic jokes. As a consequence, some individuals and groups tend to practice pluralism or multicultural approaches as an immersion in their particular cultural perspective rather than to associate or share with another culture that has been systematically projected as deficient in physical, emotional, intellectual, or spiritual dimensions. Racial myths, stereotypes, and attending racism thus act as a constraint to sharing, borrowing, and restating implied in pluralistic approaches.

Cosmetic Educational Planning

The goals of pluralism are severely threatened by values that encourage divisiveness. They are equally threatened by the failure of educators to recognize their tendency to avoid issues by cosmetic educational planning—planning that creates new titles, positions, and satellite programs in the name of "good education," but that does little or nothing to diminish racism or to stimulate the kind of humaneness needed to support the integrity of diverse perspectives.

Specifically, educators should answer the following questions in light of their potential to create humaneness and to obliterate the discomfort of racism:

1. How different are practices that advocate "prescriptive" imposition of group solidarity *from* the exclusion and aloofness exercised by those identified as the "oppressor"?
2. How different are practices suggesting a similar style, language pattern, or universal ethnic *from* the stereotypes of the "past"?
3. How different are practices that promote sporadic minority-culture events (special days and weeks) *from* the attitudes of the majority individuals who regard minority cultures as fringe expressions to be stimulated in season?
4. How different is the experience of reading *Dick and Jane* in Spanish, black English, etc., *from* the experience of reading *Dick and Jane* in Standard English?
5. How different are practices that project differences in culture as causes of the problem *from* the notions of victim blame as historically perpetuated?
6. How different is rhetoric proclaiming that minorities are "equally oppressed" *from* deceptive rhetoric of Americanization, the melting pot, and a chicken in every pot? (As stated by Weinberg in chapter 2, the fate of each minority is determined by the time and circumstances of entry into U.S. history.)
7. How different is a group direction that makes black or Chicano or Polish or native American or Irish the only legitimate perspective *from* the direction of only the "Anglo-Protestant" perspective?
8. How different are educators who see themselves as pluralists but who avoid confrontation with the real issue of racism *from* others who feign blindness to racism?

9. How can life for the oppressed minorities be improved if pluralists are unaware that they have been socialized to avoid confronting racial myths as they formulate policies to honor diversity?

Our socialization to avoid checking whether educational planning diminishes racism and enhances acceptance of diverse perspectives must be examined, lest, in this age of testing, we evaluate approaches within the aegis of pluralism, in light of inept cosmetic educational planning.

THE SCHOOL AS A SOCIALIZING AGENT

A problem educators need to consider is the narrow unicultural vision the United States has cherished. The process by which this vision was, and is, translated is one of socialization. The school, next to the home, is the major socializing agency. The individual child learns those behaviors, values, and norms espoused by the home and school; when such are congruent, there is no conflict. But when the cultural traditions and priorities of the home differ from those of the dominant culture, the school's goals—those of the majority—become imposed in a resocializing process.

The school, as a socializing agent or a subsystem of the society, has failed to respond adequately to the changing needs within the larger social system. This indictment applies particularly in the area of multiculturalism. For example, neither teacher-training institutions nor schools themselves have thus far addressed themselves seriously to the black awareness movement of the 1960s or to the emerging ethnic awareness movement of the 1970s. Our contention is that all participants (teachers, students, and communities at local, state, and national levels) are capable of renewing themselves. All that is required is the confrontation of reality, some serious searching, a bit of risk taking, as well as constructive analysis and the projection of creative strategies. Thus far, many school systems, and far too many teachers within them, appear to be ill equipped to respond to the needs of a multicultural society—ill equipped both psychologically and in terms of professional skills.

It is important to understand that the school, as an organization, has its own culture, a culture made up, to a large extent, of the relationships among different individuals, and their roles and positions within it. The effectiveness of school and the socialization process it encourages are greatly dependent on the relationships that exist among teachers themselves, between the teachers and the administration, between the teachers and the students, and between the school and its joint clientele.

Of paramount importance in attempting to modify the school to implement a multicultural approach are the willingness of school personnel to examine their own interactions, to take risks, to experiment with new ideas, and to accept the reality of their own multicultural heritage as relevant and crucial to the realities of teaching and learning.

The Unicultural Vision

To clarify the points we want to communicate, we present the following cases. They are vivid, and perhaps characteristic, illustrations of the extent of the present-day unicultural vision found among our teachers and teachers-in-training.

> In an experimental program, teachers, parents, and students from multicultural city schools met in small sensitizing groups for an extended period of time. Ron Kubic, a junior high teacher, stated his reason for being in the program: "I'm in the program because of the university credit offered by the program. . . . I have no problems teaching children of other races; in fact, if I went through my grade book, I wouldn't be able to tell you who is white, black, or Mexican-American without thinking about it.

Ron's statement represents a more or less typical example of unicultural vision and may have been overstated for effect. But the authors have encountered variations of its theme among many teachers. Overstated or not, it apparently represents Ron's ideal or reality. Ron's language-arts courses revealed no hint of a multicultural society either in his own classroom or in the world beyond. Ron was surprised to learn that nonwhite students, and some of their parents, considered him racially and culturally biased.

Ron's statement must still be taken at face value. His concern, perhaps, is with children, and with teaching in its broadest and most typically defined characteristics. What Ron fails to understand, and what the "sensitizing group" he participates in should provide him with, is the experience that in order to teach and to value all children, he must first understand himself: his own values, his own motivations for teaching, his own home and family background, his own attitudes to others around him.

A Repressive Atmosphere

If many educators are infected with unicultural vision, can schools be turned around? We feel the answer is yes. However, before schools are turned around, the interactive processes that lead to a repressive atmosphere need to be recognized and understood. This presents a special challenge to teacher education. Each school has its own culture, its own way of doing things.

Suzanne Crew is student-teaching in a culturally mixed high school in Chicago. Based on the university supervisor's observations and conversations with the students after class, two Spanish-speaking students seem to be interested in history and have copious notes in Spanish. Both are young men who started secondary school in Mexico. Because of their inexperience in English, they have difficulty communicating answers to the teacher. Suzanne believes both young men are low achievers. Suzanne's belief is reinforced for her by her coteacher.

Suzanne volunteered for this school. She wanted exposure to a different cultural milieu than she had previously experienced. Suzanne's past experience has taught her to associate classroom participation with effort and intelligence. Insecure, like most beginning interns, she relies on the experienced coteacher to interpret reality for her. Suzanne allows her own lack of language skills to be a barrier between herself and her students. A willingness to broaden one's experiences is no guarantee that the intern will approach students with an open mind or will profit from the experience.

Suzanne has been, perhaps not surprisingly, affected by the longstanding influence of achievement and intelligence testing. It has been well documented that such tests are culturally biased. To a great extent, however, they continue to be used in schools and to be discussed in textbooks. Suzanne's reaction was, then, a not unexpected one. She had been well reinforced to react thus. Her problem, then, is not one of open-mindedness. Instead, Suzanne exemplifies a much more complex problem whose manifestations are more fully dealt with in chapter 7 by Asa Hilliard.

Double Standards

The school, in its endorsement of the values of the majority, often exerts pressures on minorities to conform that become, in effect, a force for double standards. Often such diverse prescriptions for behavior are enforced by members of minorities against their own kind. Consider the example that follows.

Don Greene is a black intern and is teaching in a classroom that includes only a few black students. The rest are white. Don's university supervisor observes the following series of exchanges: A white student chats with a black friend for an extended period of time, with the black student mostly listening and nodding assent. Don tells the black student to be quiet. The next day, when a black student and a white student are causing mild disturbances, the black student is verbally reprimanded. Later in the day, two white girls demonstrate dislike for the intern by several catty remarks aimed at Don. When two black girls pick up the theme, they are quickly checked by a word from Don. Nothing is said to the white girls even though they renewed their rudeness on several other occasions.

Don was apparently unaware of his double standard until his supervisor brought it to his attention. Don conceded that he is not especially comfortable when interacting with whites. Don grew up in an urban black area of a large city and had little contact with nonblacks before coming to the university. At the university, he has avoided interaction with whites. This dialogue with his supervisor is apparently one of his first conversations with a white person about anything this personal. With the insight subsequent dialogues give him, Don is able to eliminate his double standard by the end of his internship. In addition, he is able to develop friendships with students of both races.

These examples imply that we need to analyze our multicultural society in conjunction with peers and/or students. We need to help people recognize the need for a healthy response to our multicultural society, and we need to help them recognize their place within it. Only then can concerned teaching come about.

TOWARD A HEALTHY
MULTICULTURAL SOCIETY

Several questions emerge when we consider the imperative to initiate and maintain a multicultural approach: Can it conceivably be done? Who will begin . . . and how? The first question cannot be answered now. It will be answered in practice by national, state, local, and school classroom systems. In addressing this book to teachers, we are suggesting, in answer to the second question, that they themselves begin to implement a multicultural approach.

Understanding Self and Situations

In order to move toward a healthy multicultural society, the educator must see self as a learner enhanced and changed by understanding, appreciating, and reflecting cultural diversity. This may mean trading a feeling of helplessness for experiencing intense awareness and involvement in setting goals for self and others. The role teachers play depends on choice or consensus, which may turn toward the past or future, toward paralysis or development, toward an effort to find false security by resisting change or toward the discovery of true security by taking part in progress.[4]

As expressed by Rogers, the individual who understands himself and who freely takes responsibility is a very different person from one who is simply in the group.[5] This difference shows up clearly in important aspects of his behavior. The leader who meets Rogers's prescription can facilitate a multicultural approach in which all participants are viewed as learners and worthy resources. The truer all participants are to the laws of individual nature, the nearer is self. As expressed by Faure:

> Every learner is indeed a remarkably concrete being. He has his own history, which cannot be confused with any other. His personality is determined, more or less so with age, by a complex of biological, physiological, geographic, sociological, economic, cultural and professional data which are different for each individual. How can we fail to allow for this in determining the ultimate aims, the content and the methods of education? Entering the educational process is a child (and a teacher) with a cultural heritage, with particular psychological traits, bearing within self the effects of family, environment and surrounding economic conditions.[6]

Disciplining Self to Respond to Cultural Diversity

As teachers, we may have attitudes about students that do not allow room for diverse cultural perspectives and differences as expressed in the dress, language, socioeconomic opportunities, sexual behavior, and mobility of a group of students or an individual student. To discipline ourselves to respond to cultural diversity, we must take definite steps to become—and remain—aware of our personal/professional behavior. This means being conscious of our reactions to the cultural presence of others in both the teaching and nonteaching situation. In both situations it is important to get feedback and/or reflect on whether we are:

1. indicating in the content of dialogue and assignments evidence of a multicultural society and diverse perspectives
2. drawing from stereotypes, hearsay, or biases held by self or others when referring to a group or individual
3. projecting and acknowledging an understanding of self and values (knowledge of our cultural presence)
4. extending cultural orientation through reading, observing, and listening
5. assessing the open-mindedness of all participants to diverse perspectives
6. identifying individual and institutional reactions to culture in the past and present
7. maintaining an image of what it is like to be self or other in a particular context and time within and outside the United States

Teachers Can Make a Difference

The teacher must see self and students as being participants in and products of a culturally diverse society. This implies projecting a sensitivity to what it may be like to be "me" and the "other" in the social/learning situation. Such an approach comes to grips with very subtle classroom exchanges, as well as racial, political, and economic forces within and outside the classroom. Students bring to and take from the classroom a sense of power or powerlessness that is influenced by the quality of the interaction. The teacher can make a difference. The following account illustrates this idea.

Ms. Bort, the best eighth-grade teacher at Kinley School, sat behind her desk, in a room that reflected order and response to student excellence. Student papers bordered the room. These papers were well written in good penmanship with all the important points underscored with red or blue pencil. The room was pleasantly warm, on this mid-December day, and by this time the norms of good behavior and quiet were well established. Ms. Bort's reputation for concern and respect was often the topic of students who anticipated getting her for the eighth grade.

She wouldn't take anything but hard work, sincere effort. Each student in the class felt he or she had been preselected because we could measure up. The class was as diverse as the population in Newark with every visable ethnic group. The rivalries of upmanship were drawn on ethnic lines and geographically based by black, Italian, and Polish blocks. Everyone knew the turf to which you'd return at the end of the day. There was little chance of seeing or visiting with your classmates if they didn't live on your square.

This a given, the competition in the classroom was aggressive and the play in the gym was deadly. Ms. Bort asked, "What is the term applied to warm winter days, such as the day we are experiencing now?" A couple of hands shot up, but she looked at me for the answer. I had recently completed a report that reflected the correct response and she knew my answer would be right. In looking at me she also knew that I would be reluctant to answer because of the pain of stuttering. I thought about saying "Indian Summer" to satisfy her and myself. . . . at the same time I knew the syllables would stick and my face would contort and the agony could not be compensated by her approval. I returned her glance but did not lift my hand and imagined a demerit. Ms. Bort looked away and said, "Indian Summer," as if reading what my answer would be and planning how she would, in time, discover me. I think I knew she was planning to make me her star, which I regarded as folly; yet I admired her confidence.

I had learned that in being nonverbal I could earn straight B's, a few A's, and be spared the pain of having other students stare, laugh, or mimic. Ms. Bort saw some things but even more saw the expectations of high school. We turned to our project of making a map of the United States and the forestry of the different areas. My map and trees were neat and the key was in the finest penmanship. The final project looked lovely.

From a distance, the reader could view the areas accentuated with red and blue, the neatness, and the order of the presentation. I knew this would please Ms. Bort and her desire to display the best papers. I left it on her desk and prepared to go home. In parting, she mentioned she really liked my writing style and asked me to consider writing a class play for June graduation. I was elated and began some instant mental planning.

With Ms. Bort's compliment tucked in my mind and heart I hurried home . . . past the Catholic church in the Italian ward, past the vendor selling sweet potatoes for five to ten cents . . . past the third ward alleys with threatening gangs and past the pungent smell of garlic-Italian . . . to the bridge which separated the cultures Italian and black. The bridge was the area of confrontation and passage to my turf. The bridge spanned the railroad yard and seemed so much longer than it was. I left the established ghetto inhabited by Italians (who were briefly the strongest on that ethnic collage) and Greeks, some Polish, a few southern blacks, Lithuanians. The ethnic ports were the result of struggle and heated exclamation of a culture that was strengthened by the presence of the Catholic church. The Catholic church seemed to affirm in the ritual of sporadic feasts the glory of ethnic presence in such splendor that during the festival everyone became "Italiano." . . . We'd mutter sounds that seemed like another language and move among the crowds. On my side of the bridge was Sugar Hill . . . emerging blacks with wallets padded by the post-wartime economy and feeling the good life was within reach. Nothing could stop us now. . . . Jackie Robinson had made the major leagues . . . the Brooklyn Dodgers . . . there were taxicab rides downtown . . . the Saturday movie to watch Sabu and Tarzan and all the popcorn in the world to smell and eat. Running home with Ms. Bort's compliment still fresh, my other concerns diminished. Running down the steps of the bridge many thoughts came to mind. My coat was wide open and I kept saying to myself, "Indian Summer," and wishing I had answered Ms. Bort, yet so pleased she understood. Ms. Bort seemed to *see me*. I felt she knew more about me than I had said, yet at the same time was trying to discover me. My mother would like what had happened in class, "me, being asked to write a play." That would distract her. . . .[7]

Teachers can make a difference by understanding that while all individuals seek validation, historic and current negative reactions to a cultural/ethnic presence create a situation in which some minorities need support that acknowledges their existence on intellectual and spiritual levels.

As expressed by Ralph Ellison, "You ache with the need to convince yourself that you do exist in the real world . . . that you're a part of all the sound and anguish, and you strike out with your fists, you curse and you swear to make them recognize you. . . ."[8]

Teaching and learning in our multicultural society means responding with professional and personal honesty to the valuing and rejecting experienced by differing individuals. While it is not possible to know all events that impress the student client, we have indicators from past and present behavior, attitudes of the wider society, lingering discriminatory social-economic-educational policies, and verbalized stereotypes.

The teacher begins to respond to the reality of cultural diversity by being aware of self as a resource, accessible material, and personal lack or presence of outreach orientation to extend knowledge. This awareness should be complemented by information on historical perspective, the teaching role, and teaching strategies.

Reality of Cultural Diversity

As used in this book, the term *multicultural* refers to responses to cultural differences that are intellectually honest in their recognition of existing cultural diversity. As a way of responding, this implies a sensitivity to race, religion, sex, geographic origin, economic and social status, interests, and historical perspective. A basic premise is that *the differences that characterize individuals and groups should be cherished for their worth and cultivated for the benefits they bring to all people*. The following commentary on Duke Ellington reflects this premise: "It was Edward Kennedy Ellington who took the funky staccato of Africa and the groan of the blues out of ghetto honky-tonks and into the mainstream of American culture. His band arrangements vibrated with a feeling of improvisation that came from an endlessly imaginative, but meticulous musical mind. Unlike many other successful musicians he didn't forget where he came from. He was always available to play at benefits for black organizations: his music, he said, was not jazz but 'Negro music.' "[9] The sensitivity to diversity advocated here implies the responsibility of viewing Ellington within the aegis of black culture, while honestly recognizing the influence of his sex, education, geographic origin, economic/social status, interests, and his personal reaction to the question: What has it been and is it like to be black in this society? Ellington may not have shared the isolation and frustration experienced by W. E. B. Du Bois and expressed in *The Souls of Black Folk:*

> Behind the thought lurks the after thought: suppose if all the world is right and we are less than men? Suppose this mad impulse [i.e., the demand for freedom and equality] is all wrong, some mock mirage from the untrue . . . . a shriek in the night for the freedom of men who themselves are not yet sure of their right to demand it?[10]

Further, both Ellington and Du Bois (for the sake of specific examples rather than stereotypes) may not have been stifled by the psychological milieu expressed by Richard Wright:

> Even when a white man asked us an innocent question, some unconscious part of us would listen closely not only to the obvious words but also to the intona-

tions of voice that indicated what kind of answer he wanted; and automatically we would determine whether an affirmation or negative reply was expected and we answered not in terms of objective truth but in terms of what the white man wanted to hear.[11]

The question, then, is not whether individual differences exist under the aegis of an identifiable group, but *whether, why,* and *at what costs* do we sacrifice these differences in favor of stereotypes. Although the black awareness movement of the sixties and the resurgent ethnic awareness of the seventies suggest support for both the initiation and the maintenance of a multicultural approach for social policy, which includes education, we have barely scratched the surface in implementing it.

Individuals are turning their backs on the past pressures to eradicate cultural identities. The direction of the present and future for many ethnic groups is toward the assertion of cultural identity. The intent is to rediscover and reemphasize the characteristics that are the heritage of each group, as well as the individual who is unique within the aegis of a culture.

Philosophically, the multicultural concept incorporates the ideals of equality, mutuality, human justice, and, ideally but not necessarily, brotherhood. Politically, the multicultural concept embraces the belief that people with differences can learn to live together in peace and harmony for the benefit of all. Socially, the concept holds that cultural uniqueness can enhance the quality of life for all. A healthy multicultural society, then, is one made up of more than one cultural group and one that strives to promote mutual respect, shared power, and a general dedication to the concept of cultural equality. The multicultural approach in teaching takes its direction from these basic tenets; it aims to create within the school a sensitivity to cultural diversity by creating a model of a healthy multicultural society and helping students to develop and accept diverse perspectives. The ultimate goal is to create a society that measures diversity not only by numbers of blacks, browns, reds, yellows, white ethnics, and women, but also by the presence and development of diverse approaches to loving, learning, creating, and recreating.

We're Just Beginning

One of the most visible material changes in the schools of the late sixties and seventies has been the presence and use of readers and supplementary texts reflecting ethnic diversity. However, we are far from overcoming the fixed images people hold of others out of ignorance and fear, or out of philistinism and a lack of imagination. The multicultural approach makes modifications in curriculums, pupil and teacher assignments, and programs part of a much larger change—a change away from stereotyped thinking in our national and international life. In effecting this large change the task is to actualize personal/professional objectives without the impediments of stereotypes and to expect the variety, complexity, and authenticity that can emanate from the individual's cultural perspective. A genuine conversion will be the product of frequent exposure to a variety of life patterns, tastes, and accomplishments, as well as a real appreciation for the individuals and groups who cherish and nourish the pace, lifestyle, and products of what they identify as their culture.

As a beginning, we suggest that teachers participate in the dialogue that deals with racial myths in the literature, ethnic jokes, and institutional planning, a process the contributors to this book experienced. This leads to our achieving a consensus on the reality of conflicts in the classroom that may emanate from stereotypes, discussions from our cultural and academic backgrounds, and an extension and articulation of implications we perceived from our learning/teaching.

The group or individual must become a course of study in dialogue with the other. In the process there is borrowing and a sharing that acts as a support system to develop personal and professional resources. While we have no illusions that stereotypes will completely disappear, our efforts must focus on the creation of groups that are culturally alike or diverse; capable of forging a community that has few anxieties springing from ethnic/cultural differences and that also has the confidence/support to take the risk of constructively confronting racism and honestly assessing what goes on in the name of multicultural approaches.

Complementing the various movements, innovations, and curricular thrusts of the sixties and seventies and dealing with stereotypes for educators mean developing a convincing and more humane view of our society. This begins *when* interaction, utilization, and articulation of culturally diverse perspectives are accepted and expected. Despite the proliferation of materials, an expanding vocabulary, and the burgeoning advocacy of pluralism, in practice we're just beginning.

2. A Historical Framework for Multicultural Education

Meyer Weinberg

We said we'd like the National Institute of Mental Health to set up an institute or task force to study racism or white supremacy. They didn't say they would't set up such a task force or institute. They said we will set up an institute to study minority groups. In other words, "We won't study ourselves, but we will study you." [1]

So wrote a black psychiatrist in 1973, pointedly emphasizing that a comprehensive study of racism—which must form a central part of multicultural education—must be a reciprocal exploration of majority and minority.

The American public school long ago was forced into the service of prevailing racial conceptions. For decades, in both North and South, outright exclusion of minority children and denigration of their cultures were standard practices. Today, whether by design or thoughtlessness, many of the practices still abound. A historical study can reveal some of their roots and therby provide teachers with a more realistic understanding of the dimensions of the problem.

One large group of minorities was incorporated within American society by force and violence—including enslavement and conquest. These include the blacks, Mexican-Americans, native Americans, and Puerto Ricans. Today their children make up about a fifth of all public school children in the United States. The educational fate of these children has been, and continues to be, determined largely by the relative sociopolitical power their parents exercise. Over the long sweep of American history the four minorities constituted prime sources of valuable land and low-cost labor. The dominant white community succeeded in gaining advantageous access to these resources through its control of government and armed power. Denied an adequate basis of self-support, the minority peoples were compelled to occupy a position of extreme economic dependence. Because of the localistic organization of public education in this country, the combination of dependence and powerlessness of the four minorities was translated into inadequate schooling, or the absence of schooling, wherever these minorities were found.

Let us review in a summary way the educational experiences of the four minorities. Special emphasis is laid upon black Americans. Space limitations preclude further detailed treatment.

BLACK AMERICANS

From Slavery to 1865

By 1860 more than 1.3 million slaves were children under ten years of age, while another 1.1 million were between ten and nineteen years old. Virtually none attended school. Under the rule of compulsory ignorance, it was illegal in most southern states to teach slaves to read or write. Frederick Douglass, the black abolitionist, testified from personal experience that the prohibitory laws were obeyed almost universally. A handful of slaves became literate, however, because a knowledge of letters was necessary at work, because of personal relations with the master's children, or by attendance at secret schools. Even when a slave was literate, the law forbade instruction of his or her children.

More than a quarter million free Negroes in the South fared only slightly better. Some attended public schools; in 1850, an average of about 250 black children were enrolled in each of the sixteen slave states. Even this tiny number shrank during the 1850s. A number attended secret schools that were located in many southern towns. A few private institutions were begun by blacks but foundered on the rocks of poverty and official hostility. Some free blacks learned their letters in Sabbath Schools. Even modest success alarmed slaveholders and other whites, and so after a time instruction in reading was dropped. In 1840 a total of fifteen black Sabbath Schools in the South enrolled fewer than 1,500 students. All were taught by memory rather than mastery of the written word. Apprenticeship opened literacy to some, as masters were obliged by law to instruct apprentices. During the first quarter of the nineteenth century, however, such stipulations were removed from the law in a number of states.

Free Negroes in the North, to 1865

Nearly 250,000 Negroes in the North lived in urban centers for the most part. Unlike their southern cousins, they were free to move from one place to another and were able to communicate to a much greater degree. Their children were far more likely to find the door of the public school open than were children down south. Yet, in the main, black children were excluded from the burgeoning public school system. Often, black parents paid school taxes only to find their children forbidden to attend the schools. Nothing if not realistic, black parents demanded separate schools when black children could not gain entrance to the "common" school. Even in a single northern state, policies differed: Segregation was the dominant rule in Boston until 1855, but in New Bedford the schools were truly open to all.

In Ohio, although blacks did not have the right to vote, they nevertheless conducted a successful campaign in the state legislature to force public financing of separate schools. In 1853, before the change in policy, only one-tenth of school-age black youths attended public schools; by 1862 the proportion more than quintupled. In other states, such as Pennsylvania and Illinois, legislators were adamant and resisted black efforts.

Once public schools were attained for blacks, parents advanced to an attack on the principle of separation. When the blacks of Nantucket were reminded in 1842 that they had *their own school,* they replied in a public protest meeting, "We are weary of this kind of honor or distinction."[2] Organized school boycotts by black parents pried open the schools of numerous northern communities. These included Boston, Nantucket, and Salem, Massachusetts, as well as Rochester, Buffalo, and Lockport, New York.

Wherever they were schooled, and whether or not they received any schooling, black children faced certain special problems. One was the pervasive racism that expressed itself in the form of sweeping employment discrimination. "You can hardly imagine," declared John Rock, the first black lawyer to argue before the U.S. Supreme Court, "the humiliation and contempt a colored lad must feel in graduating the first in a class, and then being rejected everywhere else because of his color."[3] Another problem was the doctrine of racial superiority that called forth feelings of self-depreciation among black children. In 1865, for example, the *New Orleans Tribune,* a black newspaper, held that segregated schools operated to "perpetuate from childhood the infatuation of the White, and prompt the Black to retaliate by enmity or envy. . . ."[4]

Black Education, 1865–1950

In the South, the end of the Civil War brought a new era in black education. The movement for education, wrote W. E. B. Du Bois, "started with the Negroes themselves and they continued to form the dynamic force behind it."[5] Blacks contributed money, labor, building materials—and countless children for whom they finally saw a realistic possibility of education. Supplementary help came from northern white missionary organizations—which contributed teachers, money, and school supplies—and the federal Freedman's Bureau, which for several years provided some school building and maintenance expenses.

By 1870, one-tenth of all school-age black children were enrolled in school, a very large increase over the 1860 figure of 2 percent. Only when black children could gain entrance to public schools in the South would the figure rise significantly. Black entry depended crucially upon the attainment of political power. From the late 1860s to the late 1870s, blacks voted and were elected to public office throughout the South. One of the very first fruits of these democratic labors was statutory provision for educating black children at public expense. By 1870 one-third of all school-age black children in the country attended public schools. This meant that more than a threefold increase had occurred during the 1870s.

With changing political fortunes, however, the direction of black public education changed abruptly. During the quarter century following 1880, blacks in the South were deprived of the right to vote; the last black member of the U.S. Congress left office in 1901; lynching became an extralegal means of terrorizing black citizens; the U.S. Supreme Court ruled in 1896 that racial segregation was constitutional (*Plessy* v. *Ferguson*) and three years later that a state might close down a black school in order to conserve funds for use at a white school (the *Cumming* case), thus effectively disabling the educational significance of the Fourteenth Amendment.

School authorities throughout the South regularly diverted state school aid from its designated use at black schools. This was accomplished by having the state legislature appropriate equal per-pupil funds, which county school boards then spent primarily on white children. By the 1920s and 1930s, southern counties spent five to twenty times more on white than on black children.

The color line was strictly enforced both for students and teachers. After Reconstruction, segregation of teachers became the rule, especially in rural areas. Black teachers were trained in institutions of meager quality. Southern states consistently refused to appropriate sufficient funds to raise the quality of such training. Black teachers were paid exceedingly low salaries, judged even by southern standards. After the 1880s their standards of employment sank, even as the enrollment of black children expanded. Consequently, they lacked realistic incentives to seek further training. In Mississippi, for example, while white teachers could attend tuition-free teachers colleges part-time during the entire school year, black teachers had available only a six-week summer school that was supported for the most part by their tuition.

Black teachers were expected to respect the system of segregation and discrimination. One black teacher who was employed to teach in a black school in Birmingham during the mid-1920s was told by a school board interviewer:

> Remember, you did not create the race problem and neither did I. But it is here, and it is here to stay. I want you to go back to Slater School and teach those little Negro boys and girls how to stay in their places and grow up to be good useful citizens.[6]

It was not unusual for school officials to select a worse-prepared applicant if he or she "would maintain the point of view of the Whites."[7] Often, influential whites would repay faithful black personal servants by gaining their appointment as teachers in black schools even though they had no formal qualifications whatsoever.

During the thirty years following 1880, Negro Americans tended to remain in the South. By 1910 only 11 percent of all blacks lived outside the South. Those who did, however, concentrated in cities and their children had unusual access to the public schools, at least in contrast to the situation in the South. Yet, racially discriminatory schooling for black children remained the rule throughout the North.

In Illinois, at the end of the Civil War, black children were not counted in the apportionment of state aid, nor did blacks receive refunds of the school taxes paid, as the law required. The legislature finally omitted the word *white* from the school law in 1872, and two years later penalties were provided for attempting to exclude black children from the public schools. In southern Illinois especially, the law meant little. By the opening of the twentieth century, radically segregated schools were almost universal in that part of the state. Neither the courts nor state school officials interfered with many of these illegal practices.

In larger centers such as Chicago, numerous schools had become predominantly black by the close of the 1920s. Devices used by school authorities to encourage segregation included the building of branch schools nearby the main building in order to direct black children away from the latter. Black teachers were segregated as well. At times they were excluded altogether from Chicago Normal College, graduation from which was a prerequisite for teaching in the city schools. At other times a quota on Negro enrollees seemed to be in effect. Black applicants for teaching positions were generally assigned to predominantly black schools. This extended also to the assignment of substitute teachers. School resources were allocated in discriminatory ways. During the 1930s, for example, numerous black children were crowded into schools that operated on a double shift, with a consequent abbreviated school day. The same pattern persisted into the 1960s despite repeated avowals by authorities that the practice had ended.

After World War II, racially based inequalities existed throughout the state of Illinois. In Edwardsville, for example, two racially separate high schools existed. The white one had a four-year curriculum—while the black one ran only three years. State authorities refused to take remedial action even though the State Superintendent of Public Instruction listed white and black schools separately in the official state school directory.

Black Population of New York City

By 1920 New York City contained the largest black population of any city. The number rose from 28,000 in 1880 to 169,000 in 1920; by 1940 more than a half million Negroes lived there. Before World War I, black children made up less than 5 percent of total enrollment. They performed as well as or somewhat below the level achieved by white students. During the 1920s, many students who were newcomers from the South and had attended short-term rural black schools there needed special help. A principal in one New York City school provided smaller classes for newcomers. In another school the curriculum was watered down, and such "useful" subjects as "millinery, dressmaking, practical homemaking, industrial art, and cooking" were introduced.[8]

Some of the discrimination in New York City was moderated by the presence of greater organization in the black community. The NAACP had its national headquarters in that city, and staff members frequently concerned themselves with school affairs. During the early 1920s, for example, the use of double-shift classes was not closely related to the presence of black children. As noted earlier, in Chicago the situation was less favorable.

During the depression of the 1930s, school problems became community-wide issues in Harlem. Complaints were heard of severe overcrowding, inadequate curriculum, discriminatory reading materials, deliberate segregation, and underrepresentation of blacks in teaching and school governance. Municipal authorities, despite their reputation for liberal politics, failed to acknowledge the seriousness of the complaints and ignored them. In 1935 Mayor Fiorello La Guardia suppressed a critical report on Harlem's schools that he had commissioned. Nearly forty years later, the report had still not been published.

Various groups rallied black parents to bring pressure upon the school board. The Junior Council of the NAACP worked toward this end in Brooklyn. It found, in a survey, that some 6,000 school-age black children out of a total of 16,000 were not in school. Teachers were accused of a lack of understanding of black students. The Committee for Better Schools in Harlem, formed in 1936, served as a means whereby many black parents learned to formulate specific demands on the school system. Large-scale delegations conferred often with school officials.

Discrimination against Negro students existed in the high schools. Three high schools enrolling large numbers of Harlem youths had opportunities for neither academic nor commercial curriculums. In 1940 a vocational guidance counselor in a Harlem junior high school charged that specialized-trades high schools were rejecting Negro students on the ground that "if we cannot place the boy in the job for which we are to train him then it is futile to give him the training. . . ."[9] Black community spokesmen objected and met with counselors in Harlem schools, but no change in school policy resulted.

RESIDENTIAL SEGREGATION

Beginning with World War I, northward migration by blacks increased from a trickle to a flood. As the newcomers entered the cities they found residential areas increasingly segregated by race. From 1910 to 1916 southern and border cities legislated to bar blacks from certain neighborhoods. After these enactments were ruled unconstitutional in 1917, other means were used, in both North and South, to reach the same ends. Real estate organizations undertook to regulate black residential expansion so as to maintain and expand a solid area of black housing. Members of such groups were forbidden to sell or rent property to a Negro if he would be the first to enter a presently all-white block.

Northern schools incorporated these same racial patterns into their organization. Attendance areas were redrawn to separate black from white children. In rapidly changing areas, school boards often created optional attendance areas with the most recent racial statistics. The grade span of predominantly black schools was sometimes extended so as to prevent children in these schools from going on to a nearby advanced white school. At times Negro students were placed in a separate room, even in the basement. Schools designed for black students were located in the growing number of solidly black residential areas. In order to prevent protest against these measures from arising within the school system, blacks were not appointed to school boards and higher managerial posts.

Between 1865 and 1950 blacks in America succeeded in creating an educational tradition in the face of extraordinary opposition. Events of these years documented lavishly Du Bois's dictum that "probably never in the world have so many oppressed people tried in every possible way to educate themselves."[10]

The mid-twentieth century marked a turning point in the history of black America. Black leadership took hold of the movement for equality, unprecedented numbers of Negroes joined in, and the movement became national in scope. Fundamental to the development was a persistent black initiative that was ubiquitous and increasingly effective. In time, these events forced a reformulation of national public policies.

Southern Schools, 1950–1965

By 1950 Negro teachers in the South had succeeded in challenging the historic racial differentials in education by court victories on behalf of salary equalization. From 1937 to 1951 the average black teacher's salary increased from 52.5 percent of white salary to 87.2 percent. During the same period, black parents filed and won numerous lawsuits demanding equalization of school facilities and programs. Southern state governments tried to deflect the movement by a rapid but highly spotty program of improvement of black school facilities. The actual change was minimal. During the years 1934–1951, for example, the dollar gap in per-pupil expenditures between black and white fell only from $53.85 to $50.15.

The failure of equalization led the black movement to challenge head-on the principle of segregation. In 1954 the U.S. Supreme Court ruled in *Brown* v. *Board of Education of Topeka* that "separate educational facilities are inherently unequal," and thus laid to rest the ancient doctrine that separate schools were constitutionally permissible so long as the facilities were equal. Unfortunately, the tribunal failed to establish a timetable for desegregation. Consequently, all but a small fraction of segregation continued in force. Efforts of black parents to press school boards to implement *Brown* foundered. Such petitioners often lost their jobs as a result; if sharecroppers, they were frequently evicted; credit was cut off. Legal evasions by states of the obligation to desegregate, on the other hand, were highly successful. In the absence of executive concern and in the face of continued refusal by the federal judiciary to enforce *Brown,* little was done. Nearly a decade after that ruling, in 1963–1964, only 1.2 percent of the South's 2.9 million black schoolchildren attended desegregated schools. More attended such schools in the border states.

The full price of southern segregation did not become evident in detail until academic achievement data were released in the 1950s and 1960s. Everywhere in the South, black children—schooled for generations in presumably equal if separate institutions—were found to lag years behind white children. When border cities desegregated schools, tracking systems were frequently introduced to perpetuate the segregation under a common roof. Black children most frequently were assigned to the lowest tracks and typically remained there for the duration of their schooling. As a consequence, both the separation and deprivation persisted.

An enduring basis for educational change was laid in the years 1950–1965 when a black-led civil rights movement arose in the South. In campaigns staffed by numerous students, thousands of adult blacks were encouraged to register to vote. The persistence of southern civil rights workers elevated the demands for equality to national levels of political concern. The North also joined the civil rights movement.

Northern Schools, 1950–1965

As of midcentury, black children in the North attended essentially segregated schools that were systematically inferior to white schools in the same communities. An achievement gap—with black children behind white children—was the rule, whether in Berkeley, California; New York City; Chicago; or Bridgeport, Connecticut.

In New York City the black psychologist Kenneth B. Clark led an interracial movement that condemned northern segregation as being as pernicious as the southern type. He charged in 1954 that inferior education in the elementary schools ensured that black children "cannot compete with other children in high school."[11] Black and white leaders organized protests aimed at eliminating deliberate and other segregation in the city's schools. Some small steps brought only minimal change. The school board resisted any further steps. In Chicago the black community protested the discriminatory distribution of school resources and low academic achievement. Large-scale school boycotts followed. In other cities, similar complaints were voiced and as little palpable change ensued.

The burgeoning civil rights movement, North and South, led in 1963–1964 to the passage of the Civil Rights Act of 1964. It placed in the hands of the executive branch of the federal government a tool of great potential in effecting change in the schools. This was Title VI of the law, which forbade the racially discriminatory use of federal funds by schools or other recipients of federal grants. Noncompliance was to be followed by a cut-off of funds.

"This legislation," wrote Martin Luther King, Jr., "was first written in the streets."[12] Action in the streets was still required after passage of the law. During 1965–1969 black children and adults participated in an extraordinarily large number of demonstrative actions on behalf of desegregation. In the South, blacks were almost always the organizing and sole participating parties. In the North, they led actions that were frequently interracial.

Black demonstrative action built a solid bedrock beneath the shifts of public polity. During the last years of the Johnson administration, devotion to civil rights enforcement lagged seriously. The new Nixon administration slowed enforcement even more. Federal courts, including the U.S.

Supreme Court, quickly adopted an activist stance and took up the slack. Between 1968 and 1973 several significant rulings extended the *Brown* doctrine far beyond the confines of the 1954 case.

In 1968 the Supreme Court ruled in *Green* that the time for "deliberate speed" had run out and that "the burden on a school board today is to come forward with a desegregation plan that promises realistically to work, and promises realistically to work *now*." In 1969, in the *Alexander* case, the Court directed the state of Mississippi to desegregate immediately. In October 1969, at the time of the decision, nearly nine out of ten black children in the state attended all-black schools. Within three months the proportion plummeted to one out of ten. In 1971, in the *Swann* case, the Court, taking judicial cognizance of residential segregation, held that desegregation plans need not be limited to neighborhood or "walk-in" schools. It was permissible to assign children to a school to which they needed to be bused or otherwise transported. In 1973 the Court decided *Keyes,* involving Denver, Colorado. Though the ruling was stated in severely limited terms, it all but eliminated the traditional defense of northern school boards that school segregation was simply a neutral response to housing segregation. Once a court found that an element of significant conscious intent to segregate had been present, a presumption of sweeping intent could be inferred. This reduced the burden of proof that had hitherto lain upon the shoulders of plaintiffs in desegregation lawsuits.

Approaching the last quarter of the twentieth century, black Americans were succeeding in placing before public schools the challenge of equal opportunity. Supported increasingly by judicial authority, they demanded revision of traditional structures that were buttressed by racially exclusionary practices. From the perspective of more than a century, black children had more practical opportunity to learn than ever before. Most of these improvements, however, resulted from the initiative of organized blacks. Few, if any, had originated with the schools or the learned professions.

OTHER MINORITIES

Mexican-Americans, native Americans, and Puerto Ricans shared one central characteristic with blacks—all were incorporated originally within American society by force. Historically, Mexican-Americans comprised a low-wage labor supply in the Southwest. Accorded the bottom rung on the social ladder in that area, their children were denied equal educational rights. During the first third of the twentieth century, a number of Texas counties failed to provide any public schools for them. In more cases, extralegally segregated schools were made available. These institutions were startlingly inferior in every major respect. In many Texas communities the black schools were in better shape than those of the

Mexican-Americans before the 1930s. Not until the 1960s, as a consequence of widespread protest movements among Mexican-Americans, did the schools begin to reexamine their practices with respect to this group.

There was no unified native American approach to schooling. Indian responses varied from that of the Cherokees, who in the nineteenth century created an autonomous school system, to that of numerous other Indian peoples who rejected outright any adaptation to white schooling. No Indian tribe, however, was monolithic in its attitude toward white-sponsored schools. Almost everywhere opposing viewpoints on the issue were in evidence. Among the Hopi, for example, the split was profound and enduring.

White society coveted the land occupied by Indians and frequently sought to utilize Indian labor for low wages. Rejected by white society was any thought of adapting to or even countenancing Indian culture. White ways were regarded as civilized, while Indian ways were characterized as savage. Dominant white society—including government, missionaries, and local business interests near the reservations—viewed education as the avenue for destruction of Indian culture. Virtually absent from white discussion was any recognition that a mutually respectful adaptation could be worked out. Only by the late 1960s did that possibility enter the realm of public discussion.

Puerto Ricans did not constitute a major presence in American schools until after World War II. During the 1940s and 1950s average annual net migration from Puerto Rico to the mainland rose sharply to 18,794 and 41,212, respectively. Between 1945 and 1962, the number of Puerto Rican migrants constituted 85 percent of all Puerto Rican migration since 1900.

Puerto Rican children and their teachers were almost complete strangers. In the early postwar years, about three-quarters of the migrant children did not speak English, but far more of their teachers could not speak Spanish. Language barriers were defined by the school system as learning barriers. Since by 1965 Puerto Rican children made up one-fifth of all public school students in New York City, the scale of academic failure was sweeping. Preliminary steps to change traditional practices that seemed to ensure failure began to be taken during the 1960s. Basic to these new currents was the formation of a new cultural and community self-consciousness among Puerto Ricans on the mainland.

As we have seen, the children of the four minorities discussed here shared certain common experiences in the public schools. It would, however, be a major distortion to equate their experiences with those of other minorities. The fate of each minority was determined in large part by the circumstances existing at the time that minority entered American history. During the late nineteenth century the American economy absorbed illiterate workers more easily than it did seventy-five years later.

The pre–Civil War immigrant typically came from northern and western Europe. While the nascent public school system kept the poorest Irish immigrants at a distance, most other immigrant children entered the schools with little resistance. After the Civil War, there was no "typical immigrant" response to public schooling. When Russian Jews streamed to the United States between 1880 and 1920, they viewed American schools from a perspective of having been officially excluded from many Russian schools. They also arrived at a time when American industry was developing numerous white-collar jobs and thereby a labor market for high school and college educated workers. In addition, by and large, Jewish students were welcome in the schools.

German Catholics who came to Wisconsin and the Midwest in large numbers between 1850 and 1890 established parochial schools that were conducted in the German language. When the state legislature outlawed the use of any language in school other than English, the Germans organized a political campaign and the law was repealed. Poles in Buffalo also conducted parochial schools in the Polish language in a largely successful effort to conserve their cultural heritage.

European immigrants were better able to provide their children with a public school education because of advantages they held over blacks, Mexican-Americans, native Americans, and Puerto Ricans. The Europeans came to occupy higher economic positions, most of them unconnected with the degree of education attained. They possessed full political rights in their communities and exercised them, although in varying degrees. And their right to attend public schools was never challenged in court. The four other minorities, however, were consigned to the lowest levels of the American economy, including forced labor. Political means to remedy community problems were denied them for many years. They were subjected to legal segregation, both by statute and school board action.[13] Asian-Americans, especially the Chinese, were somewhere in between both groups. While they were, for the most part, voluntary immigrants, they suffered from legally segregated schools in California and from extraordinary discriminations in community life.

ONE OR TWO MELTING POTS?

Once we were asked to believe that American life shaped a single, homogeneous breed of people, each equal to the other and all sharing a common culture. It is no improvement, however, now to be told that there are, after all, *two* melting pots—one for dominant Anglo whites and the other for all the minorities in American society.

The new myth of two melting pots imagines that all minorities share a common fate. They are "ethnics." Anglo whites, presumably, are nonethnics. The old myth erected Anglo culture as the measure of all others. The new one performs the same task by staking out mere footnotes and appendixes for each separate minority, while reserving the page proper for the "main" story. Such a portrayal is said to document the cultural pluralism of America. Somehow, the plurality of pots is to result in their equality.

A strong point of the older concept of one melting pot was its stress on the factual integration of immigrant and native in the general economy and, to a lesser extent, in politics. It erred, however, in believing that the absorption of minorities expanded their rights or even their dignity. Just how the minorities were absorbed—or not absorbed—has been in large part a product of history. There would seem to be no warrant in American history for single *or* plural melting pots.

Rather than draining the individuality of each minority group in an effort to create a faceless and anonymous mass, it would seem more serviceable to distinguish between minority groups and view each as embodying a distinctive set of experiences and traditions. Clearly, the experience of minority groups is differentially salient for national development. Black history is central to many basic issues in American history. The importance of Slavic workers in building American basic industries was very great, if unheralded. The impact of Scandinavian groups has been more regional and less national. And so on. Not to be overlooked are the groups that remained less than a majority but avoided the label of minority. The English immigrants apparently lost all signs of being an ethnic group.

RACISM, CULTURE, AND SOCIETY

Few immigrant groups escaped altogether the hurt of discrimination and prejudice. Religious and nationality factors provided grounds for deprivation of immigrant groups. But a special fury has been reserved for blacks, Mexican-Americans, native Americans, and Puerto Ricans. This is the fury of racism, a doctrine of racial or ethnic superiority, including advocacy of differential rewards based on presumed differences. By incorporating the allocation of differential rewards into institutions such as the economy, education, and government, dominant white society created an impersonal system that served racist purposes very effectively.

Cultural denigration of certain minorities by the dominant society formed part of the racial system. However, while minority cultures were regarded as part of the inferior group to be scorned, these were lesser targets. In American history, conquest of minorities was motivated by desire for material gain rather than by ideological hatred of unfamiliar cultures.

The proper sphere of the schools would seem to be in the cultural area, although it must be realized that the cultural aspect of minority status is not the most fundamental.

MULTICULTURAL EDUCATION[14]

Race has been part of the curriculum ever since we have had public schools. Before the Civil War, American schools accepted and perpetuated racial values. Textbooks treated blacks and other minorities as undesirables. Blacks were often excluded from public schools—North and South—and, when admitted, were frequently forced to sit in a separate part of the classroom.

After the destruction of slavery, exclusion and/or denigration of minority values continued. Except for a moment of enlightenment during Reconstruction, the years 1870–1920 were a low point in the history of American race relations.

During the past half century, interracial attendance has become a reality in many schools. Today, one-seventh of all children attend an interracial or interethnic public school. Yet the heritage of the past still weighs heavily upon the American classroom. Practices originally created to serve racist purposes linger on as thoughtless monuments to the past. Textbooks remain largely untouched by newer currents of thought. The curriculum is still inadequately responsive to recent research, especially in the social sciences. But the greatest impediment to essential change is the ethnic isolation that still characterizes the American classroom.

Over the past fifty years, interracial education has taken several forms. The *human relations* approach evolved during the 1920s and held the field, so to speak, for a generation. The method essentially was based on the concept of tolerance. It was a defensive teaching strategy, aimed principally at counterbalancing an overbearing majority sentiment that rejected equally differences of color, language, and national custom. Much attention was paid to explaining cultural peculiarities.

Interpersonal conflict was seen as a clash of single individuals. Prejudice was regarded as a failing of individuals who lacked an ability to see others as individuals. It was hoped that this lack could be remedied by the acquisition of information about the minority object, too weak to prevail against the majority; thus, the human relations approach was inevitably moralistic in its appeal.

A second approach may be called *interracial*. This method frankly acknowledged the fact of anti-Negro prejudice and distinguished it from the area of simple culture conflict. The unique role of the Negro in American life was seen as a central distinguishing characteristic of American society. Concern with individual prejudice extended now to exploration of discrimination. Disability and deprivation were found to be aspects of group existence in America. Negroes were seen as constituting a subculture with its own distinctive development. Great efforts were expended on discovering the manifold forms of group discrimination against Negroes and Indians especially. Discrimination against Negroes was found to be far more resistant than that based on religion, language, or national origin.

In the classroom, spreading celebration of events such as Negro History Week illustrated the fact of separate existence. It also signaled an affirmation of Negro accomplishment and initiative. To be sure, it was in the segregated black classroom that the celebration was most likely to adopt such a tone. Only in occasional large urban schools, integrated in some sense, were similar events celebrated.

The interracial approach was more realistic than the human relations approach, though it was also defensive in orientation. Children were taught the disability of color in American life. But they failed to learn to conceive of a world without this disability. So far-fetched did such a world seem that the possibility was not discussed.

Today, a third approach—the *human rights* approach—is in the making. This method presents group differences affirmatively, and its ideology is an unshrinking proclamation of universal equality. Essentially, it is a belief that members of ethnic groups have the absolute right to define their own ethnic status: They will be what they decide. It is neither separatism nor desegregation but pluralism with equality. The goal is not to be like others or even with others as a matter of principle.

Assimilation is rejected because it assumes lack of worth on the part of the minority. Increasingly, however, the group is viewed in terms of its dignity. (*Dignus* is Latin for "worth.") Integration as such is rejected as too prescriptive for everyone; instead it becomes one other option that some minority people can select—if they wish. In fact, of course, the option to integrate has almost always remained a white prerogative. Pluralism without equality, as Kenneth B. Clark has noted, is hardly more than a caste system, wherein each subculture has the right to exist so long as it keeps its "place."

The new movement for human rights thus strains at the seams of the traditional racial order. Even national boundaries are overtaken. If the object now is to win those rights that are common to all mankind, then a world-wide bond comes to bind all men together. The movement for human rights is therefore internationalist as well; consequently, one hears of a Third World—a combination of people in the former European colonies along with black Americans, Mexican-Americans, native Americans, and Asian-Americans.

None of the approaches discussed above is unconnected with the others. One may stress cultural distinctiveness in any of them. It will, however, take much hard thought by school people to formulate an effective response to the challenge of human rights. Some may be put off by the very newness of the subject. Alas, we cannot wait until this subject "settles down." It is up to us to examine the posture that schools have taken in considering human rights and to create instructional strategies and materials. That is the purpose of this book.

3. Our Common Humanity

Ella Griffin

The first cry of a newborn baby in Chicago or Zamboango, in Amsterdam or Rangoon, has the same pitch and key, each saying, "I am! I have come through! I belong! I am a member of the Family." [1]

THE MORAL CONCEPT

Since the beginning of recorded history, a growing recognition of the oneness of humankind has led to recurrent expressions of basic principles of equality, freedom, and justice. When Alexander the Great disavowed the assertion of Aristotle, his teacher, that slavery was an immutable and benevolent institution imposed by nature, he planted the idea of a new moral concept—that all people everywhere should be considered to be one community and one order, sharing a common humanity. And gradually, the idea took root.

Throughout the ages, more and more of the peoples of the world have endorsed this concept and reaffirmed their faith in human rights—in the equality and dignity of every human being—and have used these precepts in their efforts to bring about a peaceful and happy coexistence with their fellows. For it has always been necessary for people to define and come to agreement about universal principles, and to establish them as ideals to guide the conduct of the whole society. These agreements have become part of a universal humanitarian tradition that has found expression in various struggles for freedom and equality all over the world.

THE GROWING WORLD COMMUNITY

Present-day events are forcing people in all the nations on earth to change more rapidly than ever before. People everywhere are traveling more and are traveling farther from their homes. Consequently, they have more face-to-face encounters with an increasing variety of others.

Modern technology has stepped up the pace of communication in all sorts of ways. The top tunes on Broadway are almost immediately heard in the capital cities of five continents. All over the world young people, and indeed people of all ages, are wearing blue jeans, or caftans, or dashikis, or ponchos, or saris to suit their moods and their modes of living. A new medical discovery, such as polio vaccine, becomes available almost immediately to people everywhere. Food shortages in one country can be offset by imports from another, and everywhere people are learning to enjoy foods they never tasted until recently.

Increasingly, people who are dissimilar in their values, feelings, and behaviors are learning to respect and to live with one another's differences. Value systems are growing and changing as people learn to understand themselves better by getting to know a broader spectrum of others. Gradually, they are beginning to recognize their common denominators.

Children are aware of these common denominators to a greater extent than many teachers recognize, for children are learning through many media, and much of what they learn helps them to understand the one-human-family concept. Teachers need to be able to capitalize on the wide variety of learnings that children gain from influences such as television, movies, and travel. And teachers need to be skillful at coping with the education—and the miseducation—that children receive outside school. Actually, all of us are similarly influenced, for not only children but, to a great extent, people generally are learning that human beings everywhere confront similar problems, share like aspirations, and struggle for self-fulfillment within our growing world community.

RESTORING CULTURE TO WHOLENESS

The paradox is that while there is a growing recognition of our common humanity, at the same time there is a growing insistence by minority groups that special attention be paid to their separate and distinct ethnic identities. In response, thoughtful people, even within minority groups, are sounding a warning that understandable and valuable as increased attention to diversity may be, it could be counterproductive if taken to the extreme. Under such circumstances, Americans could come to see themselves as constituting a kind of anthropological museum rather than a single society with a common citizenship. A Chinese-American professor of my acquaintance feels very strongly that a single-directional approach to problems of ethnicity has created little pigeonholes into which we separate you and me, black and white, Asian and Caucasian, and so on. She believes that our goals should be rather to explore the commonality of life experiences.

Social scientists warn us that it may not be cultural diversity that is basically responsible for our "ethnic" problems, but rather the way that individuals regard the "others" whom they see as very different from themselves and forget the fact of our common humanity. Lee Anderson reminds us that

> to some people the very notion of common membership in the human species poses a threat, for they feel a need to see themselves and their own particular group as sharply distinct, even superior to the rest of mankind. Or, perhaps through beliefs and attitudes conditioned by racial, religious, or national experiences, they may view the concept of a global society as undermining their identity. Such feelings seldom respond to rational arguments. Perhaps all that can be said is there is a need to recognize their existence and work toward the reduction of the number who hold them by a better education at an early age.[2]

Ruth Benedict helped us to realize that if the emphasis is too much on the needs of discrete groups within a society, the individual may become enslaved by his or her own culture.[3] For no culture is static. Cultures change. They evolve from the people who live within them and, consequently, they are infinite in their variety.

REMAKING THE HUMAN INSIDE

This imperative for the schools to respond to cultural diversity, while at the same time recognizing their students' common humanity, seems self-contradictory to many of those involved. For traditionally our schools have been geared to the melting-pot idea aimed at fitting children into one mold. This has precluded the wholesome development of *every* child in terms of his own individuality.

Gunnar Myrdal feels that as we seek to recognize our common humanity and to act accordingly, we Americans need to "remake the human inside."[4] If this is true, then how can we go about remaking the human inside an ordinary American—in our case, an ordinary American teacher—so as to enable him to recognize the universal nature of every individual? How can teachers learn to cherish the differences and also the commonalities among individuals and groups of people? How can teachers learn to discover ways of using all of the commonalities as positive influences?

Humanizing Education

This is not easy, for a major problem teachers face today is how to cope with depersonalization. Teachers in the United States, as in many other parts of the world, are caught up in bureaucratic mass procedures that have dehumanizing effects on both teachers and students. The problem of promoting the idea of common humanity and acting accordingly, while at the same time regimenting children in conformance with predetermined goals, seems contradictory. Furthermore, the insistence of minority groups on special attention to their separate and distinct ethnic identities confuses the issue. Unless educators realize that cultural differences *can* be maintained, while at the same time basic standards and qualities that unite people are recognized and cultivated, they may view multicultural education as an impossible dream.

Confronted with the dilemma, many teachers feel that they are expected to steer a course between Scylla and Charybdis. This is especially true in the big cities. On the one hand, teachers are expected to follow the outmoded assimilation policy that requires all children to conform to traditional education norms geared to strictly middle-class values. On the other hand, they are expected to devise effective innovative models designed to serve the real needs of their culturally diverse pupils.

Unfortunately, many teachers find it difficult, if not impossible, to cope. For, like other people, they reflect the limitations of their environment. Nevertheless, it should be understood that special teachers are not needed for the children of various ethnic and social groups. Rather, all teachers need to be trained to work effectively with all children, and to see each child as an individual, without regard for racial or religious group or social situation but mindful of it in each case.

I have said that, in order to do this, teachers must "remake the human inside," and so learn to cope with racial problems and to understand, practice, and elicit democratic behavior. Given the two-pronged objective of helping teachers and students recognize both their human diversity and their common humanity, how can teachers work systematically to counteract the negative forces that continue to impede progress toward that goal? Actually, some teachers are already succeeding admirably, although many others feel deluged by the complexity of the problems that confront them every day. Volumes have been written about the ills of our society that gave rise to these problems. Less has been said about what teachers can do in the face of them.

Psychological Issues

I believe that *aware* is the key word. Teachers must be aware of themselves as individuals and of their own attitudes and convictions, their own prejudices and biases. Teachers need to ask themselves: Have I deep feelings—one way or another—about the common-humanity concept? Have I personally experienced a strong feeling of the oneness of mankind?

Do I *really* believe that all men are created equal? And do I understand that, by the same token, *every* person should be seen as a distinct individual with particular traits and characteristics, and that *every* child brings to the classroom—as do I, the teacher—his own culture and the particular traits and characteristics that derive from his personal experiences and from his determination, whether or not he expresses it, to be himself?

During this process of introspection, teachers need to examine their attitudes and their unguarded reactions to students whom they see as "culturally different." For example, how does the "Anglo" teacher *really* feel about the "nonwhite" children in the class? In moments of stress, has the teacher ever lashed out and shouted at a child, "You dirty Indian!" (or "black fool" or "stupid Chicano")? Or has the teacher had a strong impulse to speak that way to a minority-group child who, at the moment, is the scapegoat? Is the teacher *really* civilized?

Such self-examination helps teachers to assess their own personal integrity as well as their own capacity for the kind of fair and rational behavior that should be characteristic of all good teachers. Indeed, a key issue with reference to the acceptance of the concept of our common humanity is the extent to which those in charge of the process are themselves wholesome human beings. Unless teachers can free themselves to respect cultural differences, they will have little or no success in helping students to cope with *multicultural conditions* in schools and communities. In other words, teachers must see themselves as members of the human family in order to be able to initiate others into it.

Sociological Issues

In order to create in their classrooms an atmosphere of liberty and justice for all, teachers need to be aware of major sociological, as well as psychological, factors that condition their success. Outstanding among these conditioning factors are the characteristics of the local communities. This is especially true in big cities, with their ethnically and culturally diverse populations. Unfortunately, it is in the cities that teachers are often "sociological strangers." They are *in* the cities, but not *of* them.

Some city teachers come from small towns and rural areas, bringing with them their own parochial and chauvinistic habits and values. In their hometowns, the neighborhoods were generally almost homogeneous. But the big cities have a variety of distinct neighborhoods based on ethnic and cultural characteristics. When confronted with so many diversities in the classroom, or when isolated in the classroom with children whose cultural traits are foreign to them, teachers often become bewildered and desperate.

In the cities, the neighborhoods may stretch haphazardly across a metropolitan area, or they may be in perpendicular clusters of high-rise apartment houses, or concentrated in a few blocks. To understand the various cultures that are predominant in such areas, and to learn to relate happily to the people who compose them, teachers need to get to know the neighborhoods and to see the communities from the inside. Vicarious study may be useful, but it is not enough. Firsthand experience is vital.

The extent of the family's moral influence on children is a valid concern of the schools. Accordingly, teachers need to be acquainted with the patterns of family life within the communities they serve. However, generalizations about family life based on racial or cultural linkages are untenable. Each family has its own unique characteristics, values, goals, and human interactions that shape the lives and attitudes of its members. Many teachers of multiethnic groups who have taken time to get to know the families of their students are finding, to their surprise, more common denominators than cultural differences.

The Predominant Moral Issue

Racial equality is undoubtedly the predominant moral issue of our times. Outstanding news stories on racial prejudice and persecution are exposed almost instantaneously to the world community. It is true that, world-wide, there is on the whole an increasing tempo in the movement toward the recognition of the oneness of humankind. But prejudice based on race and color is still a pervasive influence that threatens to impede this movement.

Teachers need to become aware of the misconceptions that perpetuate prejudice. Do they, in looking at minority-group people, regard them basically as human beings—as personal and unique individuals—or do they think in terms of stereotypes? Do they see myths as myths, or myths as facts? The best way to dispel myths is to become well informed and intelligent about the issues in question—to learn the truth. Looking at the question from the world-wide point of view, in terms of people everywhere, Juan Comas of Mexico said:

> So far as can be seen, few of the physical traits used for the classification of human races have functional values for the individuals displaying them. Our own civilization attaches special importance to the color of the skin, and relatively dark pigmentation is a mark of difference condemning numerous human groups to contemp, ostracism, and a debased social status.
>
> In certain persons, color prejudice is so strong to give rise to almost pathological phobias. They are not innate, but reflect, in exaggerate form, the prejudices of the social environment. To maintain that a man is an inferior human being because he is black (or "brown" or "red" or "yellow") is as ridiculous as contending that a white horse will necessarily be faster than a

black horse. Nevertheless, however little basis there may be for color prejudice, the importance of the resultant attitudes and behavior is indisputable.[5]

President Julius Nyerere of Tanzania often serves as spokesman for all
of black Africa. He says that people of Africa and of African descent have
always had one thing in common—an experience of discrimination and
humiliation imposed on them because of their African origin. He opposes
racial thinking, but warns the world that as long as black people anywhere
continue to be oppressed on the grounds of their color, black people
everywhere will stand together in opposition to that oppression. But he
also urges all victims of color prejudice to avoid color prejudice in their
own attitudes and behavior. His rationale is that if Africans react to the
continued need to defend their position as black men by regarding themselves as different from the rest of mankind, they will weaken themselves,
and the racialists of the world will have scored their biggest triumph.

Ideals notwithstanding, ethnocentrism, the feeling of a difference between "my own kind" and "outsiders," and concomitant patterns of
discrimination persist today in our society, as we have seen, and indeed,
throughout the world. For an individual's commitment to the values and
customs of his own group, and his tendency to be prejudiced—or not—
toward members of the out-group, are developed early in life through the
influence of the home and the in-group.

Frank Jennings believes that the continuing challenge to the schools is
to provide an education as various as the diversity of the country, an
education that will allow the least advantaged, the most gifted, and the
ordinary to grow together, to learn to communicate (and to have significant experiences and feelings and opinions to communicate), to be able to
work and live in communities that are not merely tolerant of, but
genuinely hospitable to, uniqueness and even heresy. But he emphasizes
his feeling that these communities must at the same time be capable of
cherishing the ordinary and the commonplace.[6]

PERSPECTIVES

To help them meet the challenge, educators need to get new perspectives on our multicultural society by taking a Janus-faced view of history.
This is not to say that one can expect that history will repeat itself. The
futurists tell us that mainly for two reasons, we cannot replay the past,
first, because of the present world-wide shift toward social diversity, and
second, because of the accelerated tempo at which problems reach flash
point today.[7] Nevertheless, a backward look into the past often points up
the universality of humankind in terms of both time and place. Obviously,
it is impossible even to begin to discuss the many points of the past that

are of special interest to us. Each individual will have his own constellation of events and heroes that, viewed in the light of present events, provide new prospectives for understanding the universality of humankind.

All the continents on earth have nurtured conflicting races and civilizations; and wherever they wandered, the various peoples have always settled down, as they did in this country, and become a part of the larger whole. These peoples have always preferred their native customs and language. And they have always found ways of bringing about a synthesis by reconciling the particular with the universal.

More than 2,500 years ago, the Persian prophet Zoroaster said: "That nature is only good which shall not do unto another whatever is not good unto its own self." As we learn more about the religions of the ancients, we come to realize that the golden rule is universal. It is found in the doctrines of all the great religions of the world, and it is a natural common denominator for teachers in classrooms where a variety of religious groups are represented.

Many people now regard as hopelessly romantic the movement embraced by intellectuals during the Age of Enlightenment in Europe of the seventeenth and eighteenth centuries. Yet that movement's followers were concerned, as are so many young people today, with interrelated concepts of God, reason, nature, and man. Jean Jacques Rousseau, at about the midpoint of the Age of Enlightenment, stressed the fundamental unity of all people, despite their different cultures, and saw a single universal humanity above all individual societies. It was Rousseau who first sought to understand his fellow man by asking himself, "Who am I?"—a point of view reflected in the *awareness* approach that we have been discussing here. It was Rousseau who first defined the individual person in terms of his intrinsic worth. He insisted that the mere fact of being a human being gave to everyone the right to have an education, knowledge of others, human rights, and the esteem of one's fellow man regardless of origin, race, or creed. Rousseau made a vivid impression on his contemporaries by proposing a method of teaching based on respect for the child and an appreciation of his sensitivities. All of these were revolutionary doctrines in his time. It is only today that we can really recognize the universality of Rousseau's philosophy and understand clearly its implications for us here and now.

Norman Cousins has long been helping us to make bridges in our thinking about the past and the present. He believes that

despite the historians, there has been only one age of man. It is the age of primitive man. The beginning of the age of civilized man, when it comes, will be marked by his political, philosophical and spiritual awareness of himself as a member of a world species with world needs and with the capacity and desire to create world institutions to meet the needs. Humankind need not sacrifice the nation to create such institutions. It need only recognize and assert an allegiance of humans to one another beyond national boundaries, and to do those things in the human interest that the nation as an organization is incapable of doing.[8]

For years, Barbara Ward has been extremely vocal about the needs of the world community, exhorting her readers and listeners to act with the well-being of the whole human family in mind. She is in the vanguard of prescient individuals who, I believe, through their awareness of themselves and of us all as "members of a world species," mark the beginning of "the age of civilized man," as Cousins has described it. In one of her most widely read books, Ward says:

> We have become a single human community. Most of the energies of our society tend towards unity—the energy of science and technological change, the energy of curiosity and research, of self-interest and economics, the energy—in many ways the most violent of them all—the energy of potential aggression and destruction. We have become neighbors in terms of inescapable physical proximity and instant communication. We are neighbors in facets of our industrialization and in the pattern of our urbanization. Above all, we are neighbors in the risk of total destruction.[9]

Recent happenings, especially during the seventies, have accelerated a world-wide understanding of Ward's point of view, and an acceptance of the reality of man's common humanity and interdependence.

One of the strongest of the rising chorus of voices among the "vanguard group" is that of anthropologist Margaret Mead. In 1971 Dr. Mead discussed at some length her views with reference to certain agreed-upon universals that make possible the continued coexistence of the nations of the world, each of which has something valuable to contribute to the whole. She said that she believes it is possible for us to cherish the past and to save our own special and diverse traditions—our mother tongues and our culturally specialized aesthetic styles and religious visions, and the different symbols that have united men born in the same period and that still bind the generations together—if we lay enough emphasis on what all these divided groups share: a future to which we must all commit ourselves with an increasing spirit of interdependence.[10]

Early in the 1970s, when a group of students and teachers was asked to suggest the kinds of learning materials they thought would best prepare young people for life in the year 2001, two of the items they cited, within a total list of sixteen, were materials that will help maturing individuals understand themselves, and materials that will help them avoid ethnocentrism. Harold Howe II predicts that in the year 2001 the White House Conference on Education will observe that

> young Americans are arguing that rather than competing to see who can get the most for himself or his country, mankind must learn to share the resources

it has. They are strongly internationalistic in their views, and they translate these principles into the everyday affairs of the colleges they attend and the schools they want for their children.[11]

TOWARD SCIENTIFIC HUMANISM

Attention has been called to the fact that when the concept of the universality of mankind is broached as a national issue, there is still a great deal of resistance and, all too often, downright animosity. We should not expect that it will be easy to demythologize people, or to effect rapid change in deeply rooted habits and convictions. We know that attitudes cannot be legislated. But we also know that behavior can be modified, that discriminatory and inhuman behavior, whenever it is discovered, can and must be changed in accordance with the basic human rights of every individual. In this country, and throughout the world, young people are the bright hope for stepping up the pace of change for the better. And in fact, it is evident that Howe's prediction for the future is being activated to a considerable degree right now.

Someone has said that "modern man needs to be intellectually voracious in order to survive." This is so true! Teachers need to become true intellectuals, people who use the power of the mind to grasp ideas and relationships, and scientific humanists who see themselves in relation to all mankind, complementing their environment wherever they may be. Beginning in early childhood, children should develop as true philosophers— people who regulate their thinking and, ideally, their lives by the light of reason. With children this is quite natural, for all children, like the Elephant's Child of Kipling's *Just-So Stories,* have "an insatiable curiosity."

Carl Sandburg has provided us with a lyrical summary of the way in which I hope teachers of the future will view the concept of man's common humanity:

> To the question, "What will the story be of the Family of Man across the near or far future?" some would reply, "for the answers, read, if you can, the strange and baffling eyes of youth."

> There is only man in the world,
> and his name is All Men.
> There is only one woman in the world,
> and her name is All Women.
> There is only one child in the world,
> and the child's name is All Children.[12]

Part 2

MYTHS AND REALITIES OF MULTICULTURAL SOCIETIES

Part 2

MYTHS AND REALITIES OF MULTICULTURAL SOCIETIES

4. The Student as Immigrant

The Myth of Americanization

Rudolf B. Schmerl

That ours is a nation of immigrants is an observation often acknowledged but rarely explored. The champions of the social traditions of northern Europe, specifically of England, have sought to "Americanize" our increasingly diverse population through such means as immigration restrictions, segregation of the "unassimilable," political maneuvers called balancing the ticket or splitting the pie, and in particular, the educational system and its processes.

Chapter 2 of this book details early efforts to eradicate the cultural roots of minority groups, and the failure of those attempts. More recently, "Americanization" has come to include such gestures toward our diversity as Black History Week, "units" of study of Indian tribes, an occasional picture of an American of Oriental ancestry in a textbook, fuller treatment of East European immigration. But the practical significance of our intercontinental origins is still much more apparent in our electoral process than in our educational system. Our politics cultivates the immigrant and ethnic ethos as a matter of simple realism. Our education system seems to be capable, so far, of no more than cursory, half-embarrassed hints about the diversity of our origins and experiences, memories and loyalties, fears, hopes, bitterness, and pride. Cultural ties persist, despite pressures to weaken, even to obliterate them; and yet schools and teachers tend to function, not as expressions of such ties, even less as harmonious with them, but rather as the instrument of the old colonial culture, attempting to shape all students to fit a common mold.

ALL ARE IMMIGRANTS

The failure of "Americanization" is hardly a secret; the furor, rhetorically about busing and actually about racial integration, is perhaps only the most obvious proof of the concept's emptiness. But a myth's longevity appears unrelated to the evidence against it. Schools are still our society's basic device for "socialization" of our young people; "socialization" still means rounding and smoothing cultural as well as individual differences toward a preconceived goal, that of one people. I want to argue here that educators need to learn what politicians know about Americans, namely, that we are not a people at all. Further, I want to suggest, not entirely metaphorically, that the most native of American children are in a kind of immigrant status in their schools, from the day they enter to the day they leave. And I propose to be personal about this, for my credentials as an immigrant are impeccable, notarized by the Department of Justice on my certificate of naturalization.

The "New Boy"

The happiest of the circumstances surrounding my arrival in America—specifically, Ellis Island—was that I was a small boy, and therefore as malleable as Play Doh. I did not know that, of course; a child's identity seems no less fixed to him than an adult's. What I did know was that I could not speak, read, or understand a word of English, that my clothes did not look like those of American boys, and that I was very frightened. In this condition I entered the fourth grade in Princeton, New Jersey.

I learned English. It was the English of a small college town of the 1930s, by no means untouched by the convulsions occurring all over the world—what, after all, was Albert Einstein doing up the block on Mercer Street?—but still, as I remember it, gentle and placid. I was welcomed as a curiosity by both teachers and children. On my first day, my teacher assigned a boy to me—the boys all had to take turns with me each day, as with a cripple—to teach me English word by word. He took me to the nearest object and said, over and over until I had satisfied him with my repetition of it: "Radiator." That afternoon I was taught baseball in the schoolyard. I don't remember being troubled by the lack of connection.

It was not the first time in my life that I had been the new boy, but there were many more times to come. There was the fifth grade, or a portion of it, in upper Manhattan, as unlike Princeton as Europe had been. My Princeton English had to be unlearned quickly. But before I had learned the English of Amsterdam Avenue, I was in New Orleans, another foreign country. Two grades, two schools, and I was back in New York, starting high school a year before I should have, not because I was smart but because of misinterpretation of a transcript. Thirty or so years ago boys didn't wear long pants in New Orleans. They did in De Witt Clinton High School, all 6,000 of them, and my knickers attracted the comments of what seemed, that first day, more than that number. I got rid of the knickers. A little later I got rid of my version of a Louisiana drawl, also a handicap on Gun Hill Road in the Bronx. But I had no time to learn more than a New York intonation, for two years later I was in Toledo, Ohio, where I finished high school. I like to think that I was too old, by that time, to acquire a midwestern nasal twang. I know, at any rate, that I pronounce many words incorrectly—not with an eastern or southern or midwestern accent, just incorrectly. I think I learned to read English more quickly than to speak it, and so I've come to regard English pronunciation pretty much as a matter of luck.

The "New Generation"

All that was long ago. The other night my three sons, all in the same high school, were laughing at dinner about a boy named Epi. It turned out that Epi was an exchange student from Europe. My sons thought him ridiculous for his hair (too short on the neck), his raincoat (belted), and (with the contempt only teenagers can muster) his briefcase. A real briefcase, handle, lock, impossible to carry casually. Not unnaturally, I was reminded of my experiences, and to mitigate their scorn I told my knickers story, in some detail. It was a mistake. I proved only that I had always been out of it. The conversation turned to the other part of school, the part they never laugh about.

Shortly thereafter, my wife and I attended "Capsule Night" at the high school. We were given sixteen-minute versions by our sons' teachers of what they are up to in the classrooms—the teachers, not our sons. These teachers used the medical "we" when they described what "we" were learning, very much as a nurse asks a patient how "we" are feeling; but it was clear enough whom they were talking about. The teachers all seemed familiar to me. One was nice, one was surly, another was forgettable. An English teacher made fun of *The Song of Roland,* but told us that he didn't treat the poem that way in class. A music teacher had us sing a couple of bars and asked interesting questions about polyphony: "Where did man discover polyphony? Did he, as some people think, find it in the Far East?" No one interrupted to ask the teacher what kind of creatures he thought inhabited Asia. A physics teacher, breathless from working his paraphernalia, admitted that he just didn't have time to say much about Copernicus; "we" were too busy drawing charts of the movements of the planets. And a fine-arts teacher bubbled in the approved manner about her slides of the approved monuments. "Nothing has changed in thirty years," I told my wife as we left.

On reflection, I think I was mistaken again. I was not the typical American schoolboy thirty years ago, but I certainly was a type: a B student, mostly. My problems were social; more specifically, they were the innumerable adjustments I had to make to each new situation until I learned who was who and what was what. I fought when I had to, which was more often than I can believe now, and I ran when I had to, although I was often late in recognizing the need for that expedient. But with only minor exceptions, I had no particular problems in classroom after that first day in Princeton. I wasn't turned off, I wasn't alienated, and if I didn't like math, it didn't matter; I got by. There were no new kids, apparently, to the teachers.

Or so, without thinking about it, I sensed. What, after all, was more new about me in my geometry class than about the one black boy who was also in it? What was novel about my name or appearance (once I had shed the knickers) in De Witt Clinton, where I remember exactly one visibly Anglo-Saxon student? Once my English was more or less indistinguishable from that of my classmates, I was no more an immigrant than any other boy, and of course considerably less so than those who were not white. In some of my classes in the Toledo high school, there was a quiet, charming girl, a native of Toledo, who was Chinese. She was an excellent student. She was also exotic, as permanently foreign to the school as if she had been an exchange student. The black students, as always, had their own status. They produced more than their quota for the sports they were allowed to participate in—which did not include swimming—and, in the two years I was there, one black student per year was admitted to the National Honor Society. When, however, in my senior year a school precedent was set with the election of the first black captain of the football team, another precedent was broken, for he did not take the Homecoming Queen to the Sadie Hawkins Day dance. Now that I recall these antiquities from my mind's storage closet, it seems to me that it was all rather like Ellis Island, where immigrants also kept their distance from one another through the traditional barriers of color, religion, dietary habits, and notions of their social status—and, more importantly, where we were "processed" toward arrival on the mainland, where our initiation into the first phase of Americanization would begin.

A Place to Wait

Ellis Island was a place to wait. We had waited before: in Germany, where we had waited almost too long; in Czechoslovakia, both before and after Mr. Chamberlain achieved peace in our time, first in the Sudetenland and then, after a fearful night at a railway station waiting for a delayed train while the German troops marched south, in Prague, where the officials had problems of their own; and even, for a few days, in Rotterdam, for the ship that was to carry us to safety. Always there were papers;

always there were complications. The world of officialdom, like the world at large, is ill prepared to accommodate peculiarities. You are supposed to be, first of all, well and whole, so that you can be at the right office at the top of the stairs at the right time, for which you should have almost an inbred instinct. Then it helps to have acute hearing, for officialdom speaks indistinctly and hurriedly, tired to your exhaustion of repeating the endless instructions, bored to your death by what it is doing. Your memory should be nothing less than perfect, for the labyrinth of offices and corridors, streets and buildings, forms and functionaries would baffle even a Theseus equipped with Ariadne's thread. But these are merely the proper physical prerequisites. More important are the biographical ones. Our case was complicated by my mother's birth in Mexico and her father's in Russia, facts difficult for officialdom to digest within prevailing definitions of what we were supposed to be.

Learning to Blend

Looking back, I can see now how well trained I was, how eager, for the structure and order of the American school system of the late thirties and early forties. Once I could speak English, I could find a place for myself in almost any classroom anywhere. All I really had to do, East, South, or Middle West, was to wait for my novelty to tarnish, and then I could blend, more or less, with the other children, at least until the next move. Over and over again I found myself, without knowing it then, in schools like Ellis Island, surrounded by wire fences or not, a potpourri of immigrants processed by a bored officialdom toward arrival on the mainland of adulthood that shimmered across the water—for me, the wide ocean of college; for some others, the narrow channel between them and the factory's employment office.

My Americanization outside of the classroom, to whatever extent it occurred, was something intensely personal, as is true, I am sure, of the Americanization of any immigrant. But what happened inside the classroom was no more personal than the flag in the auditorium, the occasional print of Stuart's portrait of Washington, the obligatory singing (in New Orleans) of the national anthem. We were all being fitted to enter American society. The school did not, could not, "socialize" us, for we did that ourselves, on our own terms, it naturalized us. Citizenship, a notion too distant from the inmates of Ellis Island to find expression even as a dream, was similarly remote from our status in school, for a citizen is an adult. That is what the school prepared us for, and pretty much as Ellis Island did: by making us wait. And, as in Ellis Island, there were no real alternatives, not, certainly, for children desperate for order and structure.

What's left of all those endless hours in all those dreary classrooms? Transcripts, like my old passport, marking a passage, not a place; and finally, a diploma bearing a mark of musty officialdom, like that imprinted next to the adolescent portrait on my naturalization certificate. I learned quickly, I think, what I had to do to be allowed to wait with the rest and thus get my transcripts filled in—my passport stamped—at the right places at the right times. But I recall very little of the details. Had they mattered, perhaps they would be memorable.

For a long time I remembered all those schools I went to with gratitude rather than with any other sentiment. Like Ellis Island, they had let me through. Like the larger America they represented, they had made room for me. They had demanded, at least of me, only the possible, and they had rewarded me with the certificate required to search out still other possibilities. But these were the cloudy and infrequent generalities of a man inclined to think himself lucky, and they did not ultimately survive the almost daily sight of my own children under pressure. They began to walk rather than run to school, and then to come home like released prisoners. And they stared at two-columned pages when once they had immersed themselves in books. The older they grew, the more the tension mounted. I still could not remember my own term papers, lab reports, math assignments, and the infinite number of tests and quizzes; but how, I wondered, could it have been different in my generation? When so much else had remained unchanged, why couldn't I recall how beleaguered I must have felt?

Waiting for What?

What has changed in thirty years—to correct my too quick declaration to my wife, and to try to answer my own question—is not the school but the students. Much has been made of the sheer numbers of students in our schools today, and I am prepared to believe that, after some mysterious saturation level has been reached, further quantitative changes induce qualitative ones, as happens with rats confined spatially but not otherwise. But the schools I attended in New York were badly overcrowded, even in 1943. In many of our classes in De Witt Clinton we had to share our seats and desks with another boy. But we were waiting in school for life to get better—for the war to end before we would have to fight in it, for the opportunities the postwar economy was supposed to bring—and our faith in the eventual fruits of our patience was largely a matter of our self-confidence. And that, I think, is a fundamental difference between mass education then and now, for it is no longer clear what students are to wait for. If, as my teachers emphasized, a citizen is an adult, and if voting in national elections is a privilege reserved for adults, then there are citizens certified to help make the nation's most critical decisions on a November morning who, that afternoon, are forced to concern themselves with where "man" discovered polyphony.

To my mind, this is the most absurd discrepancy between the dual roles of immigrant and citizen that older high school students are asked to play. But I doubt that it is an issue troubling many of them. Far more tangible contradictions are apparent daily: in the parking lot, where sixteen-year-olds, fresh from their driver's education courses and naturalized behind their steering wheels by the same state that keeps them as immigrants behind their desks, indulge in the same ego-extension games with fours-on-the-floor that the general citizenry play; in the lounge, where they can smoke and play cards, a place where their identity is acknowledged, much like the strictly kosher table for orthodox Jews at Ellis Island; in the bathrooms, where they can exchange money for goods and services not available to children in the school cafeteria. The concessions made by school boards, administrators, teachers, and parents to young people too impatient and too cynical to wait for the privileges of adulthood—regardless of the rhetoric in whose name those concessions have been made—do not seem to have slaked impatience nor to have restored faith. Either there is something to wait for (if not self-evident, then generally agreed upon) or there is not. True maturity, it seems to me, is achieved through as personal a development as an immigrant's Americanization, and is neither hastened nor slowed by lowering an institutional barrier here while maintaining another one there. It is as if, to change the metaphor for a moment, society through its schools were hoping that virginity could be lost gradually; whereas what is at work, as students know very well, is no loss of innocence but a gain of power.

De-alienization

I don't know the details of the present process of naturalization. Perhaps they differ markedly from those I remember. America decided that our nationality was determined by our place of birth or most recent origin, regardless of what that place's government had said about it. Thus, throughout almost all of World War II, we had to register as enemy aliens. After each of my parents had completed the requisite five years of residence in the United States, they presented themselves to a judge who examined them cursorily, administered an oath, and pronounced them citizens: a metamorphosis surely as astounding as that of any butterfly. My father, it happened, had been able to arrive some months before the rest of us got here, and so became an American before we did. This meant that for some months a citizen was legally sheltering his family of enemy aliens. There was another interesting complexity. The rule was that if you were under fourteen when you arrived—as I was—you became a citizen automatically when both of your parents had obtained citizenship. Thus, my mother's achievement of that status conferred it upon me as simultaneously as my birth had made me her son. My sister, however, had been about fourteen and a half at the time of our arrival, and therefore had to become a citizen on her own, without benefit of parentage. The assumptions behind this system, even those assigning us the nationality of the country that had declared us subhuman, were all clear enough, however questionable in individual instances. Systems, of course, are not and cannot be designed for individuals. But they have to be designed for *something*, and that, presumably, is to have some relation to reality. And here my too extended analogy between the processing of immigrants and that of public school students must stop. The policies and procedures governing immigration and naturalization as I experienced them reflected American realities I came to recognize when I grew older. But what reality, American or otherwise, is reflected in the treatment of the public school student as an immigrant waiting for naturalization on the mainland of adulthood?

THE ILLUSION OF A "PEOPLE"

What *is* reflected, dimly but perceptibly, is not a reality but a fiction, at best an uninformed illusion, at worst a vicious ideology: that Americans are a people. As illusion, this fiction involves the myth of the melting pot, the notion that, however different we once were, we are becoming more and more alike. The flames heating that pot are almost always thought to include those of the public school, where the young, it is imagined, taught the same truths in the same ways by the same teachers, are welded together into a uniform alloy, however speckled. I suspect that this illusion, despite the mass of evidence against it, is alive and well throughout the country. It is no less harmful than other illusions, but at least it is not vicious, as is the concept, also rampant, that the people of America are those who put their hearts into this country and that others should get their asses out of it. This bumper-sticker ideology seems to have been specifically addressed to those of us appalled by the version of the defense of freedom that took place in Southeast Asia until very recently, but there are other implications. Among them, I think, is a bitter resentment of everyone dubious about official interpretations of this country's history, official assessments of our policies, institutions, "way of life." Perhaps the resentment even extends to the conditions inconsistent with the conventional wisdom about the greatness of our society—pollution, decay, lawlessness, corruption. These very words seem to annoy the official interpreters and purveyors of the conventional wisdom. As a result, they ask us, in one way or another, to emphasize "what's right with America," a polite way of phrasing, but not substantively different from, the bumper sticker's dictum.

Official interpretations of the peoplehood of America, and the conventional wisdom arising out of them, are a large part of the business of schools. They are not alone in conveying the message, but the schools, unlike the media, the corporations, and the government, represent the only social institution that has a legally captive audience for it. For five days a week, about nine months of the year, and for twelve years, American children learn in innumerable ways that Americans love liberty more than any other people in history; that liberty is essential to progress; that progress is measured by comfort; that comfort is achieved by subduing nature; and that America, which has subdued so much so fast, is the envy of the world. There are, admittedly, other ways to describe the cumulative message conveyed in the public schools, and the details vary. But it is the total vision, larger than the sum of parts and yet arising out of them, that is important. And that vision is not merely the abstraction of America as the greatest country on earth, but its equally abstract corollary of Americans as the world's greatest people.

To belong to the world's greatest people is a terrible burden. There is, for instance, the constant strain of having to tolerate the enormous mass of the less than best, especially when that mass exhibits no awareness of its status. At least equally irritating, I suppose, is the necessity of reconciling certain impressive particulars about other societies with the general theory of American superiority. One way to solve that problem is to ignore it, which may explain why Americans seem to know relatively little even about their immediate neighbors. When some sort of evidence about another nation's accomplishments does penetrate popular consciousness, it is frequently countered with a defensiveness hardly compatible with greatness: Russian Olympic athletes are not really clean amateurs like ours; Sweden, whatever its health-care system may be, is characterized chiefly by immorality; and so on in the unending catalog of stereotypes.

On the other hand, not to be one of the greatest people in the greatest country in the world appears to cause even more psychological discomfort. The schools still succeed, despite recent efforts to correct certain classical omissions of historical fact, in identifying the mainstream of greatness in America as a combination of the right mixture of genetics, money, and dedication to the approved ideals, and what does not originate in the mainstream somehow remains in the tributaries. The effect, like that of the bumper sticker about hearts and asses, is not only to diminish the anatomy of American peoplehood but also to identify which part is which. A currently fashionable response of those assigned to the backwaters is to assert the significance of their particular heritage within the American context, proclaiming heroes, listing obstacles already overcome, inventing symbols of solidarity. There are reasons to be suspicious of this form of therapy, partly because the therapists appear to be greater beneficiaries than the patients; partly because the substitution of one burden for another—if I may so designate all forms of ancestor worship—is not clearly a long-term gain; but mostly because the schools have no more resemblance to a therapeutic setting than to a melting pot, any more than Ellis Island did. Still, the response was long overdue, even if it does not meet the central issue.

Few Common Memories

The issue, I think, is that Americans are not a people at all. We are a nation, but that is by no means tantamount to peoplehood, and there is no convincing indication that we are even on the way toward becoming a people. Peoplehood is forged out of shared experience, including some element of tragedy, which is probably why, of all Americans, those who are not white are more like a people than those who are, and of all American regions, the South is or used to be more of a people's country than any other. Politicians have always understood this very well. This nation's voters have no common memories of Bunker Hill, the Alamo, Gettysburg, Little Big Horn; they do not remember the *Maine*, nor do they believe in making the world safe for democracy, or that all they have to fear is fear itself. Our national memories, I suggest, are fragmented beyond repair in the public schools. If they exist at all, they exist in vistacolor and are interrupted by beer commercials. And if there is a vision of our country as a whole that Americans, regardless of their personal perspectives, are to have, it is probably that of seeing the U.S.A. in their Chevrolet. So politicians, seeking our votes or our confidence, appeal to those realities they think we can confirm out of our experience, realities far deeper and more personal than those represented by our passage, however recent or long ago, through the public schools.

Politicians—and I include union leaders, spokesmen for corporations, advocates of the interests of groups ranging from welfare mothers to the Daughters of the American Revolution, from migrant workers to the American Medical Association—do not for a moment pretend that we are a people. "Race will not be an issue," declare both white and black candidates for office at the beginning of a campaign, confirming once again that race is the pivotal issue. Mr. Nixon's unexceptional promise "to bring us back together again" was mocked soon enough in the nation's press, which also made certain that we were all fully informed about Mr. Agnew's ethnicity and Mr. Kissinger's origins. Questions of legalized abortion and even sex education are surrounded by religious animosities. Irish revolutionaries have marshaled support for their cause among their

American "brethren." Memories of Russian oppression in Eastern European countries, and concern for relatives remaining there, influence votes for candidates for national office in this country. There can be little doubt of the support rendered Israel by large numbers of American Jews, nor of the hostility that support (called, by its opponents, "the Jewish vote") has engendered among those convinced that Arab oil embargoes are at the root of our oil shortages. Americans a people? Only in their public schools, where they are all immigrants.

Searching for the Unique

I have not yet traveled as much as I would like to in the United States. Perhaps I never will. Unless you are going from one place to another because you have to—a situation too fraught with anxiety to allow you to pay attention to anything but directions—traveling can confer a freshness of vision, not necessarily in what is to be seen but in seeing. Travel is sharpening. Before you go, your acquaintances tell you of places to see along the way, restaurants, views, monuments. When you return, people want to know what you saw, whom you met, what experiences you had. You will probably have quite a bit to tell, perhaps to show as well, and there you are, writing that old paper again—"What I Did on My Summer Vacation." The assumptions, yours and those of your audience, are exactly the opposite of those surrounding the immigrant's experience. You are to share the novelty; the immigrant is to lose his.

The tourist trade is big business, and it's hard to go far without encountering an invitation to sample the local flavor. A country store will carry picture postcards of a stream, presumably nearby, meandering through a quiet pasture. Magazines listing current attractions are placed in guest rooms of hotels in big cities. Pamphlets and brochures guide the visitor to locations of historical interest; plaques instruct him; everywhere there are souvenirs stamped with the local name and symbol. Grant the obvious and undisguised element of commercialism, subtract it from what you see, and there still remains, almost always, a sense of identity, a community of an area or a place asserting its origin and its being, eager to answer where it came from, proud to say who and what it is.

I would never advocate a chamber-of-commerce approach either to history or to society. But inasmuch as youth *is* a passage to adulthood, and since the schools are the only social institutions we have devised in which that passage is to occur, it might be worthwhile to speculate what changes in the public schools could be brought about were they to treat students as welcome visitors to knowledge rather than as immigrants to be processed through a system. Such changes would be ideological, for schools, in this context, would support rather than suppress the differences between peoplehood and nationality. They would be organizational, so as to instill cohesive and comprehensive perspectives of where we are and how we got here. And they would be humane, designed to accord each student citizenship upon entrance rather than exit. But these are goals, not means. The question confronting our schools is how to improve what exists: in the present context, how to enhance each student's self-respect by demonstrating that the fact of his birth makes him both inheritor of and contributor to the human experience.

In our multicultural society, it is necessary to affirm not only that there are different ways of being an American but also that each is an essential element of the whole. It should be the teacher's task, not the student's, to carry the burden of that affirmation. Public schools as organizations and teachers as individuals must accept the obligation to learn and understand as much as possible about what it is that students bring into their classrooms. What is to take place in those classrooms, after all, is the growth and development of the students. That requires enhancement of their self-respect. And that, in turn, requires the school as an organization and the teacher as both a professional and a person to respect whatever stage of development the students have reached on the day they enter the classroom, to see them not as immigrants who should lose their accents but as citizens who should learn to hear others. Let me assume perceptive and dedicated teachers of good will and sensitive imaginations. Let me assume, further, schools that encourage experimentation, helping teachers to find the most productive ways—for them—to teach the students as their students. Then what needs analysis and ultimately new syntheses, in a continual process of renewal, is the curriculum.

I have no case to make for "teaching children, not subject matter," nor for the more contemporary version of that position, called "relevance." The chief characteristic of a fashion of the moment is that it is precisely that, ephemeral, and curriculum committees contorting their imaginations to find the next recipe for a "unit" seem to be modeling themselves on those television executives who rise and fall with their Nielsen ratings. Still, reasonable people can agree that questions of what to teach and how to teach it had better remain open.

Now, what I think is remarkable is that, while more and more people, reasonable or not, are in fact agreeing that they can give only tentative answers to those questions, the news of their humility does not yet appear to have reached the curriculum itself. If, as I see no reason to doubt, the high school my sons attend is more or less representative of most American high schools of its size, then high schools generally are purveying a kind of knowledge about both man and the world he lives in with little indication either of how limited our knowledge is or how slowly and painfully we have acquired it. It is simply not enough, in a "unit" on American Indians at the beginning of a course in American history, to acknowledge that Columbus "discovered" this continent only in the sense that he discovered European ignorance. It is not enough to "cover" evolution in a course on biology (where it is "covered" in two weeks) without any significant examination of its import in a course on the humanities. And—to dredge up a memory from elementary school—it is not enough to teach children the Latin alphabet without teaching them that ours is but one of many sets of symbols for yet other sets called sounds.

The materials for a truly multicultural approach to what should be a multicultural curriculum are all around us: in our names, our families, our towns and cities, our aspirations, and our memories. In their conjunction lies the hope of building a sense of community. The school's opportunities to contribute to that effort are practically limitless. Perhaps the most obvious example is the teaching of history.

BUILDING A SENSE OF COMMUNITY

Not long ago, shortly after a Michigan high school, caught in the passions of the times, was confronted with demands for courses in black history, a sarcastic letter appeared in the local newspaper from a man who evidently thought that he could show this demand's absurdity by claiming equal time for his ancestors: Germans. In this area of Michigan, he argued, there are far more descendants of German immigrants than of African slaves; therefore let us first have courses in German-American history, let us enumerate the names of German-Americans who helped to build this land, let us study their ways, acknowledge their culture, keep alive their memory. Teutonic blood-and-irony dripped from his pen. A friend of mine was moved to anger. "I thought of writing an answer to the paper," he told me, "in which I would have said: yes, let us do all that for German-Americans—but first let us equalize the need to do it. Let us begin by shipping German-Americans back to Germany, where slave traders shall buy them. Let them be sent as slaves to this country, and let the voyage be murderous. Let them toil as slaves for 250 years, during which time they shall be regarded by both law and custom as chattel, with no families, no languages, no names, no identities but those assigned them by their masters. Let them struggle for another century as slaves freed only of their iron shackles, still despised, poor, thwarted, brutalized, humiliated day and night, all the while fighting in this nation's wars, helping do this nation's work, singing this nation's songs, including 'The Star-Spangled Banner' and 'America the Beautiful.' Let them then say, if they still can, *Enough: we are men and women: give us our past so that we may have a tomorrow.* And then I would say, why, yes, let us have German-American studies in our public schools. But not until then!"

The conflict epitomized by these perspectives should be of interest, I think, to most teachers of history, especially in states like Michigan. The beginnings of the states of the Midwest are not enshrined in national mythology. Their place names echo the diversity of European explorers and settlers as well as the variety of Indian nations who preceded us. If the Civil War was a turning point in their history, it would be hard to show an equivalent significance in its impact on the psychology of their present-day citizens. Those citizens are free, then, of such burdens as the citizens of Massachusetts and Mississippi must carry, free to assess the degree to which the meaning of their history—that is, official interpretations of it, especially in their schools—is identified with its substance, which is not so much what happened, but rather what, and how, we choose to remember. For meaning is everywhere entrusted to officialdom—teachers, journalists, ministers, politicians, and especially commencement speakers. But substance lingers on elsewhere, in suitcases and diaries, in farm implements and tombstones, in a barbershop or at a riverbank or in a hardware store founded a hundred years ago—most of all, perhaps, in the stories families tell their children.

If this distinction between the meaning and the substance of history is valid, it will be plain that one of the differences between the letter writer and my friend is the writer's acceptance of officially espoused meaning and my friend's contrary knowledge of officially ignored substance. I have no desire to point out yet another "gap" in our contemporary social topography. Still, the frequent lack of relationship between our public and our private memories may have much to do with the lack of a sense of community in our communities—*Gesellschaften* but not *Gemeinschaften*. "Community" has come to mean two entirely different things: a psychological sense of belonging or not belonging, depending on the ethnic (or comparable) modifier preceding it, and a geographic area in which one man's pride is another's fear. Cleveland, Detroit, Indianapolis, Chicago, Milwaukee, Minneapolis, Omaha—everywhere there are black and white communities, Polish, German, Italian, Jewish communities, country-club and bar-on-the-corner communities, whose nature is tied to memories that have nothing to do with civic boundaries. Yet somehow Cleveland, Detroit, all of them, are asked not only to survive as democratic political entities but also to become aware of themselves, to become, that is, communities with a sense of community.

My conviction is that much of the trouble starts in the schools, which not only teach history upside down—beginning, generally, with what is far away, chronologically and geographically and so, of course, conceptually—but which also teach it as if it had no life of its own. A waxworks museum, with neither dust nor cobwebs, can inspire no true understanding, for age, as children know, has wrinkles. What children get of history in school is too often dispensed in odorless doses, just so much at a time, resulting in crayon impressions of pioneers and Indians in the lower grades and encyclopedic regurgitations in the high schools. (But not so encyclopedic as to come to grips with real pioneers and Indians, past or present, to say nothing of all those of whom nothing is ever said!) Twelve years of this medication may produce loyalty to slogans (or to counterslogans), but not a sense of community, not an awareness of the past as a process to which this generation, too, is a contributor—through what it neglects as well as through what it does, through its dreams as well as its machines, and most of all through its children, carriers of pride and sorrow that they themselves are already transmuting on their way into the last quarter of the century.

There is much that teachers of history might do to stimulate a sense of community. There are science fairs, local, regional, state-wide; there could be history exhibits, not for purposes of self-glorification but to nurture, and to reward, a similar joy of discovery. All children could try to discover what has survived—a Lutheran church in the country, surrounded by cemetery markers with German inscriptions; an old man's recollection of horses on Main Street; an antebellum underground railroad station; a racial restriction at a private club downtown—and the older ones might try to discover why. Schoolchildren could be encouraged to dig into the past themselves, so that they might learn how their city grew rather than merely that it did grow. And they could learn what happens when a village grows into a town and then into a city, what happens to its water, its streets, its neighborhoods, its buildings, and what goes on inside them—and why. Above all, since there can be no sense of community when neighbors know nothing of one another, ways should be found through which memories can be shared. Every child an oral historian, chasing octogenarians with tape recorders? Not necessarily, although I think both might enjoy it. But surely we need not continue to erect walls between yesterday and today, between the schools and our real lives, between ourselves and our children. On the contrary, the walls must come down, for they block our vision of our horizons.

5. "You Know the Rules!"

Myths about Desegregation

James Deslonde

The racially isolated, all-minority public school is quickly disappearing from the educational scene. For instance, in 1968 an HEW school census[1] reported that 57 percent of all minority students attending schools in the southern states were enrolled in 100 percent minority schools. In 1970 only 12 percent of minority students were attending such schools in the southern states. On a national basis attendance by minority students in all minority schools was reduced from 29 to 10 percent during this two-year period. It appears that the shift in minority attendance is toward the 0–49.9 percent minority school. In the South, minority attendance in such schools increased from 21 to 38 percent and from 30 to 37 percent on a national basis. Whereas the courts are not in agreement on the percentage definition of a desegregated school, it appears that eventually the norm of a desegregated school will be one that enrolls no more than 50 percent minority and 50 percent majority students.

Although these rough population shifts may hearten the supporter of school desegregation, one should be cautious about interpreting these figures as signs of progress. In the same report, if one collapses the HEW categories to get composite figures, close to 50 percent of the minority population (on a national basis) attending public schools in 1971 were enrolled in schools with 90 percent or more minority population. A more conservative view is that desegregation is occurring, but at a very slow pace.

The small, yearly shifts of minority students into desegregated school environments are not occurring through the good will of the local populations concerned. If violent, conflict-ridden protests do not accompany such a changeover, the resistance from the white majority often manifests itself in other, more subtle and disguised forms.[2] It is this *quiet protest* against school desegregation that this chapter will attempt to document. The intent of this chapter is not to focus upon the overt protests against school desegregation: the burning of school buses in Pontiac, Michigan, the jeers of angry mobs in New Orleans, and the outright lawlessness in Boston are familiar news stories. In spite of these overt objections to school desegregation, thousands of youngsters are "peacefully" bused into many communities each day to attend desegregated schools. What happens at the end of the bus ride is often complicated and defies simplistic labels such as "racist actions," "defense of the neighborhood school," "unmanageable costs of busing," "unfair federal dictates upon local processes." What follows is an attempt to aid the reader in establishing frameworks for analyzing desegregation processes at the school and classroom levels. •

HISTORICAL-LEGAL GOALS OF DESEGREGATION

In the 1800s when various state legislative bodies began providing tax support and policy procedures for the establishment of public schools, separation of the races was an often debated issue. By the time Radical Reconstruction began in the South, the question was settled in most of the northern states. A few of these states devised crude formulas for determining the relative amount of tax money that would be set aside to support the schools for children of African descent (and other groups of color, such as Asians, Mexicans, Indians, mestizos, when and if they were present). Other northern states provided clauses that left the decision to local districts where and when the race question presented a problem.[3] However, as Meyer Weinberg has shown in chapter 2, the predominate mode of legal provision in most of these states was not characterized by ambiguity and sidestepping the question; the races were legally separated through provisions that created an unequal dual system that was never intended to be equal.[4] Even before the collapse of Radical Reconstruction "a bitter opposition from quarters not desirous of the education of colored children"[5] set the stage for the South's dual and unequal system.

As early as 1871 black parents began petitioning the courts for the legal interpretation of the rapidly forming segregationist school policies. When the Fourteenth Amendment was involved, the courts assured the plaintiffs that separate schools were not in violation of such rights provided for in the amendment. Throughout the early 1900s the courts were continuously forced to rationalize segregation practices scuh as gerrymandering, attendance zones, special transfers, unequal expenditures, the neighborhood school concept,[6] shorter school terms for blacks, unequal hiring practices, and racial testing and placement; the state of Arizona even provided segregation by petition and vote.[7] The continuous legal pressures to desegregate schools during this almost one-hundred-year period rested upon the conviction among black Americans that segregation was inextricably associated with inferior education and was in violation of equal protection of the law. With this contention the 1954 court decision agreed. However, the language of the decision introduced the extralegal notion of the psychological damage of segregated schooling on black children:

> Such considerations apply with added force to children in grade and high schools. To separate them from others of similar age and qualifications solely because of their race generates a feeling of inferiority as to their status in the community that may affect their hearts and minds in a way unlikely ever to be undone. . . . Whatever may have been the extent of psychological knowledge at the time of Plessy v. Ferguson, this finding is amply supported by modern authority.[8]

Thus, from the perspective of the court, not only are black children to be granted equal access to educational opportunities because it is their right, but white society, by finally allowing desegregation, is also offering them psychological therapy. The paternalistic overtone of this decision has created a persistent ideology among the majority group in control of education: school attendance with whites will correct feelings of inferiority held by blacks. On the other hand, the courts unknowingly challenged the schools to provide free, open access to all racial groups as well as to account for its *effects* on such groups. In addition to the problems of logistics, organization, and gathering community support for desegregation, the average classroom teacher (and administrator) in a desegregated school is faced with the serious dilemma of discarding anachronous, simple notions of "helping poor minority students" and replacing them with goals of equality that go far beyond mere access to schooling. The lack of clearly articulated, equitable goals for a classroom, school, or school district can create an environment that is confusing and at worst damaging to minority and majority youngsters. The courts have naturally been reluctant to tackle the deeper issues of equality. The issues involved are often not legal.

TWO SCHOOLS: DISPARITIES OF EQUALITY

To highlight and illustrate the emerging issues involved in contemporary desegregation processes, I shall describe visits to two desegregated schools. The desegregation plans in both schools were "peaceful"—there were no violent community clashes, no court orders, no visible resistance from school officials. The schools are in two different states in moderately large urban centers. In each school the concept of multicultural education has not been discussed before the visit.

Valencia School[9]

In a bright, sunny kindergarten classroom, Mrs. Jones, the teacher is just settling down with a small group of youngsters. The focus of the group's attention is a scale model of a typical middle-income home with four bedrooms, three baths, living room, dining room, family room, and attached two-car garage. Scattered about the carpet are various pieces of dollhouse furniture. Mrs. Jones tells the youngsters that they will take turns placing the proper pieces of furniture in the correct rooms. Bobby is first; he places the car in the garage. "Good, Bobby!" says Mrs. Jones. Alice is next; she places the stove in the kitchen: "Very good, Alice." Eddie is next; he selects the bed and places it in the living room: "No, Eddie! Beds don't belong in the living room, they belong in the bedroom."

This classroom happens to be in a school that has been desegregated for five years. The Chicano and black youngsters are bused in from neighborhoods that house low-income families of color. Even though the homes surrounding the school are near-replicas of Mrs. Jones's scale model, no such homes appear in Eddie's neighborhood. Eddie happens to be black.

Mrs. Sutton has only twelve youngsters in her room by the time I arrive. It is reading time. She explains that because of the wide range of reading abilities in the third grade, the primary teachers instituted the "early and late readers" program. Early readers arrive first, and they are the youngsters reading below grade level—and incidentally, many in this group are also severe discipline problems. The late readers arrive forty-five minutes later to begin their day with reading. Of the twelve early readers observed in Mrs. Sutton's room, ten are either Chicano or black, two are Anglo. Mrs. Sutton explains that these forty-five minutes alone with the early readers give her a chance for intensive remediation and individualization. When the late readers arrive, the early readers continue their reading—primarily seat work; so in essence the early readers get a double dose of instruction. "All right, group, let's look at our sight word list—Billy, don't squirm in your seat, face Mrs. Sutton—that's right. Repeat after me: far—*f–a–r*." (Broken responses from the group.) "No, no, all together in one big voice; far—*f–a–r*." (More unison this time.) "Good! Now let's go to the next word. Away—*a–w–a–y*." The monotonous drone of drilling the sight word list lingers in my ear as I walk to the next room.

Behind me a teacher is scolding a little black boy in a harsh, very annoyed voice. I turn, and there in the breezeway is a red-faced teacher pointing a menacing finger in the face of the child: "And if you EVER say those dirty words again you'll be sorry." The child has tears streaming down his face and is gasping for breath. The teacher grabs his arm. "Well, what do you have to say now? Do I have to phone your mother AGAIN?"

"No, no!" cries the boy.

"Well, do you apologize?"

"I'm sorry, Miss Green, I won't call you a bitch anymore."

"OK, young man, you'd better watch your mouth, and you sit on this bench until I tell you to come back into the classroom."

I must remember to visit Mrs. Bronson's room. The principal has especially asked for my advice. Mrs. Bronson has complained of several hyperactive black and Chicano youngsters disrupting her fourth-grade class. Since I am black the principal thinks my observations might reveal special insights into Mrs. Bronson's problem. I enter the room, nod to Mrs. Bronson, who is expecting me, and quietly take a seat in the back of the room. My eyes sweep across the room; neatly arranged rows are all facing the teacher's desk.

"All right, class, clear your desks; let's prepare for spelling." Noise, chatter, four youngsters are up out of their seats looking at something on the floor near me. "Children, children! Quiet! Clear your desks." Four children return to their seats. "Now take out your spellers and turn to page thirty-two."

Two little black girls are whispering and giggling. Mrs. Bronson chastises them. "Mrs. Bronson, we did page thirty-two last week!" they protest. Mrs. Bronson is clearly flustered by the remark. Nervously twisting a tissue in her hand, she walks back to her desk. Then, after going over to the bulletin board and back to the desk, she flips through her lesson plan book. By this time her face is almost as red as her lipstick. A little Chicano boy is out of his seat; a little white girl out of her seat drops a note on another child's desk and quietly returns to her seat.

"Carlos! Will you PLEASE sit down! . . . I'm sorry, class, I meant page thirty-eight, not page thirty-two." Chatter, groans, paper ruffling. "Marcella, one more groan from you and on the bench you go." The lesson starts; some books are open and some remain closed. "Marcella, since you haven't opened your book, maybe you'd better go sit on the bench outside until I decide to come and talk to you." Marcella stomps out. That makes two black youngsters on the bench in the breezeway.

The tour is now returning to the principal's office. I see Mr. Perrilli on the playing field; he seems to be organizing a softball game among the sixth-grade boys. After five minutes of idle chatter with Mrs. Tanner, the principal, the secretary comes in looking rather flushed. "Mrs. Tanner, I think you'd better come into the outer office."

Mrs. Tanner returns shortly with a slight nervous smile and says,

"Glad you're here, you can get a firsthand look at some of our problems. If you don't mind, I'll let you sit in on this." In walks Mr. Perrilli and four of the sixth-grade boys. "Well, Mr. Perrilli, why don't you start from the beginning," says Mrs. Tanner.

"As you know, we are trying to organize the softball team so we can play a game against Washington's team. I selected a captain, Darrell said he would not play, and the other three joined him. They walked off the playing field," Mr. Perrilli quickly reports.

"Well, what seems to be the problem?" asks Mrs. Tanner. All four boys start talking at once. "One at a time, boys. Darrell?"

"Well, Mrs. Tanner, you see, Mr. Perrilli, he's not fair about the captain."

"What do you mean?"

"Well, he's just picking his favorite to be captain!"

Mr. Perrilli quickly interrupts and explains that he had just finished telling the team that he would rotate the captainship among several boys and that whoever did not get it this time would have a chance for the next game. Apparently Darrell resisted his explanation because he wanted to be captain the first time.

"You always pick the white boys!" says Darrell.

Mr. Perrilli flushes and in a cracking, nervous voice denies Darrell's charge. Mrs. Tanner interjects: "Now, boys, I've known Mr. Perrilli for many years and I can assure you he would never do anything like that! Mr. Perrilli, are you sure the boys understood your plan?"

Mr. Perrilli, calming down, nods and says, "I'm not so worried about the softball game as I am about Darrell's remarks on the field. He called me a racist!"

"Well, you picked the white boy," says Darrell.

It was clearly a standstill situation. Darrell stuck to his side and Perrilli held strong the proof that he wasn't a racist. After ten minutes of fruitless debate, Mrs. Tanner dismissed all of them. She told Mr. Perrilli to continue his ball game, the boys to sit on the bench. She would finish this with them in a few minutes. As the boys were filing past my chair, Darrell mustered all of his energy to hold back a smile. The victory was clearly his. As he passed my chair, I heard him whisper to his Chicano buddy, "At least we don't have to go to our math class!"

A while later, as I walked through the school grounds to my car, the recess bell rang, and I stopped to observe the youngsters on the playground. As I continued to the car I could still hear the yard duty teacher shrieking and blowing her whistle: "All right, girls, you know the rules about bouncing balls in the breezeway. Boys! boys! You know the rules, only one person at a time at that water fountain. You girls stop that running, YOU KNOW THE RULES!"

Garrett High School

The soft voice of Mrs. Washington on the other end of the phone had just convinced me to come to Garrett High School. Her plan was to institute a Human Relations program for Garrett. She wanted a comprehensive program that would touch base with all factions in the school—teachers, administrators, students, parents, and even custodial staff. She was distressful and desparately needed outside help. Her intensive three-month effort to start the program had met with one roadblock after another. I agreed to Mrs. Washington's request to meet the Garrett faculty.

Garrett was more than I expected. It had recently been desegregated by "transferring" approximately 250 black students to a student population of 1,200. Up to the time of the transfer program, Garrett had definitely been an upper-status school. The plaques in the hall attested to this. There were awards for excellence in athletics, pictures of merit scholars from each graduating class since 1960, huge trophies for the state championship debating team, and all-city football. There were even a few pictures of Rhodes scholars who had been Garrett alumni and photos of the bright shining faces of pompon girls from each year since 1955.

"I really don't think our problems are so great," Mr. Vance, the principal, was saying. "Mrs. Buckley [one of two black teachers] has done tremendous things with her black literature class. We do have a few old timers who have a hard time understanding what the black students want. But you'll get to judge for yourself tomorrow at the in-service meeting. By the way, I hope you understand that I could not mandate this meeting; so we won't have one hundred percent attendance."

"We've had several meetings with the students, and feel as though we really have a comprehensive idea of the problems," said Mrs. Washington. "We've prepared a formal document to present our side of the problems. This is on the agenda to follow your presentation." That afternoon I sat glued to my chair as Mrs. Washington read the report from the black students.

The report stated a chronology of events that had prompted Mrs. Washington and the other black teacher to call an informal meeting with a group of black students. In essence, they felt that the faculty should discuss the following concerns with an intention of taking immediate actions:

> We are concerned with black student participation (or lack of it) in the student council, the pompon girls, the fraternities and sororities, the debating team, and the drama guild. We are concerned about the low number of black graduates gaining scholarships to four-year colleges, the fights in the girls' restroom, interracial dating and its repercussions. We would like the faculty to discuss the low enrollment of black students in the chemistry and physics

classes, the large number of black students failing tenth-grade English, the basketball team being all black, and the swimming team being all white. In addition, there seems to be a disproportionate number of black students getting suspensions and expulsions; there are interracial fights on the school grounds, shakedowns for money, drug pushing in the boys' john, and a lack of "soul food" in the cafeteria. And, finally, we are deeply concerned about the lack of black faculty in all departments of this school.

The in-service discussions went well, even though a few people got "hot" under the collar. The faculty finally agreed, after more than an hour of discussion, that the root of the problems could be solved with a more rigorous diagnosis of the academic strengths and weaknesses of the black students. They recommended the immediate institution of a testing center in the counselor's office. When the students finished their testing, the counselors would then assign them to appropriate skill development modules for an intensive five-week tutorial. The students completing the tutorials successfully would immediately be placed in a college prep track. After the meeting, Mrs. Washington shared her feelings with me: "It's a compromise to the breadth of our original concerns. I think the problem is probably incapable of solution; I'm discouraged and feel like quitting."

Each of these schools has several positive factors in its favor. The multiracial make-up of the student body indicates the community's commitment to the value of an interracial school experience for their children. Regardless of how the student body ratio was obtained, such schools also indicate some level of commitment from the school district to bring about equal education opportunities in a multicultural setting. The schools are also in a favorable position to make positive use of the rich and diverse backgrounds of each ethnic group within the schools. Another advantage—one that is not exclusive to such multiracial schools—is the fact that multicultural education can become a strong viable force for change in these schools. These schools also offer the opportunity to extract general principles that can create and guide an educational environment that is suitable for *all* youngsters.

OPERATIONAL GOALS FOR MULTICULTURAL EDUCATION

The case of Mrs. Jones illustrates the need for teachers to be not only extremely sensitive to and knowledgeable about the cultural backgrounds of their students, but aware of how their own assumptions of what is right or wrong may conflict with what the students perceive as right or wrong. Unless the teacher is dealing with factual, cognitive information, there are few, if any, "rights" or "wrongs" about the way people live, feel, think, or behave. Mrs. Jones should also weigh these concerns very carefully as she plans for the youngsters and selects materials for them. Uppermost in her thinking should be the question, "Will this artifact, this lesson, this planned experience in any way put down the students who are different and make them uncomfortable with their differences?" When we communicate to any youngster that he is wrong for being different, then we risk having that youngster denigrate his background and himself.

This particular school district did, in fact, hold a one-day workshop the day before the first buses began the desegregation plan. I was further informed that the workshop focused on "increasing the sensitivity of the teacher to minority cultures." Obviously the one-day in-service approach did not help Mrs. Jones. Sensitivity and awareness are human skills that need constant nurturing and reassessment. For classroom teachers, developing sensitivity alone is not enough; the connection must be made between the new awareness and how it applies to selection of curricular materials as well as how it can modify the behavior of the *teacher*. Teachers who have been trained in new sensitivities must be given many opportunities to try out the new awareness in many situations. They should be provided opportunities to objectively view their new behaviors, and they *must* feel secure and comfortable with the new set of behaviors. Without this type of extensive, ongoing sensitivity training, the Mrs. Joneses should not be permitted to teach culturally different youngsters.

Mrs. Sutton's concern for her "slow readers" expressed itself in a situation that may invite negative feelings about racial and intellectual differences. Her instructional organization may encourage invidious comparisons between the children in her room; it sets the stage for negative labeling to occur. Most important, these "slow readers" may never see themselves as anything else but slow readers. Situational factors contrived by the teacher that physically separate youngsters because of their intellectual or cultural differences are not compatible with egalitarian notions of multicultural education. In a multicultural school setting the faculty should continually assess the effects of their instructional strategies and organizational patterns. Resegregation after a long bus ride may be more than many parents can tolerate.

The incidents with the "dirty words" and the softball conflict seem to indicate that this particular school staff is not comfortable with the presence of the minority youngsters. The extreme reactions of the teachers to certain aspects of the children's behavior may be interpreted by other students as proof that the teacher gives differential treatment to the minority youngsters. Such reactionary teacher behavior may also communicate the fact that harsh, negative sanctions are reserved primarily for deviants. With relatively few children of color in the school, skin color may be one of the deviant characteristics perceived by other children.

By the time minority youngsters in such situations as these reach the upper grades, they have accurately sorted out the interpersonal dynamics of the school and have concluded that they can *control* the teachers with slanderous remarks, swear words, flaunting of the rules, and other "deviant" acts. Darrell's remark about math is illustrative of this point. Such controlling behavior left unchecked on the part of any of the students may well create a false sense of power: "To manipulate people, simply perform a deviant act!"

Such interpersonal processes depress and stultify the entire atmosphere of the school. The rules in Valencia School are so numerous and extensive that it may be difficult for any child to get through an entire day without breaking one of them. The "benching" and isolation of "deviant" youngsters may well impress upon their young minds the feeling that the teacher rejects *them* as persons, not their behavior. Unless the distinction between the person and his behavior is made clear to students when punitive constraints are employed, many may feel totally rejected in their school.

The quality of interaction among students and adults must also be continually reassessed as a vital part of any multicultural education program. These interaction patterns *or processes* must be the target of planning that is equal to any of the other curricular areas of the school. Schools are not the place to teach deviant behavior that society penalizes.

Mrs. Bronson's classroom problems are not entirely the students' fault. It may be that the students are fidgety and unruly simply because they are imitating her fidgety, nervous behavior. As Mrs. Bronson's eyes sweep across the room, the color of the black youngsters impacts on her visual field more than other stimuli. As a result, the behavior of the black youngsters appears more prominent to her than that of the white children. In this situation it may benefit to modify the teacher's behavior before attempting to change the students.

Garrett High School is faced with an array of problems that are probably not entirely unique to multiracial, desegregated schools. Before desegregation in this school, few, if any, concerted efforts were made to modify the school environment or curriculum to accommodate the new population mixture. However, the most shortsighted and obvious flaw of Garrett High School is that the faculty believes that problems with grave socioemotional bases can be solved by intellectual, nonemotional means. To offer an academic-intellectual solution to a social-conflict problem is diversionary and ineffective. It may drive the problem underground, but is not likely to solve it.

What does this mean for multicultural education? One obvious and general principle that can be extracted is that schools and the people who run them *must change* substantially before the schooling process can become equally rewarding for students and teachers alike. Hunter suggests that change in schools should take place along three dimensions:

structure, content, and process.[10] Unless change occurrs along all three dimensions simultaneously, certain innovations are doomed to failure. Hunter defines innovations in structure as "those that involve the ways schools and classrooms are organized." In both of the cases cited, the addition of new students of color to previously all-white schools is a structural change; so is Mrs. Sutton's instructional reorganization. Content changes are "those that introduce subjects not previously dealt with in schools or the revision of old subject areas in new ways." Mrs. Buckley's black literature class was certainly a content change for Garrett High School. Process change "has to do with human interaction" patterns. The examination of how persons interact in schools, an analysis of the consequences of such behaviors, and the resultant change in the way people behave would be considered as process change. The major problems in the two schools visited were that unplanned changes were introduced into the setting, the planned changes were usually isolated exclusively on one dimension, and all three dimensions were not being simultaneously planned for. The operational base for any multicultural educational program must include all three components. It is when structure, content, and process are changed to enhance a positive appreciation of cultural diversity that multicultural education has begun.

Curriculum Content and Multicultural Education

A multicultural educational program is characterized by _content_ that reflects an awareness of ethnic diversity in American society. The content to which young children are exposed should help them understand both the negative and positive aspects of what ethnic diversity means in America. They must explore such concepts as racism, poverty, and inequality in housing, income, and health care. Institutional inequality must be understood before students can fully appreciate the American ethnic experience, which is characterized to a great extent by group reactions to structural inequality. The content should foster active social analysis and social-problem–solving skills among the students and teachers. Dickeman speaks most strongly about this general content objective:

> . . . there is the aura of rosiness, of unreal prettiness and cuteness which so often pervades the school. Not only in the area of social relations has our curriculum traditionally denied the ugly truths of life; the painful, the brutal, the existence of conflict and evil has been rooted out of the standard curriculum, whether in literature, history, biology, geography or social studies. Surely we may ask whether there is not some relationship between the rosy utopia of smiling faces which the school projects, and the function of the classroom as a place in which the student is initiated into the most traumatic social conflict of her early life. . . . A school free of ethnocentrism and racism must be a school new in function, profoundly new.[11]

The rosy prettiness to which Dickeman refers is not to be totally eliminated from the school curriculum: it is the "unreal" aspect of this view that is harmful.

This aspect of content dictates that the school curriculum should not only project new intellectual or cognitive concepts but that emotional (or affective) content should receive equal emphasis as well. Epstein emphasizes that this dual aspect of the curriculum is inescapable:

> Every subject must be explored not only on the cognitive level but also on the affective level. Often, we struggle and fail in our attempts to help children "achieve" in school because we are ignoring their strong feelings that must be dealt with before they can cope with "facts." There is no subject that can be taught legitimately without concern for the learner's feelings. Thus, feelings about self need to be part of the classroom material before mathematics becomes important for some children, feelings about adults need to be explored before information about drugs can be internalized, and feelings about race need to be expressed before history and civics take on any real meaning.[12]

Process Content for Multicultural Education

This affective dimension of the curriculum has direct implications for the manner and quality of student-student interactions as well as teacher-student and teacher-teacher interactions. According to our criteria, *process* changes must accompany new content relevant to multicultural education. From the tour, we may say that in a multicultural environment, a youngster is not made to feel ashamed of his differences. The school has a relaxed, warm atmosphere with a minimum of rules and punitive sanctions. Reactionary behaviors on the part of teachers are absent, and limits are set within reason and applied equally to all youngsters. Teachers are critical (in light of cultural and ethnic differences) of any structural changes that isolate and separate youngsters on the basis of intellectual or ethnic differences. The environment supports and encourages a variety of friendship patterns among the children, and interracial or interethnic conflict is contained through active problem solving by teachers and students. There is a minimum of extreme competition and invidious comparisons among the students and evidence of a balance of cooperation. In addition, Hunter recommends that process changes might also include

> changing the questioning patterns of teachers [and the use of] questions calling for imagination and thought on the part of the pupils rather than mere recall and retrieval. . . . Still other changes would affect the entire pattern of pupil and teacher talk in a number of ways: expanding the amount of pupil talk, increasing the amount of pupil-to-pupil talk, acknowledging and dealing with the existence of feeling and decreasing the amount of controlling and censorious talk on the part of teachers.[13]

Structural Components of Multicultural Education

In a school or classroom that is ethnically or racially homogeneous, one necessary structural change is to provide the teachers and children with face-to-face interactions with culturally different groups through meaningful curricular activities. If we expose children to content stressing ethnic diversity but do not offer them contact with others different from themselves, then we are depriving them of practical situations in which to apply the newly acquired skills. If, however, such contact is difficult to arrange in the classroom, the teacher should explore other means through which the students can apply their problem-solving skills. The "classroom," then, cannot be confined to the walls of the school. Throughout the community there are problems relevant to the application of problem-solving skills. Letters to the local newspaper, the city council, the mayor, or the school board and visits to local agencies concerned with combating inequality in society can be useful. The generous use of visitors to the classroom as resources is another structural change worthy of exploration.

Ethnic content must be liberally sprinkled with small-group tasks that require cooperation rather than competition among the group members. Simulations and games, dramatic role-play, and other exercises that encourage the sharing of feelings should be employed. The surrounding community must be considered as a laboratory in which the children can test their assumptions, hypotheses, and problem-solving skills. The curriculum should be as vibrant and as different from mainstream content as the ethnic groups treated in the curriculum. Very often a structural change can give ethnic content the spark needed to capture students' imagination and to motivate them.

THE TEACHER AS A CENTRAL EQUALIZING FIGURE

The teacher, by virtue of his sustained contact with students, is a vitally important link in any multicultural effort. Numerous research reports offer ample grounds for considering the teacher as a central element of concern when educational innovation is planned. Rosenthal and Jacobson show that teacher expectations can have powerful effects on student performance.[14] Rist argues convincingly that the teacher can unknowingly perpetuate the same patterns of social inequality in the classroom that exists in society.[15] Henry provides evidence that the teacher may unknowingly create an atmosphere that encourages destructive, "witch-hunt" behaviors among the children.[16] Rosenfeld's ethnological study illustrates ways in which the teacher's behavior with minority youngsters may be destructively racist.[17] And the work of Valentine suggests that the biculturality of youngsters, if ignored by teachers, may become a serious source of antagonism and distrust between students and teachers.[18]

The concerns prompted by these writings seem to be magnified in a desegregated school. Many teachers, when faced with the very serious problem of accepting the culturally different child from a perspective based on norms of *equality* rather than *deviance*, find themselves riddled with confusion and doubt. If the "problem" persists with no resolution, the teacher may become extremely punitive toward "deviant" cultural characteristics in an attempt to make the child "act like everyone else." Some teachers may draw heavily upon the deficit-pathology literature to explain away cultural differences. Others may find a comfortable niche through refusing to recognize the existence of cultural-conflict problems. Still other teachers may become hostile and angry because they have been placed in such an awful situation.

The following transcript, which reveals the teacher's perspective on desegregation issues, may help illustrate the points mentioned above. This concentrated transcript represents a cross-sectional report of six full days of open-ended group interviews with approximately sixty teachers from Valencia School and another nearby school.[19]

This group consists of five teachers in a group problem-solving session. The task of the group is to identify the most pressing problems faced by the classroom teacher in a desegregated school.

DISCUSSION LEADER: I have just outlined for you a description of what multicultural education might consist of. I inevitably referred to problems which teachers face in such situations. Do these adequately express your problems?

MISS JONES (*after a long pause*): Well, everyone seems to make such a fuss about race. Children are children, white, blue, purple, or black. I have never made any distinctions. Thus, I don't see the need to talk about changing things just because of desegregation.

MRS. EDWARDS: I disagree. Partly, I do have some of those same problems in my classroom. Let me tell you about Essie Mae Banks.* She came to school one morning in the worst-smelling and worst-looking dress I have ever seen. You see, her mother is on ADC, and she told me one day after the other children left for lunch that her "uncle" had beaten her mother that night because her other uncle had been there the night before. Well, to make a long story short, this child is simply neglected. How can you expect a child from that kind of home to learn anything when she has to cope with all those problems at home? At least we seem to get along together. She is always asking to help me after school. I just feel sorry for some of them. And those kinds of problems really make it hard since desegregation occurred.

* For those who have trouble attaching ethnicity to names: Essie Mae could only be black.

MR. SMITH: Well, now that you mention it, you would think that the superintendent and all those other downtown people would have had enough insight to know that those kinds of problems would come up. What do they think we classroom teachers can do about all the Essie Mae Bankses in our school? I just think the administration should provide some buffer in the plans for handling these problems. But of course, those guys haven't been in a classroom in years. They have their heads in the clouds. In fact, the other day I asked the assistant superintendent of instruction about that order of spelling books I gave him five months ago for the fifth-grade team. (I'm team captain for the ungraded upper.) He told me they would be here next month, but "in the meantime I'm sure you've been innovating without the spellers all this time." And they're paying that guy twenty-two thousand a year to screw up the system!

MISS TAYLOR: Well, now, wait just a minute, Ed. We really don't need those spellers anyway. They are nothing more than an extension of the Dick and Jane series anyway, and my Chicano and black youngsters would laugh me out of the room if I gave them those books. I have managed quite well so far—you know about my creative writing units which incorporate spelling. In fact, I have Darrel Banks—Essie's brother, who you will know was the terror of the school—and he wrote a beautiful haiku poem after our lesson on the assassination of Martin Luther King. You simply have to break away from those tried and traditional methods if the minority youngsters are going to have any success in school—segregated or desegregated!

MRS. BAKER: Well, Dorothy, everyone knows that you, Edna, and Laura had that summer workshop last year. Even though you've been trying to get me to coordinate in my primary program, I still don't think those black and Chicano kids are being helped. After all, they've got to learn the traditional way sometime!

MISS TAYLOR: Well, have you tried it? If not, don't knock it!

MR. PALASKI: Well, I did try it. You remember I told you about trying to get those high school youngsters to come into my class one day a week to work with my slow readers? Well, after three weeks of planning and letters, phone calls, and two trips to the high school, I finally got these three very nice young ladies to come. I gave them the slow group and they took them out on the lawn to work with them. Well, those girls had to bring Manuel and Roosevelt back because Roosevelt called the girl a white sucking bitch and Manuel was asking her for a date. I just told the girls to forget it, I couldn't expose them to that kind of abuse. However, one still comes over one evening a week—I just let her help grade papers, though.

LEADER: Well, it seems as though I am getting several reactions, all somewhat different. Some of you definitely do see some racial problems which interfere with learning in the school. What about that, Miss Jones?

MISS JONES: Well, as I said before, I love 'em all—they are just children to me!

MISS TAYLOR: Well, you know the fifth-grade teachers tried last year to bring Dr. Matthew into the school to do some sessions on black history, and you primary teachers [block] voted it down because you didn't think we needed it.

MISS JONES: Well, after all, Dorothy, we are *second* in the district with our achievement scores. And we had an African dance on the talent show last spring. If we are second on the Iowa Reading Exam, we can't be doing that much harm to them.

LEADER: Well, you know the research and evaluation office in their report last spring showed a tremendous gap in achievement for the Anglo and black and Chicano youngsters in the district.

MR. PALASKI: Jim, surely you didn't believe in all that evaluation junk! You saw kids on the playground the other day—did you see any race riots erupting? If we could just get them some breakfast in the morning, those black kids would make the all-city track team!

LEADER: Yes, Palaski, you're probably right!

MR. PALASKI: Well, you sound sarcastic!

LEADER: Well, I am a little disturbed, because I don't know where you are coming from with that statement. For instance, if you believe that the black students can be all-city track stars because of hereditary advantages, that's one thing. But if you think their potential rests upon environmental conditions, then that's something else, and . . .

MR. PALASKI: What's that got to do with it? Jeeze! I won't say anything anymore about the black kids.

LEADER: Well, Palaski, if you believe black youngsters make good runners because of some hereditary advantages, then I think you may be conditioned to believe that they don't learn as well as white kids.

MR. PALASKI: Well, I made it the hard way. If they wanted to, they could also!

LEADER: Well, it's about time for us to adjourn. Miss Tucker, you've been awfully quiet. Don't you have anything to say?

MISS TUCKER: This has been a tremendous eye-opener for me!

LEADER: In what way?

MISS TUCKER: Well, I . . . I think we should do it again.

MISS TAYLOR: I agree! Then maybe we can start coordinating our social studies program with you primary teachers.

The teachers began leaving. Miss Tucker lingered behind and heaped praises upon the leader for the good job he did in handling the group. She went on to tell me that she went to high school with colored children in Brickstomp, Indiana, and that she would be most interested in cooperating in making some of the changes that the project wanted, but she didn't think the group (the primary teachers) would approve.

LEADER: Well, Miss Tucker, I really admire you for the wonderful experiences you had in high school. I am sure because of these you can be of far greater help to the children in your classroom. Why don't you invite me to see them sometime?

MISS TUCKER: OK, anytime. It would be nice for the youngsters to see a colored success model!

LEADER: Let's hope not!

TOWARD THE PROCESS COMPONENTS OF TEACHER BELIEFS

Obviously, part of the problem was the wide variance in views and feelings expressed by the teachers on school desegregation and multicultural education. A first step in approaching the problem, then, was to look for some classifiable way to plot attitudinal differences found in each school. From numerous conversations, faculty meetings, anecdotal records, and questionnaires these attitudes were known to be varied. Teachers, of course, may differ radically within a school, but I was looking for evidence that one school, when compared with another, approached more closely a state of true integration and thus was ready to institute multicultural educational changes rather than simply exist in a desegregated condition.

This dimension of the desegregation process at the *school level* somewhat confirms portions of the Purl hypothesis, which states:

> The [integration] process seems to progress through several stages. First, there is resentment and hostility, not so much toward the low-achieving pupils as toward the power structure that brought the situation about. Secondly, there is an emphasis on discipline and behavior. Having the situation in hand behavior-wise, the next stage is ignoring the achievement problem, or at least assuming no responsibility for it. Next comes a half-hearted attempt to individualize instruction and finally an all out attack on the problem. . . . Arriving at the final stage is done only after many defenses have been employed. Not all teachers arrive at this point, but the resistance either becomes less or becomes unconscious. The process is long and difficult, but it is the process that is important. The final solution if applied without the process would be meaningless.[20]

Thus, the process in terms of teacher attitudes seems to be as follows:

Component 0: (Miss Jones)	Teacher oblivious to difficulty; refusal to recognize that problems require differential responses. "I haven't changed my standards in twenty years and I am not going to start now!"
Component 1: (Mr. Smith)	Expressions of hostility toward authorities who brought situation about. "How could they do that to these children; it isn't fair to them!"
Component 2: (Miss Tucker)	Positive action underground. "Those children really work for candy, but I couldn't use that on the others."
Component 3:	Stiffening resistance, delaying tactics, stall-

(Mrs. Baker)	ing. "Those children are going to have to learn the traditional way; otherwise, how will they succeed?"
Component 4: (Mrs. Edwards)	Focus on deviant characteristics of children as rationale for difficulties. "They just can't help it; look at the homes they come from!"
Component 5:	Token actions taken. "And if a child dictates 'Damn,' I write down 'Damn'!"
Component 6: (Mr. Palaski)	Cleavages develop among teachers as positive actions become better organized, more important. "If they want to try that new-fangled stuff, they can; but you notice I took no part in it."
Component 7: (Miss Taylor)	Negotiations and information dissemination between interested faculty and administration. "Let's get together, guys, and see what we can work out."
Component 8:	Plans formulated, outsiders brought in, experimental programs begun. "Let's get Dr. Matthew to give us an in-service session for our cultural awareness unit."
Component 9:	Resistance goes underground. "I can't go along with it, but I guess the administration likes it."
Component 10:	Wholehearted acceptance or resignation. "Well, it seems to be working out after all."

INTERPRETATION AND USE OF THE MODEL

In this school, it was difficult to assess accurately the teacher beliefs without detailing certain organizational factors (such as components 6, 7, 8). Cleavages among the staff over ideological or multicultural issues are a healthy sign that some teachers are ready for change. To use such data for planning purposes, a comparison must be made with a nearby school in the same district: Arroyo. This staff essentially had the same format for discussions as the Valencia staff, which provided an important frame of reference for the comparison.

Valencia

Teachers at Valencia, in the upper-middle-class community, generally presented a picture of relative satisfaction with school programs. When questioned at length regarding progress made by minority children in the school, a few teachers reacted in a rather defensive, emotional manner. Their behavior toward the children was well rationalized in a highly intellectual manner. They seemed to view their jobs as requiring the inculcation of white middle-class values. While these teachers were surely not racist in the usual sense of the word, they were having some trouble getting their program across to children who might not be clean, docile, and alert to the nuances of middle-class disciplinary measures. The teachers conveyed a general quality of aloofness and emotional distance from the ethnically different children who behave in "ways we don't understand." Their statements seemed to reflect the feeling that these children come from foreign cultures that need to be translated and formally taught. Strong emphasis was placed on the deviant nature of the ethnically different child. The teachers were not satisfied with their disciplinary program and had repeated difficulties with specific individuals known by name to the entire staff.

In general, the teachers presented a unified picture. There were no severe criticisms of fellow teachers, and much defending of shared opinions. When some of the program staff members attempted to relate the special nature of the black experience to Valencia teachers, several resisted the impact of what was being said by relating their own struggles to achieve. They seemed to be conveying the notion that blacks and browns could not be expected to be tolerated as equals in American society until they had assimilated Anglo middle-class values. The conservative nature of their values was pointed up by the concern that the Valencia teachers had regarding the possibility that the incoming university students and professors would be "radical." That the school would stand as a bastion against onslaughts from without seemed clear.

In a few isolated cases, individual teachers approached the discussion leader privately and replayed the notion that they personally would be interested in cooperating in making various kinds of changes in the school. These incidents have a rather clandestine quality, as if the teacher realized that most of her colleagues preferred things to remain as they were. No important cleavages were observed among this school's members, and a few of the conditions necessary for progress were noted during the sessions.

In the process model, the school could be said to be located along points one to five. Needless to say, at the conclusion of the session, the program staff was, rather disinclined to hope that new programs would be undertaken at Valencia in the near future.

Arroyo

If the meetings with Valencia faculty were basically unproductive, those with Arroyo were quite the opposite: sessions did "buzz" with the exchange of ideas and even hoped-for plans. Here, obviously, was an entirely different situation, as it became clear that there had been a history of both administrative and faculty attempts to attack the achievement-level problem in the school. The atmosphere and productivity of any one of these groups was also contingent upon effects generated by the interaction of teachers, administration, and even project staff between sessions. The sessions became forums, in some instances, for problems that had developed over a considerable period of time and that underwent redefinition during the sessions.

Given the larger number of teachers from Arroyo, it was not surprising that every variety of attitude toward the integration process was represented. Reactions to multicultural education ranged all the way from "I treat all minority children exactly as I do white children; I always have and always will," to "I can't wait to get started!" Distinct cliques and cleavages already existed among the teachers of this school. In contrast to Valencia, resistance to change was largely underground and not readily apparent to most staff members. It may also be significant that the teachers had few compunctions about criticizing their fellow staff members. Some even implied that they would rather spend extra time with the students than "some of those teachers we have." Specific objections were never revealed. However, personal risks of many kinds were taken during these sessions as teachers freely expressed their hopes and feelings. Negotiations and communication designed to implement program changes were common in the later sessions. Several sessions even had a "brainstorming" quality. Many of the teachers at Arroyo seemed to have an enthusiastic approach to their work and took obvious delight in the exchange of ideas. While a few teachers expressed feelings of emotional distance from individual students, there was less of a "we-they" attitude at Arroyo. The general impression was that many of the teachers appreciated the minority children as projections of certain of their own desirable characteristics, such as simplicity, strength, and dignity. The Arroyo group thus presented behavior classifiable as belonging in components four through nine of the process model.

In summary, the positions of the schools could be pictured as in figure 1, on the following page.

Thus, the Valencia staff had a greater distance to travel in terms of attitude adjustment. They also showed a greater tendency to reject any proposal based on strong desires to modify the Valencia academic program or attempts to incorporate activities that would reflect and support the multiethnic make-up of the student body. In contrast, Arroyo seemed quite ready to begin programs of change.

With such unified resistance at Valencia it would be disastrous to introduce new programs of a multicultural nature until more Miss Taylors could be introduced into their circle. In other words, Valencia's problem

FIGURE 1.   The Single School Integration Process

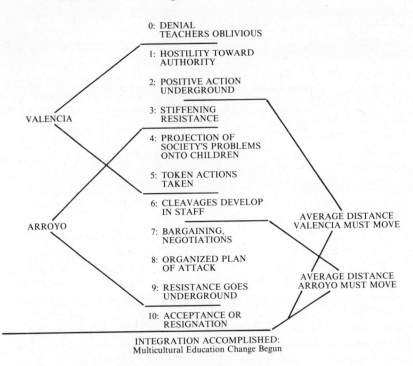

0: DENIAL
   TEACHERS OBLIVIOUS

1: HOSTILITY TOWARD
   AUTHORITY

2: POSITIVE ACTION
   UNDERGROUND

3: STIFFENING
   RESISTANCE

VALENCIA

4: PROJECTION OF
   SOCIETY'S PROBLEMS
   ONTO CHILDREN

5: TOKEN ACTIONS
   TAKEN

6: CLEAVAGES DEVELOP
   IN STAFF

ARROYO

7: BARGAINING,
   NEGOTIATIONS

AVERAGE DISTANCE
VALENCIA MUST MOVE

8: ORGANIZED PLAN
   OF ATTACK

AVERAGE DISTANCE
ARROYO MUST MOVE

9: RESISTANCE GOES
   UNDERGROUND

10: ACCEPTANCE OR
    RESIGNATION

INTEGRATION ACCOMPLISHED:
Multicultural Education Change Begun

was closely linked to the staff. Other problematic components of this school are really manifestations of the central staff problem.

With Arroyo the problem was to mobilize the faculty around systematic approaches to change and selection of desired programs of invention. Less emphasis on staff interaction was needed here.

Several approach choices and strategies are available to the multicultural program planner. An individualized approach using clinical strategies to impact individual teacher attitudes is one choice. This strategy would hopefully result in implementation of program changes, new instructional strategies, and so on by the teachers themselves. Another approach focuses on supporting and rewarding those teachers whose actions place them on components 7 and 8. The object of this is the creation of several tailor-made programs reflecting individual teacher characteristics and desires, rather than a total school program. Yet another choice might be to use the observational data presented here (as well as other more or less empirical data)[21] and to introduce a total school program based on the diverse skills of the faculty. This approach would focus on program rather than teachers, and the artifact of program development could have the desired effect on impacting teacher beliefs.

Two strategies were selected for these schools; for Valencia, the individualized, clinical approach; for Arroyo, the program approach. At the end of the first year, few changes were noted at Valencia, except that the faculty voted the program out of the school. In essence they refused to participate in a follow-up year and totally rejected any concepts of multicultural education. On the other hand, the Arroyo faculty voted for a follow-up year and seemed relatively pleased with themselves as they noted the numerous aspects of program changes they accomplished in the pilot year.

As a result of these experiences, I am extremely cautious in recommending individualized in-service strategies focused on teacher attitudes. Impacting a school with a carefully planned program of change requiring the skills of all the teachers seems to hold more promise. This approach is task-oriented and less threatening to those teachers who feel that defenses must be employed to explain their behavior. The program approach has the decided advantage of requiring new behaviors on the part of the teacher; the attitude-value change is then a private personal affair for each teacher.

The concept of multicultural education offered here[22] goes far beyond the mere inclusion of activities or content focused on food, dance, music, and so on. Multicultural education has to be more comprehensive than the celebration of ethnic holidays and/or one meager ethnic studies course. If the promise of a cultural democracy in the United States has any chance of beginning, the schools must play a large role in preparing us to live this new life. Multicultural education is closely linked to America's promise of freedom for all.

6. Children's Language and the Multicultural Classroom

Rae Moses, Harvey Daniels, and Robert Gundlach

Over the past few years, language has emerged as one of the major issues in the drive for multicultural education. Educators have generally recognized that language is a principal aspect of cultural difference, and linguists have made strong arguments for a relativistic view of such differences. The result has been a vigorous debate centering largely on the place of "nonstandard" speech in American public schools and in the society at large. The debate has been valuable because it has raised a number of important questions about the role of language in education. Still, the controversy has yet to yield much of use to the classroom teacher. Perhaps this is because most of the discussion has involved wide-ranging political, social, and moral perspectives on a very narrow linguistic issue—the common dialectal features of the speech of black urban Americans.

The purpose of this chapter is to examine children's language in a broader linguistic context, as a first step toward making current linguistic insights more useful to the classroom teacher. First we will discuss the process of language acquisition—the ways in which children learn the language around them. The fact that children do acquire the speech of their parents and peers requires that we next consider the matter of dialects. We will then take up the issue of speech styles—the ways in which a speaker adjusts his language to suit the social context of an utterance. And, in turn, we will go on to consider function, or the purposes to which a speaker puts his speech. By surveying these broad linguistic issues, we intend to establish a firm foundation for our analysis of the multicultural classroom as a language environment.

LANGUAGE ACQUISITION

The child's ability to acquire the language that he hears is only one of his remarkable system-acquiring abilities. Temporal, spatial, and quantificational systems are probably acquired in about the same way. The feat of initial language acquisition has long amazed scholars, not to mention parents. Kornei Chukovsky, the Russian author of children's poetry, expressed this amazement nearly half a century ago, in his volume *From Two to Five:*

> It is frightening to think of what an enormous number of grammatical forms are poured over the poor head of the young child. And he, as if it were nothing at all, adjusts to all this chaos, constantly sorting out into rubrics the disorderly elements of the words he hears, without noticing, as he does this, his gigantic effort. . . . The labor he thus performs at this age is astonishing enough, but even more amazing and unparalleled is the ease with which he does it.[1]

By the time he reaches school age, the child has acquired the major structures of his language, and a large and very expressive vocabulary. Those who have grappled with a foreign language are aware of the measure of this accomplishment. This self-propelled pedagogical step is phenomenal not only because of its size, but also because a child takes it without lesson plan or pedagogue.

How, then, is this remarkable language-learning feat accomplished? First, a child starts listening very early. Babbling usually begins during the second six months of life, and seems to be a universal precursor to the development of speech. The first meaningful utterance occurs imitatively at about the age of one year, and by the time a child is two years old, he is putting two words together in a nonimitative and expressive way. Studies of early child language suggest that while the child acquires the specific language variety he hears around him, children all over the world appear to acquire their speech in approximately the same way and at about the same speed. Though severe language deprivation, such as deafness or isolation, takes a linguistic (and probably cognitive) toll, language acquisition from child to child, from culture to culture, and from language to language, occurs inevitably and follows the same general pattern.

A child's language acquisition is controlled more by the rules the child seems to generate from the language "data" he hears than by the "facts" of the language. For example, when Sammy says, "She comed home and then goed out again," *comed* and *goed* are forms that Sammy has probably not heard; instead, they are based upon a rule that when you want to put a verb into the past tense, you add *ed*. Sammy is speaking ungrammatically only by adult standards. *Comed* and *goed* are, for the present, the only way his individual rules of grammar will allow him to render the past tense of *come* and *go*. Since, in the language variety that Sammy hears, the past tense of these verbs is rendered as *came* and *went*, the child will, in his own good time, restructure the rule to accommodate the irregular forms. Curiously, no amount of correcting or prodding by adults appears to affect the child's usage. Only when he is ready will he make the change in his rules that produces the correct, adult form. Chukovsky, again anticipating today's scholars, noted the child's apparent insensitivity to correction: "I have been convinced many times over of how well the child is armored against thought and information that he does not yet need and that are prematurely offered to him by too-hasty adults."[2]

This observation has been confirmed recently by Roger Brown, who investigated the effect of different types of verbal responses to the utterances of children.[3] According to Brown, there are three ways in which parents and children's caretakers respond to a child's utterances: (1) they repeat what the child has said without change; (2) they repeat what the child has said, changing all nonadult forms into adult forms, and adding any words they think may have been left out; or (3) they add semantic information to what the child has said. So, for example, if Lisa says, "Daddy car," the adult response might be (1) to echo the child's utterance; (2) to say something like "Yes, that's Daddy's car"; or (3) to add some contextual information such as "Yes, Daddy's in the garage" or "It just looks like Daddy's car." Brown's work suggests that the way adults respond to child language is not an important variable in language acquisition when judging what is learned or how fast it is learned.

In another study reported by Brown, the order of acquisition of ten different child-language structures was charted and compared to the frequency of structure types in the language of the child's environment. The frequency of any given utterance did not seem to affect the order in which the child acquired the structural features.

We can see that the way in which children acquire language runs counter to some widely held, commonsense notions about language learning. Children *should* learn by imitation, but in important ways they don't. Children *should* be affected by language differences in the kinds of "training" situations they encounter in the linguistic environment of early childhood, but in important ways they aren't. Researchers' evidence suggests, then, that language is acquired rapidly, easily, and without direct "teaching." This is only a part of the process. There is a less verifiable but perhaps more profound aspect of language acquisition. The child, as he learns to speak, is undergoing a learning process that is probably as central to his overall development as the acquisition of the structure of his language. He is learning about the identity and magic of his own voice. Language is a human characteristic, and so, too, is the tendency to find special meaning in one's own voice. We talk to ourselves, almost as if to keep ourselves company. We plan our day, commend our own virtues, and condemn our own foibles in language. Since our language helps to control the way we think about the world, our own voice is probably as intricately associated with self-identification as our own image in the mirror. Each of us is sensitive about his language. We are probably aware quite early that our language is as much a part of us as our smile.

LINGUISTIC VARIABLES

While a child is learning the structure and use of his language, he is probably also learning to have a special regard for his *own* language and for the varieties of language he hears about him. It is to these variations in language that we now turn our attention.

There are at least three significant linguistic variables: dialect, style, and function. *Dialect variation* is the set of differences in the sound system, word choice, and syntax that occur because of the social or geographical distance of the speakers. In the United States, such dialects as "New England" or "rural Appalachian" are examples of such language subgroups. By *style,* we mean that all speakers have ways of adjusting speech to suit different situations; that they have acquired certain sociolinguistic rules that may affect their lexicon, phonology, or syntax in response to changing relationships between speakers and listeners. By *function,* we simply mean that people use language for different purposes at different times, and that their language will change according to the function it is intended to serve. Whenever someone speaks, he always does so in a particular dialect, in an appropriate style, and with a given purpose.

Dialect

In the United States, the geographical distance between northern and southern speakers is apparent in the pronunciation of words such as *pin/ pen* and *lint/lent:* the southerner does not make a distinction, while the northerner keeps the pairs separate. The lack of agreement among Americans about what to call a carbonated drink (soft drink, pop, soda, or tonic), or the name of the long piece of furniture used for sitting (sofa, couch, davenport, or settee), is a reflection of geographical differences. A speaker who makes a distinction between the seond-person singular and plural (*you* versus *you-all*) has revealed his geographical roots.

Many dialect differences that arise from geographical isolation become stereotyped both by the speakers and by others. For the speakers, the dialect features become marks of solidarity and cohesion. We need only look at the uses of dialect features in the media to understand how easily and uniformly we allow them to become symbolic markers of socioeconomic and ethnic groups. The Brooklyn boy is tough and poor. The Boston lady is aloof and well-born. The southern politician is down-to-earth, but a bit of a racist.

In recent years many studies have been made of the various dialects found in our schools in an effort to assess their impact on the learning process. What has been learned is that dialects are natural, rule-governed versions of a language that are produced by a combination of isolation and language change. Our classical conception of a dialect is basically geographical; we realize that spatial isolation will eventually produce language differences between groups. More relevant to current problems, though, are social dialects, which may be rooted in geographical isolation, but are perpetuated through social separation.

Labov, Stewart, Dillard,[4] and others have shown that "black English," for example, is a perfectly respectable speech form, as capable of a full range of expression as "standard" English. Moreover, the process by which a dialect like black English comes to be disvalued has nothing to do with its linguistic integrity, and everything to do with the tastes, fears, and prejudices of speakers of other dialects. There is no cognitive, intellectual, social, educational, or creative deficiency built into the language of black people.

Schools have had different ideas on this subject. They have been the willing carriers of the mythology of correctness, and the cheerful eradicators of "substandard" forms. By their refusal to admit different languages into the business of the classroom, the schools have helped to draw the battle lines where they currently stand. And, unfortunately, they continue to stand against children whose normally developing speech does not suit prevailing tastes.

Style

A second dimension of language that must be considered, if we are to understand the language of children, is style. Every utterance is conditioned by the speaker's understanding of the social situation. People acquire sociolinguistic rules that govern language in varying situations. In order to consider this aspect of language, we shall examine the classic hierarchy of styles described in Martin Joos's *The Five Clocks*.[5]

Joos postulates five basic styles of speech: intimate, casual, consultative, formal, and frozen. The *intimate* style "fuses two separate personalities,"[6] and can only occur between individuals with a close personal relationship. A husband and wife, for example, may sometimes speak to each other in what sounds like a very fragmentary and clipped code, the meaning of which is discernible only to them. The main characteristics of these intimate utterances are extraction and jargon. Extraction refers to communication by means of "extracts" of potentially complete sentences. Jargon is a personal code built of implicitly shared and private meanings. The intimate style, in sum, is personal, fragmentary, and implicit.

The *casual* style is also based on social groupings. When people have shared understandings and meanings, certain adjustments may be made in the way they talk to each other. The earmarks of this style are ellipsis and slang. Ellipsis is the shorthand of shared meanings; slang often expresses them in a way that defines the group. The casual style is reserved for friends, acquaintances, insiders, and those we choose to make insiders.

The *consultative* style "produces cooperation without the integration, profiting from the lack of it."[7] In this style, the speaker provides more explicit background information to the listener because he is not sure he will be understood without it. This is the style used by strangers or near-strangers to get things done—by coworkers dealing with a problem, a buyer making a purchase from a clerk, and so forth. An important feature here is the participation of the listener, who acknowledges his understanding frequently during the speaker's remarks. This is most often seen in interjections such as "yeah," "uh-huh," and "I see" into the utterances of others speaking to us in the consultative mode.

The element of participation drops out of the *formal* style. Speech in this mode is defined by a lack of participation by the listener, as well as by the opportunity for the speaker to plan his utterances ahead of time, and in detail. The formal style is most often found in speeches, lectures, sermons, and the like.

The *frozen* style is for print, and particularly for literature. The distinctions of this style are that it can be densely packed and repacked with meanings by its "speaker," and that it can be reread and reconsidered by the listener. What is lost is the immediacy of interaction between speaker and hearer, sacrificed, presumably, for the permanence and elegance of the final product.

While other linguists have developed different scales of style, most of them share similar considerations. Joos's scheme, when applied to children and schools, raises many points. It takes little perception to note that schools do not operate in any balanced way in terms of language styles. Schools in general tend to favor the formal and frozen modes. Teacher-centered classrooms, where the participation of children is not called for (even on the consultative "uh-huh" level) continue to be the norm. And, needless to say, a preoccupation with the frozen style of literature is virtually a defining characteristic of the school. What consultative and casual language does occur in schools is generally between one child and another, rather than between teacher and child, and is often considered illicit by school authorities.

All of this is not to say that there is anything wrong with frozen and formal speech. They are a part of our range of language styles and a part of our lives. The frozen word can educate and uplift us; formal speech can inform us in special and important ways. But the other styles of speech are equally important and just as integral to our lives. The main question raised by the style prejudices of schools is one of balance. Our instincts, and all available evidence, lead us to the conclusion that schools should accept and foster the use of all speech styles, just as they should accept and foster all dialects.

Function

People use language for different purposes at different times. Beyond this basic proposition, we can get a sense of what is involved in the functions of language by considering the work of the British linguist Michael Halliday.[8]

Halliday has observed that in the speech of young children the categories of function interact less often than in adult speech, and are therefore more clearly identifiable. One result of Halliday's study is a list of seven early speech functions: instrumental, regulatory, interactional, personal, heuristic, imaginative, and representational. The instrumental function is for getting things done; it is the "I want" function. Close to this, the regulatory function seeks to control the actions of others around the speaker. The interactional function is used to define groups and relationships, to get along with others. The personal function allows one to express what he is, and how he feels; Halliday calls this the "here I come" function. The heuristic function is in operation when a speaker is using language to learn, by asking questions and testing hypotheses. In the imaginative function, a speaker may use language to create his own world just as he wants it, or may simply use it as a toy to make amusing combinations of sounds and words. In the representational function, the speaker uses language to express propositions, give information, or communicate subject matter.

As Halliday carefully notes, these neatly defined categories are applicable in a strict sense only to the language of very young children. We can describe a young child's solitary monologues as simply imaginative, or his repeated question "Why?" as purely heuristic, but we know that the speech of adults rarely partakes of only one function per utterance. For example, when we call our boss to discuss a given matter, we may use language to communicate information he does not have, and at the same time try to interact and get along with him winningly, personally to let him know how capable we are, and so forth.

In many classrooms, there is an imbalance in the kinds of language functions fostered. Some teachers behave as if the representational were the only language function worthy of attention. As Halliday points out, most adults (presumably including teachers) seem to think that their language is predominantly representational, even though they constantly and importantly employ the other functions every day. Many schools do not foster an open attitude toward imaginative, personal, and certain kinds of regulatory, heuristic, instrumental, and interactional speech. Again, it is apparent that we are making a mistake in denying the exercise of the wide range of language functions in the schools. By restricting the range of language used we are, at the very least, creating a linguistically unnatural environment in schools, and there is little to suggest that children, who acquire the various skills of language naturally and without formal teaching, will gain much from such a situation.

As we look at the dimensions of language variation we have a picture of great complexity and uncertainty. While progress is being made toward the description of certain dialects found in our schools, we still know very little about language styles and language functions, and almost nothing about the way these variables affect the speech of a given speaker. Beyond this, even less is known of how the interaction of these phenomena fits into the language development schedule of children, and how the schools may enhance or obstruct this natural process.

CULTURAL ADAPTATIONS

So far we have set forth a good deal of information about children's language. We have discussed language acquisition and shown that all children are naturally impelled to learn and speak the language around them. Contemporary research in language development confirms what Chukovsky suggested long ago. First, a young child performs complex and subtle operations in learning language, and these rule-hypothesizing operations are conducted on a nonconscious level. Then, a child acquires language in a structural sequence and at a pace that is not determined by the particular adults in his life (or even by the culture into which he is born). To put it another way, a child learns to listen, to make sense of what he hears, and to speak—a very complicated process—without being taught.

We have also discussed the linguistic variables of dialect, style, and function. When a child acquires the language of his family and his community, he is learning a dialect. Because his dialect represents his geographic and social origins, the dialectal features of a child's speech are a part of his cultural inheritance. The features of the various dialects in the United States are continually changing as people from different parts of the country and different social communities interact. Certainly the proliferation of commercial media, particularly television and radio, is having considerable impact on the evolution of dialects, though perhaps the greatest effect is in the range of forms people are now accustomed to hearing. Studies have shown that people understand a spectrum of speech forms broader than the range they employ in their own speech. For example, Roman Jakobson reports: "People usually display a narrower competence as senders of verbal messages and a wider competence as receivers. . . ."[9]

The issue here is not only whether a speaker is *able* to use forms that are not part of his native dialect; we also need to ask whether he *wants* to. Most children are aware, if only half-consciously, that the way they speak represents a bond with family and friends. Thus, the asymmetrical relationship between language comprehension and production can be partly attributed to a speaker's sense of his social and cultural identity.

We have also discussed the variable of style: the ways a speaker adapts his language to the immediate social context. A speaker takes into account where he is and to whom he is speaking as he gives form to what he has to say. Again, this process if often nonconscious. Martin Joos has established a scale of levels of formality to help explain this phenomenon, and William Labov has shifted the focus somewhat to show that the form of an utterance is affected by the speaker's perception of the power-authority relationship between himself and the listener.[10] Some linguists find that adapting speech to social context is a systematic process, governed by sociolinguistic "rules." Labov has suggested that there is cultural and subcultural variation in sociolinguistic rules, and that

> though native speakers of a given dialect show an extra-ordinary ability to interpret the grammatical rules of another dialect, they do not necessarily show the same ability in dealing with the broader aspects of communicative competence. The rules of discourse tend to differ . . . in the interpretation of the social significance of actions—difference in the forms of politeness, ways of mitigating or expressing anger, or of displaying sincerity and trust.[11]

Next we took up the important—and too often ignored—variable of function. Viewed in the context of a child's experience, purpose, and not the resulting form, is what is important about language. As Halliday puts it, "Language is 'defined' for the child by its uses."[12] We think it is crucial for teachers to consider children's speech from this perspective because it draws into sharp focus what should be an obvious fact: when an adult, or any listener, responds to a child's utterance, he is unavoidably responding to the purpose that motivates the speech.

WHAT WE DON'T KNOW

Before we consider what all of this suggests about children's talk in the multicultural classroom, we need to concern ourselves for a moment with what we don't know. In the final paragraph of *The Language of Primary School Children,* Connie and Harold Rosen note, "As scholars themselves would be first to admit, the process of understanding how children come to master their mother tongue is still at its early stages. As for understanding what does and should happen to children's language in school, that is at an even earlier stage."[13] Concluding a chapter on communication styles in her comprehensive book, *Child Language and Education,* Courtney Cazden poses the problem for people interested in promoting multicultural education: "We do not yet know how to best use children's indigenous strengths in the classroom if our goal is to encourage them to retain their own culture while at the same time teaching them to function in a wider social context when and if they wish to do so."[14] We don't know, for example, the extent to which school-age children are still engaged in learning the structure of their native language. Thus, it is unclear what effects the classroom, as a language environment, might have on that process.

It is difficult to determine which specific features of the "nonstandard" dialects spoken in this country stand clearly outside the bounds of "standard" spoken American English in 1976. We certainly do not know which features will be clearly "nonstandard" ten years from now. And of those features we can identify as currently "nonstandard," we do not know which require alternate "standard" forms in order for a speaker to "function in a wider social context."

We do not know how, or at what age, sociolinguistic rules are learned. Cazden suggests that "the way we learn about appropriate and effective language use may be quite different from the way we learn language structure."[15] While Labov has suggested that different subcultures have different sets of sociolinguistic rules, we have no precise description of these variations. Indeed, we do not even know if the notion of "rule" is the most useful one in describing the ways a person's speech forms are affected by immediate social context.

Halliday and others have given us an idea of the human purposes to which talk is put, but we do not know very much about *how* a speaker's purpose affects what he says and the way he says it.

IMPLICATIONS FOR
MULTICULTURAL CLASSROOMS

Where do all these unanswered questions leave us? First, they make us skeptical of curriculums that purport to impart isolated speaking "skills." We simply do not have enough information about linguistic variables or about the advanced stages of language acquisition to give us much confidence in curriculum materials that are said to extend a child's ability to speak. In fact, what *is* known suggests that less emphasis should be placed on curriculum development, and that more energy and thought should go toward creating a rich sociolinguistic environment in the classroom. Cazden, Baratz, Labov, and Palmer put it simply: "The first step in extending each child's verbal abilities is to create a school setting which stimulates each child to use all the language he has."[16]

In general, a rich sociolinguistic environment describes a place where (1) a lot of talking and listening goes on, (2) the natural dialects of all speakers are respected, and (3) the full range of language styles and functions can come into play. For different people, in a culture-related way, different speech situations are sometimes more comfortable and natural than others. The goal for the teacher in a multicultural classroom is to create a variety of different contexts for student talk.

Perhaps the best way to get a sense of the possibilities is to consider classroom relationships in structural terms. We will consider four basic structures for speech interaction in the classroom. Our discussion is based on S. Phillips's model of classroom "participant-structures."[17]

First, there is the situation in which the teacher conducts a discussion involving the whole class. The speech interaction here is closely controlled by the teacher, who chooses when to speak and when to listen, and who may demand talk from a student whether or not the student has anything to say.

In the second arrangement, the teacher addresses and listens to students in small groups (while the class is working on group projects, for example). Here again, the talk is controlled by the teacher, and what a student says usually follows, both in function and style, from the language the teacher uses for the particular interaction.

In the third structure, individual students initiate conversation with the teacher. Here students are working independently and either approach or summon the teacher, seeking to ask a question or to share an accomplishment. In this situation the student sets the function and (within the range he thinks the teacher will accept) the style of his own speech.

The fourth structure involves situations in which students are interacting with other students without the direct involvment of the teacher. Here the activity, rather than the teacher, sets the range of useful speech styles and functions.

Let us take a closer, critical look at these arrangements, starting with the first two teacher-student interaction structures. In conducting a discussion with a whole class òr a group of students, the teacher's purpose is often to assess what the students know, or to build a lesson from students' contribution of information. When either of these is the case, students are expected to use language almost exclusively in its representational function. Furthermore, the representation of knowledge is being made to an adult listener who probably knows more about the subject than the speaker does. Certainly there is nothing inherently wrong with this situation. Students are often eager to show what they have learned. If the discussion is a relaxed one, the talk may vary between formal and consultative styles and may even become casual. In a discussion that truly engages many participants, bits of speech serving several language functions can also enter. Still, it is important to note the limits imposed on students' speech when the central purpose of the interaction calls for just one kind of talk.

A teacher can broaden the language possibilities, even within these structural arrangements, by acknowledging and seeking the development of what may at first seem to be peripheral student remarks, and by encouraging students to respond to what other students say. Thus, what to an outside observer might seem to be less than a controlled and "productive" discussion may actually be very productive. A relaxed discussion that brings into play several language styles and functions can be productive for students as listeners as well as speakers, providing them with rich and varied language "data" that they can incorporate into their own speech styles as they see fit.

The third structure also involves the teacher as a participant. Here one-to-one interactions are initiated by the student, and the teacher's role is to listen and respond. Probably the main restriction on the student's speech is a perception of the "politics" of the situation—the unequal power relationship between adult and child. Also, cultural conflict can occur when a student feels that his natural way of speaking is unacceptable to the cultural authority that the teacher represents. In interactions with individual students, especially in the multicultural classroom, a teacher needs to be alert to these factors. To minimize restrictions on what the student says, the teacher must act as a careful and sympathetic listener. It is also important that the teacher focus his response on *what* the student says rather than *how* it is said. By suggesting this, we are not merely recommending a "be kind to students" policy; rather, we are asserting that a student is more likely to use his full language ability—for his own purposes and in his natural style—when he believes that the teacher will listen carefully and will share the speaker's concern for the meaning he is trying to convey.

Too often students do not have this faith in their teachers. One result is that a student will sometimes distort his speech in an attempt to meet what he takes to be the teacher's expectations. In the process, communication is subverted. Another common result is a defensive strategy whereby the student will say as little as possible. In neither case does the student have the chance to use his full facility with language, and to explore ways of extending it. Even in one-to-one situations, where the teacher listens and responds with interest and sensitivity, many students will feel the pressure of the unequal power relationship, and this may limit the language they use. We believe that to allow students to use and expand the full range of language possibilities, abundant opportunity must be provided for them to interact directly with other students.

This brings us to the fourth kind of situation: students talking and listening to other students. This deserves special attention, both because it is a structure in which children can exercise their language ability to its limits, and because it is a structure found far too infrequently in today's schools.

In an article addressed to day-care center personnel, Cazden, Baratz, Labov, and Palmer identify three speech functions that for children speaking to other children "seem particularly important as incentives for complex language."[18] They are speech for self-aggrandizement, language for explication, and language for aesthetic pleasure. These are roughly analogous to the language functions that Halliday identifies as personal, representational, and imaginative.

It is not surprising that the language of boasting is often complex. Children and adults (including teachers!) can be counted on to be linguistically inventive when presenting themselves. It is important that a relaxed, friendly environment be created where students feel free to present themselves openly. This means that the teacher must make clear that the student is not being officially evaluated on what he says, and certainly not on how he says it. In fact, it is probably best for the teacher not to intrude on the situation at all. As Cazden, Baratz, Labov, and Palmer note, "The most language is produced when there is no one present of superior status: in other words, when nothing the child says can be held against him." The teacher should recognize that a student might use language for self-aggrandizement during almost any activity. And while a student speaking to this end may seem to be wandering from the task at hand, he is engaged in "language arts" work nonetheless. In a multicultural classroom where an attitude of cultural acceptance prevails, students can learn much about the cultural backgrounds of their peers simply by hearing how people from various backgrounds choose to present themselves. It is worth adding that when students are directly interacting with other students, there is no room for a teacher's correction of a student's speech forms.

The time-honored elementary school tradition of "show-and-tell" can also be extended to provide opportunities for students to explain things to other students, using language for the purpose of explication. In one school we visited recently, show-and-tell had been redubbed "drag-and-brag." The new phrase indicates that the traditional activity, if conducted in an environment where students are truly interested in each other's presentations, offers an opportunity for students to use language for several purposes. Indeed, any activity that prompts one student to need or want to explain something to another student is potentially a language-learning activity for both. This kind of activity is especially suitable to the multicultural classroom, because it offers students a chance to learn how peers from different cultural backgrounds approach and deal with a variety of situations. As noted above, the teacher's role is to promote interaction among students, rather than to operate on the forms a student's speech takes.

Finally, children sometimes use language for aesthetic pleasure: simply to please themselves by playing with sound and meaning. This will occur in an environment where students feel that bursts of speech-play are permitted and appreciated by those around them.

What is the value of creating classroom situations in which there is room for students to play with their language? First, Cazden, Baratz, Labov, and Palmer find that when children play with language, they sometimes "demonstrate skills which go far beyond any current program of instruction." Second, play is a kind of exploration, a kind of trying out. Language play can be viewed as an exploration of how sounds are made, how meaning can be arranged in various word combinations, and how listeners will respond to unusual statements and questions. Third, Courtney Cazden has recently suggested that language play is also related to the development of a metalinguistic awareness—awareness of language itself rather than regard for it only as a "transparent" medium through which meaning passes. In turn, it is thought that metalinguistic awareness may be linked to a readiness in learning to read and, perhaps, in learning to write.[19]

If language play is of value, then two kinds of activities—both within the structure of students interacting with other students—can be encouraged. Teachers can arrange for a variety of organized activities that involve language play, ranging from creative dramatics to commercially produced word games. But since a child's natural inventiveness sometimes defies the best-laid adult plans, general classroom conditions should be such that a student feels free to play with what he is saying.

AN OPEN ENDING

Recent scholarship presents teachers with a first step in promoting language development in the multicultural setting. This first order of business is to create a combination of classroom situations and activities that will allow a student to have confidence in his own language, and to explore and extend what he is able to do with it. This is what contemporary linguists point to in educational policy. Still, for two reasons, our conclusion must be open-ended.

First, it is not clear at all what the long-range goals of current school language policy should be. Part of this uncertainty is due to a shortage of sociolinguistic knowledge that would lead to long-range recommendations. But the uncertainty is also caused by the larger, unresolved issues involving all our social institutions. If we were to make a list of what seem to be the societal goals in the United States today, we doubt whether a multicultural approach would be among the high-priority items. We hope the time is near when such a goal will clearly emerge as top priority, because it is unlikely that a multicultural concept can be effective in schools if other social institutions are guided by conflicting, culturally hierarchic values.

There is also a more positive sense in which we leave our ending open. We believe that today's classrooms can be made into rich language environments where students from many cultural backgrounds can learn together. We conclude with an invitation to teachers to use the information and suggestions we have presented to develop practices that will make their classrooms truly multicultural.

7. Intellectual Strengths of Minority Children

Asa G. Hilliard

Cognitive deficits in minority children have been assumed, described, and *then* explained. The "evidence"—direct and indirect—has been mounting to suggest a genetic cause for achievement differences between racial groups. It is the purpose of this chapter to present an overview of this "evidence." Analysis will also be made of relevant, but often over-looked, research. The focus here is on research pertaining directly to the black child and adolescent. The points developed, though, are relevant also to any racial ethnic minority or economically powerless group. I intend to illuminate the findings of a variety of ethnic and racial studies.

RACISM AND RESEARCH

Research, like any other aspect of our lives, reflects prevailing cultural values. Myrdal has treated the problem of objectivity in social research in incisive fashion.[1] From his exposition on subjectivity in social research and Levenson's treatise on "the fallacy of understanding,"[2] one gets a better perspective on how uneven systematic inquiry in the social sciences can be. By the time the tools of research are applied, there is much room for error and distortion. When institutional and individual racism are present, then the problem is compounded.

Assessing Minority Abilities: Aspects of the Problem

A visit to classes for the retarded in any large urban area will tell a dramatic story. The conditions found in such cities were described by Williams:

In St. Louis, during the academic year 1968–69, blacks comprised approximately 63.6 percent of the school population, whereas whites comprised 36.4 percent. Of 4,020 children in Special Education, 2,975 (76 percent) were black, only 1,045 (24 percent) were white. . . . In San Francisco . . . although black children comprise only 27.8 percent of the total student population in the San Francisco Unified Schools, they comprise 47.4 percent of all students in educationally handicapped classes, and 53.5 percent of all students in the educable mentally handicapped classes.[3]

Such patterns of placement are fairly common in other large cities. There also tends to be a disproportionately low representation of blacks and other minorities in classes for the "gifted." Both genetic and environmental explanations have been given for class placement distributions like these. If the genetic hypothesis were true, this discussion could be ended quickly. However, disturbing irregularities would have to be explained. For example, *why are the overwhelming majority of pupils in classes for the educable mentally retarded male?* Even Jensen, father of the genetic inferiority controversy currently in progress, points out that earlier findings showing differences between male and female average IQ in the general population were false.[4] He asserts that evidence for this conclusion was based upon sampling errors caused, in turn, by a failure to account for differential dropout rates for male and female school populations.

The explanatory power of the Jensen IQ and genetics hypothesis is feeble. An alternative explanation is that environmental conditions account for performance differences between minority and majority group members. If there are more "gifted" minority children and fewer "retarded" minority children than have been identified in most schools, then the process of assessment must itself be assessed. Why are minority children misassessed? Who is competent to assess?

A discussion of the assessment process must take into account the fact that teaching and assessment are highly complex processes. "Standardized testing" *alone* cannot yield the significant answers educators seek. Yet, a review of placement practices reveals that little else is used to make far-reaching decisions. Black-and-white solutions are inadequate for technicolor problems.

Professional educators love language. It is hard to think of another professional discipline in which the language is so picturesque, and at the same time so loose. In education there is the appearance of precision and the assumption that something real and substantial is being described. This sloppiness in the use of professional language creates a basic problem when professionals begin to do assessment. Words such as *gifted, retarded, intelligence, curriculum,* and *creative* are never precisely defined. This ambiguity of meaning permits unconscious individual or institutional bias to intrude into judgments. The lack of precision in professional terminology permits those who run programs for "gifted" students to use the

Stanford-Binet IQ score as a primary selection criterion for programs that purport to have "creative behavior" as a programmatic goal. But the correlation between IQ and creativity often tends to be low. Many teachers who work in programs for the "gifted" are unable to describe the goals of the program clearly. What then is the basis for excluding students? Little more can be said here except to note that one immediately enters a professional wasteland when talking about most specific problems in education. Soft constructs make the job of analysis difficult.

Historical Failures of Assessors of Minorities: Errors and Predisposition

Cross-cultural assessment is routinely contaminated by observer bias. This is clear in the literature of social science and should be the grounds for a healthy skepticism and caution among educators who do assessments. Valentine makes a telling point:

> Among the sources of ethnographic method was a keenly felt need to overcome the limitations of other observers who often preceded the anthropologist in describing life among alien and exotic peoples: explorers, conquerors, traders, missionaries, and imperial administrators. With few exceptions, the observations of these men were external and superficial. Moreover, it was inherent in their viewpoint that they should see social order mainly in whatever they could discern that seemed analogous to western institutions and patterns. To them, more often than not, all else was either bestial savagery or natural—i.e., cultureless nobility. . . . As we shall see, there are analogous problems in the study of the poor in our own society today.[5]

A further example of observer bias in cross-cultural settings is offered by Myrdal:

> Whenever I turned, I found that any statistics available had to be scrutinized most severely before being used; at best they were highly uncertain and not as specific as the analyst would desire. Most of the general figures so confidently quoted in the literature, such as those pertaining to trends in income, population, literacy, and school enrollment, proved to be no more than extremely crude guesses, often palpably wrong.
>
> . . . I found myself engaged in a study where the main concern was methodological—how to cleanse concepts and discard theories and then state problems in a logical and realistic way—and where the results were very often merely a demonstration of our ignorance and a clearer statement of what we do not know. It is in this way that the work on the study became to me personally a destiny, the course of which I had not foreseen or planned from the beginning. I sincerely believe that at the present stage an important contribution to the advance of knowledge about these countries is the negative act of destroying constructs that we have rapidly put together and exposing to criticism masses of more or less worthless statistics collected within the framework of

these constructs, which we are using all too confidently. I believe this because these constructs and statistics now stand in the way of scientific progress.[6]

Myrdal's concern in studying other cultures should be the concern of any responsible professional who attempts to assess cultures different from his own. The potential for error is great. This same matter has been treated from a philosophical-sociological perspective by Berger and Luckmann, Mannheim, and others.[7] These men present the field called the "sociology of knowledge." An absence of doubt in the judgments of these professionals, who assess those from cultures other than their own, is frightening.

Negative distortions are also fed by selective perceptions born of a racism ingrained in our culture. McDermott carefully analyzed the dynamics of selective perception when he compared the perceptions of "hosts," or dominant majority members in a society, with the selective perceptions of "pariah minority" children.[8] In McDermott's analysis, hosts saw what they wanted or needed to see when they observed the behavior of pariah minorities. The consequences of this "seeing" by a teacher from a dominant part of the culture seldom facilitiates learning for a pariah minority student.

The track record of "expert" assessors of minority children has been notoriously incompetent. If the pay of these assessors were "competency based" or "performance based," some would go hungry. White assessors of minority students have included the best talent available. It is important that the "skill" of some be placed in proper perspective. Thomas and Sillen cite several of our top "experts." They quote Lewis Terman, father of the Stanford-Binet, as follows:

> . . . a low level of intelligence was very, very common among Spanish-Indian and Mexian families of the Southwest and also among Negroes. Their dullness seems to be racial . . . the children of such persons are uneducable beyond the merest rudiments of training. No amount of school instruction will ever make them intelligent voters or capable citizens in the true sense of the word. Judged psychologically, they cannot be considered normal.[9]

From G. Stanley Hall, first president of the American Psychological Association, they offer the following quotation: "Africans, Indians, and Chinese are members of primitive or adolescent races in a stage of incomplete growth." And Carl Gustav Jung, the renowned psychiatrist and a self-proclaimed student of races, is quoted as saying: "Blacks have a whole historical layer less in their racial unconscious than the White man and Black childishness is contagious." More recently, "scholars" such as Jensen, Shockley, Jencks, Moynihan, Bernstein, and others have written in the same vein. What is troubling is that their views have the aura of scholarship, and are influential. But one cannot find any of these notables working from a data base considered valid and reliable.

Thomas and Sillen interpret Arthur Jensen of the University of California at Berkeley and William Shockley of Stanford as follows:

> A most frightening issue raised by Jensen is the ideology of eugenics applied to Black people. It is hard to believe—so soon after the Nazi nightmare—that proposals are again being advanced to restrict reproduction on a racial basis. Yet this is clearly the implication of Jensen's concern about the danger of a decline in "our national I.Q." resulting from a higher birthrate among Blacks than Whites. He raises the specter of "dysgenic trends," which he links with "current welfare policies, unaided by eugenic foresight." The same fear has been expressed by physicist William Shockley, one of the most persistent agitators on the subject of Black genetic inferiority: "Can it be that our humanitarian welfare programs have already selectively emphasized high and irresponsible rates of reproduction to produce a socially relatively unadaptable human strain?"[10]

Thomas and Sillen point out that such thinking in the past has had drastic policy consequences. As recently as 1914, psychiatrists succeeded in adding a provision excluding the "constitutionally psychopathically inferior" onto an immigration bill. Later, state after state adopted sterilization laws (which were often used selectively against blacks). Even today, reports of "voluntary sterilization" and experimentation on black subjects with syphillis remind us of the dangers present in this strange scholarship. The student in education must question all research, all researchers' motivations, all methods, all data, and all interpretations. The same people who distort research also influence policy positions, such as Moynihan's recommendation of "benign neglect" for blacks and other poor.[11]

We know, for example, that Jencks set out to reassess the data from the Coleman report. But his detailed Appendix A is a radical departure from Coleman's study. It presents information on the same old haunting theme, "IQ and Heritability." *Why here? What is the real Jencks agenda?*

As a sidelight, it is interesting to note that neither Jencks, Jensen, Shockley, nor Moynihan has established credentials as a teacher of younger children. These "scholars" would be more credible if they worked with children. Unfortunately, a look at the financial support for public education suggests that the "scholars" are making their point with policy makers.

In Spite of It All, the Subjects Misbehave

In spite of "expert predictions" of low minority aptitude and achievement, there have been many surprises. In the United States, studies of infant IQ by Bayley, Anastassi and D'Angelo, Pasamanick,[12] and others have shown that there are no differences between races up to the age of two years. Jane Mercer found that many Mexican-American children were inappropriately assigned to classes for the retarded in California schools.[13] The Bay Area Association of Black Psychologists found that "retarded" students in a school in San Francisco were similarly labeled and placed. Cross-cultural studies of aptitude in other countries have developed interesting findings, especially when considered against a popular conception of the "noble savage." Kleinfeld has written about the complex mental skills that are required for survival among the Eskimo.[14] There, the environment determines the content that will be utilized and the skills that will be needed.

Claude Levi-Strauss clinches the point. He cites examples of classification among "primitive" peoples.

> Products which Siberian peoples use for medicinal purposes illustrate the care and ingeniousness, the attention to detail, and concern with distinctions employed by theoretical and practical workers in societies of this kind . . . such as contact with a woodpecker's beak, blood of a woodpecker, gobbled egg of the bird kookcha (Iakoute, against toothache, scrofula, high fevers, and tuberculosis, respectively).
>
> . . . The real question is not whether the touch of a woodpecker's beak and a man's tooth does in fact cure toothache. It is rather whether there is a point of view from which a woodpecker's beak and a man's tooth can be seen as going together . . . and whether some initial order can be induced into the universe by means of these groupings. Classifying as opposed to not classifying has a value of its own, whatever the form classification may take.[15]

Among the Aymara Indians of Bolivia, Levi-Strauss says, "over two hundred and fifty varieties of maize are still distinguished in native vocabulary and the figure was certainly higher in the past." Among the Fulani of Sudan, he says, "classifications are not only methodological and based on carefully built up theoretical knowledge. They are also at times comparable from a formal point of view, to those still in use in zoology and botany."[16] Two examples are given by Levi-Strauss of the failure to appreciate the use of systems of classifications by observers whose ethnocentrism was a problem.

> When he began his study of the classification of colours among the Hanundo of the Philippines, Conklin was at first baffled by the apparent confusions and inconsistencies. These, however, disappeared when informants were asked to relate and contrast specimens instead of being asked to define isolated ones. There was a coherent system but this could not be understood in terms of our system, which is founded on two axes: that of brightness (value) and that of intensity (chroma). All the obscurities disappeared when it became clear that the Hanundo system also has two axes but two different ones. They distinguish colours into relatively light and relatively dark and into those usually fresh or succulent plants and those usually dry or desiccated plants.

It was a professional biologist who pointed out how many errors and misgivings, some of which have only recently been rectified, could have been avoided, had the older travelers been content to rely on native taxonomies instead of improving entirely new ones. The result was that eleven different authors between them applied the scientific name "canis azare" to three distinct genera, eight species and nine different subspecies, or again that a single variety of the same species was referred to by several different names.[17]

Taken together, these studies of other minority groups tend to demonstrate an equality in cognitive capacity across cultural lines. But when the observer's frame of reference is imposed on the experience of people alien to him, confusion and invalid interpretation are almost certain to result.

This condition is directly analogous to the ordinary condition in which many teachers find themselves. *Most teachers are monolingual in a bilingual or a bicultural situation. As such, it is the teacher who has the deficit. The bilingual or bicultural student who meets an untrained, ethnocentric, monolingual teacher is unlucky indeed!*

CRITICISMS OF BIASED RESEARCH

Why are intelligent readers so easily satisfied with what passes for significant research on minority people? The classic examples of efforts gone astray are the Coleman report on equality of educational opportunity,[18] and the Jencks reassessment of that study.[19] Approximately two million dollars was appropriated by Congress for the Coleman study alone. Amid high congressional expectations, and with the help of prestigious professionals from the National Center for Educational Statistics (NCES), the U.S. Office of Education, the Educational Testing Service, and outstanding universities, a study was designed and conducted. Because of its origin and the caliber of researchers involved, the study was widely received as valid. The findings of Coleman and Jencks have had a dramatic impact on public policy in education and public thinking in general. Their influence is clearly undeserved. Many writers have developed vital points in criticism of the work of these two men and their helpers.[20] While space will not permit a detailed summary of significant criticism here, a few points should be made to illustrate why such studies as the Coleman report are dangerous.

Sample Bias

Apart from the question of numbers that are required for a representative sample, several major cities chose not to cooperate. From what we know of the uniqueness of the problems in urban areas, a disproportionate representation here may well have been the source of a biased estimate. Further, of those who participated in the study, many chose not to answer sensitive items. For example, Guthrie points out that in a sample of about three hundred elementary schools in the Northeast region, *over one-third of the principals failed to answer one or more questions regarding their views about the racial composition of school faculties.* What does the response of the remaining members of the group mean on this significant question? What does the nonresponse mean where the first group was concerned? Any valid inference requires, first and foremost, a representative sample, especially on significant variables. Here Coleman fails. *What, then, is Jencks reassessing?*

Inaccurate Data

When one looks at the variables that were measured, it is clear that certain data should not be accepted at face value. As Guthrie properly points out, a district-wide average figure on per-pupil expenditures masks the fact that there is generally a range of expenditures by schools within most districts. Further, these differences within districts tend to favor those who are nonminority. This kind of averaging can explain why the differences that resources may make in the growth of students and their subsequent achievement were not discovered. Other examples are presented by Guthrie.

Irrelevant Variables

The most serious shortcoming of this study of "school effectiveness" is that few if any of the important things about schools were measured. The study examined such variables as the following:

1. access to certain classes
2. access to special school facilities such as laboratories
3. access to special personnel
4. teacher background variables such as training, professional standing, and morale
5. type of curriculum
6. test score information
7. accreditation

It takes the "nose counting" variety of social researcher to settle for a study of school effectiveness that deals only with such superficial variables. It is very interesting that even Mosteller and Moynihan spotted the following key information:

As much as could be was also made of the findings that a child's sense of "control of his environment" correlated strongly with his educational achievement. Of all the variables measured in the survey, the EEOR reported, including measures of family background and all school variables, these attitudes showed the strongest relation to achievement. . . . Negro students who had a strong sense of control of environment did better than White students with a weak sense.[21]

Where is the inquiry into what causes a student to experience a "sense of control of his environment"? It would seem that school-effectiveness researchers would have designed a study to get at such interactions. Reassessors of Coleman data should be interested in what the data may suggest by way of explanation for this. People who understand schools would have anticipated the need to build appropriate inquiry techniques into the basic design of the study to explore this phenomenon and others like it. Charnofsky, Fanon, Freire, Zahn,[22] and many others have not been silent on this concept. Instead of taking the power-and-learning relationship into account, we are treated to an examination of the "number of books in a library" or an inside peek at "salary schedules." The real resources of successful schools are virtually ignored. Therefore, along with sampling bias, the variables *themselves* are irrelevant. No "reassessment" can correct these fundamental flaws. What does an elegant statistical treatment of data that has the value of garbage yield? Computer experts tell us that if one puts "garbage in," after processing, one gets "garbage out." They even have a word for it: GIGO.

It is clear that many of those who write about the aptitude and achievement of the "disadvantaged" usually are long on experimental method and statistics, and short on experience with children, especially those classified as disadvantaged. There is seldom, if ever, any history of researchers' having had success in promoting the growth of the minorities studied, or even having attempted to do so. From where, then, do their hypotheses for research come? At best, their hypotheses are naive guesses, apparently stemming from their reviews of questionable journal articles. The "scholarship" of the Jensens and Jenckses wilts and withers under the onslaught of true scholarly criticism such as that by Kamin,[23] who has provided a devastating analysis of original studies of twins by such notables as Burt, Shields, Newman-Freeman-Holzinger, and Joel-Nielsen. Such truly objective analyses show clearly why some so-called scholars are really pseudoscientists. Many of these pseudoresearchers are like the man who looks for a lost coin under a streetlamp—rather than in the dark, where he lost it—because the light is better under the lamp. Clearly, *the proper study of growth must concentrate on an examination of growth itself, not on the archives of educational minutiae.* There seems to be no study of blacks that starts from a basic understanding of what the black environment is. That research must be done. One can start by looking at the hundreds of thousands of black and other minority children whose outstanding progress cannot be explained by deficit projections from regression equations. A look at the following data will leave one with some nagging discrepancies to explain. If the Jensens and Shockleys are right, then how do we find children who function the way these do?

EVIDENCE OF INTELLECTUAL CAPACITY

Unexplained Growth and Intellectual Strength

The following is a sampling of studies or projects that show how blacks in certain environments have performed as we would expect them to in a facilitating environment. These studies represent *observed behaviors, not theories*. If the assumption of genetic differences between racial groups is postulated, how can this happen?

When IQ test differences between blacks and whites are found, they usually favor whites. We know now that language, motivation, and other variables affect test scores and are themselves affected by the condition of opportunity. What happens before these influences have a chance to act unevenly on racial groups? Bayley found the following:

> It would appear that the behaviors which are developing during the first 15 months of life, whether they are motor skills or the early perceptual and adaptive forms of mental abilities, are for the most part unrelated to sex, race, birth order, geographical location, or parental ability. The one possible difference is in motor development in which the Negro babies tend to be more advanced than the whites during the first 12 months. Although there is considerable overlap of scores among whites and Negroes of the same age, a genetic factor may be operating. That is, Negroes may be inherently more precocious than whites in their motor coordination.[24]

Golden and Birns studied black children at twelve, eighteen, and twenty-four months from a group of parents one-third of whom were on welfare, one-third lower class, and one-third middle class or above. The tests involved Piagetan sensorimotor tasks. There were no social or class differences in "object concept" development.[25]

Wachs investigated "object concept" and "means ends" behavior in infants up to the age of twenty-two months. Half of the infants were lower class, mainly blacks, and half were middle-class whites. There were no essential differences between the groups on these measures.[26]

Palmer found that up to three years, eight months, low socioeconomic urban blacks did not score differently on tests of intellectual skills from middle-class whites.[27] Similarly, Anastasi and Pasamanick[28] in different studies, came to the same conclusion regarding the lack of differences on intellectual tasks between blacks and white middle-class subjects during infancy.

What happens after infancy? Ginsburg summarizes the evidence.[29] He indicates that after infancy, poor children receive lower IQ scores. Black poor receive even lower scores. This seems to suggest a connection between *poverty and scores* rather than *race and intelligence.*

IQ scores may change for blacks in general, but there is strong evidence to support the notion that the IQ is an artifact of cultural bias in measurement. For example, Templin found no differences in the production of sentence types between lower- and upper-class white children, if one accepts "functionally complete" but "structurally incomplete" sentences. It should be clear that the concept of structure in language is culturally determined. Baratz was able to demonstrate the same thing in her study: black children could communicate the *sense* of a standard English sentence when they were permitted to respond in nonstandard English. The potential source of some of the errors of judgment that are made about black children is illuminated by Baratz.

> These are but a few of the many instances where Negro nonstandard sound usage differs from standard English. It is no wonder then that Cynthia Deutsch (1964) should find her assessment of auditory discrimination that disadvantaged Black children did not "discriminate" as well as White children from middle-class linguistic environments. She administered a discrimination task that equated "correct responses" with judgments of equivalencies and differences in standard-English sound usage. Many of her stimuli, though different for the standard English speaker (e.g., *pin–pen*), are similar for the Negro nonstandard speaker. She attributed the difference in performance of disadvantaged children to such things as the constant blare of the television in their homes, and there being so much "noise" in their environment that the children tend to "tune out." However, Black children make responses on the kind of language they consider appropriate. In the same way that *cot* (for sleeping) and *caught* (for ensnared) or *marry* (to wed) and *merry* (to be happy) are not distinguished in the speech of many White people (so that they would say on an auditory discrimination test that *cot* and *caught* were the same), *pin* and *pen* are the same in the language of ghetto Blacks. The responses that the Black child makes are on the basis of the sound usage that he has learned in his social and geographical milieu, and do not reflect some difficulty in discriminating.[30]

Language, while not a test of intelligence in the formal sense, is definitely an integral component of intelligence. In that light it is important to consider the work of Labov.[31] In making the case that nonstandard English is equivalent in complexity to standard English, he indirectly supports the notion of the equivalence of aptitude between blacks and others. Ideas of substance translate readily from one "language" to another. The authors of chapter 6 have pursued the development of language, specifically, how children develop a range of language styles for different situations.

Mercer, in a study of children who were labeled mentally retarded (IQ below 70), found that Mexican-American and black children who were labeled retarded were less subnormal than Anglo children who were so labeled.[32] Further, the Mexican-American or black child was likely to be so labeled when an IQ score was the only evidence. Of those who scored below 70 on the Wechsler Intelligence Scale for Children, but had "passing adaptive behavior," all were black or Mexican-American. In further study, Mercer showed that when social background factors were held constant, no differences were found between the measured intelligence of Mexican-American and Anglo or between black and Anglo subjects.

Self-concept

One area of study in which there is much myth and little fact is that of black self-concept. Typically, writers have assumed that there was one black experience and one black response to it. In fact, there is much to learn, as the following studies suggest, if we are to understand motivation and achievement.

Jones found that black children rejected the label "culturally deprived" when referring to themselves.[33] In a study of black college students, he found the same thing. The idea of black self-hatred must be reexamined in light of these and other findings that follow. There are simply not enough data here to understand the variability of results from one study to the next.

Powell, with an interracial team of investigators, used the Tennessee Self-Concept Scale on a sample of black and white students in a northern and southern city.[3] Powell found that blacks in the southern city had significantly higher self-concepts than whites or blacks in the northern city. This is very different from previous findings on the same subject. Powell's description of the cities and the times during which the study was conducted helps to explain the change. However, few, if any, studies have been designed to explore the reasons for higher self-concept among southern black children.

Trowbridge found similar results using the Coppersmith Self-Esteem Inventory.[35] She found that low socioeconomic-status (SES) black and white children from eight to fourteen years of age scored higher than middle SES children.

Thomas Hilliard studied black college students in Chicago.[36] He found that the activists among them were psychologically healthier than the nonactivists. In light of assessments made of aggressive students by college administrators, this is an interesting finding indeed.

The importance of these and other studies in the area of self-concept is that self-concept and achievement are positively related. If self-concept is in fact high, the teachers and other helpers have a good base from which to facilitate students' growth.

Achievement

This discussion would be no better than those I have criticized if it did not cite studies beyond those dealing with potential. A look at the *actual achievement* of black students is required. The same kind of evidence is available as for any other ethnic group.

Judith Anderson reported on the Special Elementary Education for the Disadvantaged project (SEED) in Oakland, California.[37] Fourteen black students and one Oriental student from poverty areas in a fifth-grade class demonstrated their knowledge of logarithms, equations, gamma signs, and variables. Professor William Johntz, a former mathematics teacher from Berkeley (California) High School, also directed SEED nation-wide. *Studies of Project SEED students show that they scored "precisely like middle-class white students on conceptual reasoning tests."* The children also improved in reading and regular arithmetic according to evaluations made by the Cal Tech mathematics department. Does good teaching make a difference?[38]

Stephen Strickland reported on a special project involving slum children in Milwaukee.[39] An interdisciplinary team from the University of Wisconsin selected an area of Milwaukee that, according to census data, had the lowest median family income, the greatest population density per housing unit, and *the most dilapidated housing* in the city. It yielded *the highest rate of mental retardation* among schoolchildren when compared to other areas of the city. For four years, starting in 1966, a total of forty mothers with IQs of less than 70 participated with their newborn children in the Infant Education Center Project. All mothers who were asked if they wanted to participate in the program quickly accepted. Two-thirds of the babies were in an experimental group and one-third in a control group. Special parent-education programs and education-stimulation programs for the children were conducted. *After 42 months, children in the active stimulation group measured an average of 33 IQ points higher than children in the control group. Also, the children in the experimental group were learning at a rate that was in excess of the norm for their age peers generally. IQ improvement was approximately 50 percent for most youngsters, with some achieving IQs as high as 135.*

In Dade County, Florida, black students scored above the national average in mathematics.[40] These are not examples using special kids, *only special teachers.*

Bradfield, Hilliard, and others reported on the Behavioral Evolvement through Achievement Management (B.E.A.M.) project in San Francisco.[41] A group of more than eighty blacks was selected from the student body of an all-black junior high school in a low-income neighborhood. For one year, these seventh- and eight-grade students were given a special program in reading, counseling, and "cultural enrichment" by high school and college tutors. Most of the students were bordering on failure in school, had marginal attendance, were reading nearly three or more years below grade level, and were on probation with the juvenile courts. After thirty-six hours of reading instruction with other supporting activities, there was an average gain in reading scores of nearly three years; the attendance patterns for the group became higher than the school average; and the recidivism rate in delinquency dropped from the city's average of nearly 50 percent to 4 percent. Teachers and counselors in the school indicated that they could recognize B.E.A.M. students by their improved performance.

Cole and Gay have shown how Kpelle children in Liberia, when tested *using the categories of thought growing out of their experience,* are able to perform on certain tests at levels superior to their U.S. counterparts.[42] Levi-Strauss has developed extensive cross-cultural data to demonstrate that intelligence is complex for all of the world's people.[43] People apply their complex intelligence to the unique experiences their environment permits.

Putting aside the question of political ideology, it is interesting that Malcolm X had extreme difficulty in school and yet later proved to have a superior intellect. Ruchell McGee, a prisoner in San Quentin, was diagnosed as mentally retarded and this was used as an argument to keep him from acting as his own attorney. Yet he has been able, largely on the basis of self-taught law, to confuse and at times immobilize court proceedings. There are many similar cases reported throughout the literature. However, one searches in vain for researchers who have pulled such information together for systematic scrutiny. Rather, we have the Colemans, Jenckses, Jensens, Moynihans, Shockleys, and others who continue to receive financial support and who seem able only to develop explanations for "deficits" among minority children, *even while the children are achieving.*

Why Assessors Fail to Find Talented Minority Children

It should be clear that, in general, the talents of minority students tend systematically to be underestimated. A brief examination of the school context within which assessments take place shows why assessors are unable to discover many talented minority students. The following description, while far from complete, seeks to provide a feeling for the dynamic assessment context, and to illustrate why one or two "standardized tests" under conditions of "standard administration" may yield invalid results.

In the situation where assessments are made, *someone measures a student* with an *instrument* or *process* for placement in a *school setting*. Important variations are associated with each of the four elements of the assessment context listed above. These variations affect the outcome for minority students in significantly different ways than for mainstream students. Each element will now be examined more closely.

Someone Measures. The person or persons who are responsible for assessment are not benign ingredients in the whole process. On the contrary, they have a major impact on the assessment, the data, and the interpretation. Alien assessors have expectations for minority students. Often the expectations are low. Experimenters have shown how a teacher's low expectations tend to "produce" low performance in students.[44] Assessors may be more or less ethnocentric. The more ethnocentric they are, the less likely they are to perceive the cues that mark aptitude in another culture. The assessor may feel superior to the minority student. This attitude can be detected by the student, and will affect his or her performance. The assessor may have personal preferences among students. He may dislike poor students or students who have limited capacities. These attitudes can affect student response. Even the assessor's developmental stage in life will affect his or her attitudes and responses to students and will therefore have an impact on a student's performance. Bess gives an example of such dynamics:

> For some men, especially in the helping professions, there is an early and perhaps premature development of vocational interests. . . . For these men, there may be later disillusionment and a tendency to develop interest patterns more characteristic of persons who prefer to work with ideas rather than with other human beings.[45]

Bess cites other studies to show that with increasing age people tend to be less inclined to take risks, to have less tolerance for nonconformists, and to exhibit lower levels of permissiveness. After age 55 older people tend to agree more with clichés, are more rigid in their behavior patterns, and are reluctant to take risks even when personal judgments are certain.

As assessors move through various developmental stages in their personal lives, their predispositions toward others change. What is the effect on the assessment of minority students by an adult who retreats increasingly to the world of ideas, and away from human beings? Is he less open to behavioral cues? What effect does a teacher's decreasing tolerance of nonconformists have on his assessment of minority children, many of whom may, from his point of view, be considered "nonconformists"?

What if the gifted child described below were a minority child who tended toward nonconformity?

> As with gifted children in general, the mathematically gifted tend to be curious, persistent, highly intelligent, and equipped with good memories. They are also reluctant to accept the obvious, and manifest a positive dislike for repetitiousness and routine. . . . In elementary school they are typically well-adjusted, flexible and realistic, but highly independent and frequently unconventional in their thoughts. But when their independence of thought and action is threatened, they tend to respond with hostility and self-assertion.[46]

Hostility and self-assertion from a nonconforming minority child are seldom regarded by a white teacher in the same way as similar behavior from a white child. In the assessment situation, the results can be damaging for the minority child.

Often the goals for the assessor tend to be more academically oriented than people-oriented. For example, if a teacher teaches primarily for the love of the subject, its beauty, harmony, and stimulation, he or she may be interested only incidentally in student growth. If this is the case, little care may be given to attending closely to the student's behavior. The assessment will therefore be superficial.

The person who assesses may be a stranger to the person being assessed. The degree of estrangement from the culture of the person being assessed may affect the accuracy of the assessment. The alien assessor may not be able to understand the information that he or she collects.

Many minority students see the teacher as a symbol of a general oppression that they experience and feel deeply. As such, the teacher will have extreme difficulty in establishing the requisite rapport for getting essential data.

While teachers may be poor assessors of minority-student aptitude, some minority students are not so poor in assessing their own aptitude, and that of others. Therefore, when the assessor inappropriately places a member of the student's reference group in a category higher than is deserved, the minority student will respond negatively, often to his own detriment.

Many other factors affect the person who conducts assessment. In fact, an accurate description of the assessment process could show clearly that *the assessor is really the "instrument."* An assessor is not objective, does not perceive clearly, and will make imperfect interpretations. This fundamental fact must always be in mind in order to treat information with appropriate caution.

The Instrument or Assessment Process.   Another element can be seen as contributing to variable results in the assessment of minorities. Most standardized tests tend to be biased in favor of white America. Most have extremely low validity, especially low predictive validity, and especially low predictive validity where minorities are involved. Many universities tried "open admissions" programs a few years ago. Often statistics show that test scores have been very poor predictors of minority-student achievement. One department in a large university in the San Francisco Bay area stopped using a standardized test of aptitude for screening students for admission to their program when they learned how poorly the national examination that they were using correlated with minority students' success.

Perhaps the worst thing about the use of some instruments for selection is that the constructs they purport to measure tend to be unclear and often unrelated to the aims of programs for which they are used as screening devices. The constructs also come more from armchair speculation than from analysis of the required behaviors. An example of what should happen follows. Krutetski went into classrooms and observed closely the responses of Russian schoolchildren as they worked to solve mathematics problems.[47] From his observations, the following components of mathematics ability were isolated: formalized perception of math material, generalization of math material, curtailment of thought, flexibility of thought, striving for economy of thought, mathematical memory, and spatial concepts. Assuming that his observations were skilled, and that these are the main components of mathematics ability, where is the test or instrument to measure these items? If other components are the real ones, how were they determined? Since IQ tests are usually used for selection, and since correlation with the un–factor-analyzed Stanford-Binet is often one measure of validation for any other test of ability, what is the proof that the components measured by these tests are related to what students will be required to do? The best that can be heard from most test makers is something about the mystical factor of "g" or "general intelligence." It sounds good, but explains little.

Most teachers talk about program objectives, rather than about goals. But goals are implied by what is measured in standardized tests, which are used to screen and place students. The following is the set of artists' criteria from the School of Performing Arts in New York City:

1. The work shows a fresh viewpoint or insight.
2. The technique shows individuality and initiative.
3. Persistence is shown in solving problems in detail or broad pattern.
4. The work is not imitative but shows a fresh sensitivity to possibilities.
5. The work shows more than patient practice and conformity to a given model.
6. There is some sign of protest against custom.
7. The work would have been done without external motivation.
8. The artist has the capacity for self-criticism, self-evaluation, and subsequent independent improvement.

If these goals are really close to what teachers seek, then it should be easy to see why most tests are not helpful at all in selecting students who work in line with the goals above. How does a test like the Stanford-Binet help to find students who function creatively? By accepting such tests as diagnostic devices, teachers tend to develop curriculum concepts that fit the test's dictates.

The Student Who Is Assessed.   The assessor and the instrument for assessment are themselves dynamic processes. So is the student who is to be assessed. The minority student comes to the assessment context with expectations developed from a long history of experience with people who are different and with systems that seem to act forcefully and negatively upon him or her. An invitation to testing is seen by many minority students as an invitation to one more opportunity to be judged negatively. It is thus difficult for them to be eager and enthusiastic participants. If motivation for school is already low, then motivation for being assessed is even lower. Under these conditions, few teachers or assessors will be perceived as helpers. Many minority students have learned to feel powerless with respect to the formal school setting. And yet, the sense of power to do something about one's environment is directly related to the possibility for learning.[48] Any true assessment of minority potential, therefore, must be preceded by an atmosphere wherein a student is permitted to be potent and to feel his potency. *Student advocacy* by concerned and respectful teachers will be an essential ingredient in this environment. It is unlikely that this can be achieved by teachers who have shown no knowledge of, interest in, or identification with the culture of the minority students they serve.

Much has been made of the unique values, or special cognitive styles, of specific minority students. When basic values and cognitive styles differ from those of mainstream America for a given minority student, he may be unable to "show his stuff." For example, a major research corporation proposed to measure the success of a major government program for young children. The majority of the children in the program were black. One of the tests for cognitive gains was to be a test of the child's ability to understand puns. Incredible! The pun is definitely not a part of the style of black humor. Puns and one-liners are a part of the white American tradition. Humor among black Americans more often involves nuances of delivery or milking a bizarre situation, preferably with some audience participation. Few alien teachers or assessors even have the ability to detect or deliver this kind of joke for a black audience.

In addition to a unique style of humor, the following hypotheses are presented as potential dimensions that would in general differentiate one kind of black style from mainstream white America.

1. Black people tend to prefer to respond to and with "gestalts" rather

than to or with atomistic things. Enough particulars are tolerated to get a general sense of things. There is an impatience with unnecessary specifics. Sometimes it seems that the predominant pattern for mainstream America is the preoccupation with particulars along with a concomitant loss of a sense of the whole. There is the belief that anything can be divided and subdivided into minute pieces and that these pieces add up to a whole. Therefore, dancing and music can be taught by the numbers. Even art is sometimes taught this way. This is why some whites never learn to dance. They are too busy counting and analyzing.

2. Black people tend to prefer inferential to either deductive or inductive reasoning. This is related to item one, above.
3. Black people tend to prefer approximations to accuracy to "fifty decimal places." This is also related to item one.
4. Black people tend to prefer a focus on people and their activities rather than things. The choice by so many black students of the helping professions, such as teaching, psychology, and social work, cannot be explained by job availability or ease of curriculum.
5. Black people have a keen sense of justice and are quick to analyze and perceive injustice.
6. Black people tend to lean toward altruism, a concern for one's fellow man.
7. Black people tend to prefer opportunities for stylistic display within the parameters of what the reference group thinks is hip.
8. Black people tend to prefer novelty and freedom. Witness the development of improvisations in music, styles in clothing, and so forth.
9. Black people in general tend not to be language-dependent. That is to say, there is a tendency to favor nonverbal as well as verbal communications. Words may be used as much to set a mood as to convey specific data.

As stated earlier, these are merely hypotheses regarding a few aspects of one black life style; they come out of the author's own observations, and would certainly require experimental validation. However, if only some of these parameters characterize the unique style of many black people, it can be seen immediately why assessment of black students is often negative. Schools tend to be places of conformity, particulars, exactness, individualism, and worship of arbitrary standards. The issue is not that the minority student should change the school, or vice versa, so much as that the teacher or assessor must recognize that something may be occurring inside a minority student that cannot be understood in terms of the teacher's limited framework. This lack of understanding can be the cause of inaccurate assessments. Values will be negotiated or accommodated in a series of transactions between the students and the schools. Teachers and assessors must respect the need for these transactions, and try to give up their stultifying ethnocentrism and learn to participate freely in both negotiations and accommodations.

A word must be said about the creative minority student, in light of some research findings on the relationship of creativity to IQ in general. Gold compared students with high IQs with those who had high creativity scores on the way that they ranked eight qualities for themselves.[49] The high-IQ students ranked a sense of humor last, while the high-creativity students ranked it second. For high-IQ students, there was a .67 correlation between their values and what they believed to be the values of their teachers. *For the high-creativity students, the correlation was −.25.* For the high-IQ students, there was a correlation of .91 between their values and what they thought were the values that make for success in life. *For the high-creativity students, the correlation on this was .10.* Overall, Gold found the correlation between IQ and creativity to be .40. For students whose IQs were over 120, the correlation dropped to .10. Something different was definitely happening with each of the two groups of students.

The issues are these: How can IQ tests be used to select students for programs geared toward creativity? For the minority student, what are the consequences of behaving according to the above description of creative students, in terms of the response that is likely to come from teachers?

Assessors do not have to fail in finding minority talent. The first step in finding that talent is to understand the dynamics of the assessment process.

What Needs to Be Done to Develop Assessment Skill

Teaching and assessment require *clinical skills* of a high order. It takes hard work to develop these skills. There is no one-week workshop, or professional "injection," that will give the serious teacher or assessor instant skill. There is no "instrument," other than the teacher or assessor who is properly prepared, for the assessment of minority talent. What does it take to establish a fair and equitable context for the assessment of minority children?

Assessing the Assessor
1. Does the assessor have the requisite basic skills in assessment and, in the case of assessment for gifted students, is the assessor gifted?
2. Is the assessor's own life rich and creative, and does the assessor exhibit a propensity to inquiry?
3. What is the assessor's reaction to divergent thought and action?
4. Has the assessor demonstrated valid asessment skills? (Compare results with those obtained by skilled assessors.)

5. Does the assessor have an intimate understanding of the cultures with which he or she must work?
6. What is the assessor's response to disorder, control, error?
7. Does the assessor identify with his or her clientele?
8. How well does the assessor understand the basic constructs in assessment such as IQ, intelligence, creativity?
9. How well does the assessor understand the relationship between power and learning?

Assessing the Context
1. Review each item in any standardized test to determine if the test is valid for the program that is in operation.
2. Develop a shared definition, among professionals who operate a program, of precisely how the program is unique. What is the actual difference between a program for the gifted or for the retarded when compared with any other program? How is teaching behavior different? How is student behavior different?
3. To what extent does the staff reflect the cultures of the community served?
4. Assess community expectations for the program and the degree of community impact.

Special Assessment Techniques
1. Look for evidence of talent in unconventional places (use of humor, etc.).
2. Get the child's own assessment.
3. Assess children in free situations.
4. Use unobtrusive measures in observation.
5. "Response contingent testing" is required in cross-cultural settings. This is an individual test where the "items" would be determined by the response of the student. Skilled assessors are required.
6. Where the staff is not ethnically representative, assistance must be sought from qualified minority professionals and certain skilled paraprofessionals.
7. Arrange for new assessors to observe minority youth and talented assessors at work.

When all this is present, the clinical judgment of the "clinical" teacher is superior to any known instrument. This will take much hard work, but the very survival of human beings depends upon that work. If there are to be special programs, then the damaging effects of misassessing minority children must be overcome. Any teacher who cannot develop the requisite competence level must not be permitted to malpractice.

The skilled eye comes in all colors; so can the blind eye. As a professional:

1. You look harder if you know talent is there.
2. You look better if you are clear about its manifestations.
3. You look more clearly, with less bias, if you know how perspective can be contaminated.
4. You look more urgently if you are identified with the children.
5. You get hooked on looking when you find a pearl!

We have just examined the problem of assessment as one way of understanding the complexities of cross-cultural education, and cross-cultural teacher education. The question may arise: Is cross-cultural teacher education possible? Can a teacher work effectively with students from cultural backgrounds quite different from his or her own? The answer is, of course! The professional literature is filled with examples of teachers and researchers who have negotiated the difficult waters of cross-cultural understanding and cross-cultural professional practice. Researchers such as Mercer, Labov, Levi-Strauss, and Baratz, are but a few who have managed to do an excellent job of bridging the gap between cultures. The point is that simple expertise in understanding an academic area, or simple expertise in professional practice, in a monolingual or monocultural setting, gives no automatic guarantee that the professional will have the skills necessary to function cross-culturally. Special experience, training, and commitment are required to enable a professional to serve the needs of those from cultures different from his own. At the same time, it must be noted that there is no automatic guarantee that a professional can serve members of his own group effectively just because they share a common culture. This is also the case for those who serve different cultures; a professional who serves his or her own cultural group members must have a commitment to serving students and to identifying with them, and must have the requisite professional skills.

Teaching students from different cultures is not a problem because of "who" the students are. African teachers have no trouble teaching African children in Africa. Eskimo teachers have no trouble teaching Eskimo children in Alaska. Indian teachers have no trouble teaching Indian children in India. Students do not suddenly lose the ability to learn just because they happen to live in America. Their capacity to learn remains intact.

What does change is how teachers reach out and support learning. For that reason, it becomes critically important that we learn how to diagnose learning environments in order to identify skilled and unskilled teachers, in terms of their ability to work effectively with students from cultures different from their own. It is important to pinpoint evaluation of teachers and their individual assets and liabilities, so that teacher training can be planned appropriately. Teachers, like their students, are individuals with different needs and capacities. Programs of teacher education must also be individualized. There still is a way to keep minority students achieving. That way is to keep teachers achieving.

DIRECTIONS FOR RESEARCH

I believe that the needed research for solving educational problems of minority children and adolescents must take new and important directions. Among these are at least the following:

1. *Identification of teachers, schools, or programs that consistently produce dramatic growth in minority children.* The programs should be analyzed and the information widely disseminated.
2. *Identification of teachers, schools, or programs that consistently produce negative results in minority children for the same reasons as indicated above.*
3. *Representation of black and other minority perspectives at levels where research priorities are determined, where research proposals are evaluated, where research is conceptualized, where it is implemented, and where the results are evaluated.*
4. *Further research in the area of teacher behavior and student change.* Rosenthal and Jacobson, Beez, and others should have their experiments replicated or extended. We know that teacher expectations, attitudes, emotional health, and other factors directly affect student growth. However, when much of this research is presented, certain researchers seek the safety of arguing over minute errors of design or statistical analysis, rather than designing and executing a proper study.
5. *In-depth studies of minority people who have achieved at high levels despite severely oppressive conditions.* This may provide some clues as to what can be salvaged from our present programs of help.

CONCLUSIONS

There are too many examples of minority growth, often in the face of overwhelming odds, for us to be satisfied with a situation where national educational policy is overly influenced by excuse-makers whose research is detached from significant reality, and whose understanding of what it takes to help minority children grow is nil. There are people in this country who know how! It is from *this* group that educational policy recommendations should be sought. It is *this* group that should receive full support of public and private funds. It is *this* group that should be made more visible to the profession, so that our new professional talent can see exciting, productive alternatives to the despair expressed by many who ought to know better. The group to which I refer consists of *those who have a track record of success* with black and other children. All of our children, minority or majority, have what it takes. *They deserve the professionals who also have what it takes.*

Fundamental educational change in America has been difficult to achieve. This difficulty is due in part to the inability of educators to develop *clinically valid* conceptualizations about the process of education. It is also due to a failure to examine all relevant information in a given context of education. Many popular and professional writings give testimony to these points. Philosophical, often poetical abstractions, such as those in Leonard's *Education and Ecstasy,*[50] engage teachers in hours of rapture. At the other extreme, Jensen, imprisoned in a simplistic mechanical model, makes professional "hay" by treating poor information with impeccable statistics. He generates another kind of abstraction. While all of this is going on, children who would have no trouble with complex learning in countries from which they originated, or in their neighborhoods, continue to fail in American schools. Change *can* come. All children *can* learn. However, the teaching task will require levels of teaching skill and understanding far beyond those that are often seen.

The fundamental problem for American education is how to make the system work for the multicultural mix that characterizes most schools. How can this be done when the schools are themselves an integral part of a total culture that withholds its benefits from its minorities, while granting them to mainstream white America? Multicultural education and multicultural teacher education must deal with a fundamental problem that goes far beyond a minimal concern for sharing information about the history and cultural patterns of ethnic groups in the world. Multicultural education, and multicultural teacher education, must focus upon the dynamics of person-with-person and institution-with-person interactions, as these interactions give clues to oppressive and facilitative behaviors. To do this, educators must leave the comfortable world of abstractions. Educators must lift the veil and deal directly with experience.

8. Multicultural Objectives
A Critical Approach

Terrence N. Tice

Myths about multicultural education shape objectives that people set for schools. Such distortions are illustrated by the multiplicity of themes that characterize different approaches to "multicultural education." In North America the rich mosaic of immigrant experiences poses a major theme. So does the rapid expansion of frontiers depicted in such works as Conrad Richter's classic trilogy, *The Trees, The Fields,* and *The Town,* and in the unceasing barrage of new frontier literature, from William Dean Howells's 1885 domestic tale of a self-made manufacturer, *The Rise of Silas Lapham,* to the urban studies and the gadget-filled science fiction of today.[1] Both the injustice visited upon the oppressed and their own deep influence on the American mind mold still other themes of paramount importance—themes that pervade our popular music, our church life, our ways of making economic decisions, and our preoccupation with oft-told varieties of the American dream.[2]

In addition to the more substantive themes such as these, there are also the more formal themes concerning our general grasp of the concept. If, for example, we ask how we are to conduct multicultural education in the face of such great variety, we must also inquire about what the proposal means. If we ask how we are to find agreement on what we are talking about, we must also wonder what such agreement might consist of. If we then ask how we are to set appropriate objectives, we must also consider how criteria of appropriateness are to be derived.

My task here is chiefly to consider some of the more formal themes. I propose to view some basic problems and procedures that are involved in addressing the questions just mentioned and to consider what structure is to be found in any genuinely multicultural experience. I shall also discuss multicultural experiences in schools, and indicate some corresponding

121

modes of setting multicultural objectives. As the reader accompanies me in this discussion, I suspect that we will both realize more clearly that our topic is open-ended. Our best expectation can only be to set up a continually opening critical approach to the problems. The task of developing genuinely multicultural objectives in education is an ennobling endeavor. As such, it admits of continuing insight as we attempt to understand even the more general aspects of multicultural experience.

SOME BASIC PROBLEMS AND PROCEDURES

As individual selves, we are made up of all the relationships we have ever had. Several features of these relationships are useful to keep in mind as we think about their effect on subsequent cultural experience. First, some relationships—notably those with our parents or parent surrogates and others who influenced our early family life—are more generally determinative than others. Second, although some relationships are more fantasied than real, distorted images enter into our original perceptions and subsequent memories of them all. Third, to each relationship we contribute our own interest, motivation, self-awareness, thoughts, perceptions, rules, preferences, values, anticipations, and feelings; but without the distinctive presence of others, their language, habits, knowledge, and modes of relating, we would be nothing at all, humanly speaking. In recognizing these features, we realize that one of the basic problems to be considered in an inquiry into the meaning of "culture" is that of understanding how each person becomes the individual he or she is.

Capacities for Cultural Experience

The interpersonal character of our life histories can be "roughed out" by distinguishing four sets of capacities we all have. Each set must be taken into account in designing a genuinely multicultural approach to education.

Congenital. Although our congenital capacities are almost totally hereditary, physical environmental conditions both in the womb and from infancy on greatly affect which native capacities will be accessible to development. Formation of the infant's congenital activity type can also be markedly determined by mother-infant interaction in the first few days or weeks of life. Furthermore, both the infant and the mothering adult influence each other's styles of relating from the moment of birth.[3] In a sense, therefore, cultural experience has already begun at this level. A genuinely multicultural curriculum must hold these features in view.

Inherited.   Our biological inheritance as persons is not simply derived from isolated physical properties such as eye color and bone structure. To a considerable extent, these characteristics emerge from the family setting. A tightly organized network of relationships is formed there that may go back several generations. This historical process becomes strikingly apparent when things go wrong, as R. D. Laing showed in the case of Paul, a young schizophrenic of twenty-three whose nuclear family network was traced back to the great-great-grandparents.[4] In biographical shorthand, this is what had happened:

> His mother thought she could be a better husband and father than his father. And his father thought he could be a better wife and mother than his mother.
>
> In his view of his mother's view of her father, and his mother's view of her mother's view of her husband; and his father's view of his mother, and his father's view of *his* wife, there had never been a real man or woman in the family for four generations.
>
> Paul, through his internalization of this tangled set of relations of relations of relations, is tied in a knot, whereby he is effectively immobilized.

Laing poignantly summarized: "His body was a sort of mausoleum, a haunted graveyard in which the ghosts of several generations still walked, while their physical remains rotted away. This family had buried their dead *in each other.*"

Healthier networks generally, though not invariably, produce healthier people. For better or for worse, where family ties are strong they are the primary carriers of culture and of personal identity, and they are not lightly given up.

Others close to the family—relatives, associates, and other figures of relatively constant importance to family members—participate in the relational network that is inherited. As individuals, we too contribute in varying degrees to family patterns, not least through our own reactions and defenses. In later life we may also discover ways to broaden or to escape from some of these influences. The inherited network, however, remains a significant part of who we really are, especially of the cultural memories, feelings, fantasies, and biases that bear powerfully upon our relation to people of backgrounds different from our own.

An authentic multicultural curriculum must recognize the distinctive coloring and tenacity of inherited capacities. Decisions must be made as to which of those capacities are to be affirmed and encouraged, or gracefully tolerated, or supplemented and transcended through alternative experiences.

Acquired.   Each of the four categories overlaps with the others in actual experience, if for no other reason than that each begins early. Nonetheless, it is a sign of cultural growth that individuals move out of their inherited setting into a fuller, less narrowly controllable social world and acquire further capacities for relationship there. This we do through a broadening scope of occupations—aesthetic activity and play, work toward specific ends not necessarily shared within the family network, further social identification, moral and political engagements, friendships and acquaintances, and the like. As we take in new capacities from our cultural surroundings, we move out more effectively "on our own," which principally means away from the family. If all goes well, we will also be able to participate in a manner more and more distinctly our own.

In recent American tradition, schools have played a primary role at this level, both in extending the family influence and in disengaging children from it so that they could enter fruitfully into the larger society. Schools have always done multicultural education of a sort, though often with misguided judgment.

Attained. The etymology of the word *acquire* refers to a process of gaining-to-oneself by seeking things from the outside world. In contrast, that of *attain* refers to a process of gaining some end by reaching out, as if to touch, and by one's own distinctive efforts. Although meanings of the two words overlap in ordinary usage, what we acknowledge here is that some of our capacities go beyond acquiring what is already available in our environment. We reach goals and achievements not so much because of what our environment provides but because of who we are, and by our own distinctive effort. We contribute our own bit to human culture, thus sharing, if only in minuscule fashion, in the continuing creation of mankind.

Experiences in art often display these attained capacities most impressively. Every other domain of human experience, however, is likewise open to the spontaneity, the imaginativeness, the flexibility and self-releasing qualities of creative action. A multicultural curriculum must include opportunities for personal attainment in art and in other areas of creative expression. Otherwise it will chiefly serve as a purveyor of what is already known, not as an agent of cultural experience in the fullest sense.

Summary

In sum, the quality of any instance of multicultural education is to be judged by the mixture of these four sets of capacities presented within it. Accordingly, a useful component in a procedure for forming multicultural objectives would be to view the educational setting, process, and aims or products from all four perspectives.[5] Generalizations about cultural identity or multicultural education that do not take these complex relations into account are bound to go awry, adding additional chapters to the mythology of educational objectives.

Cultural Capacities	*Multicultural Experience*
Congenital	Educational Setting (physical, interpersonal,
Inherited	social . . .)
Acquired	Educational Process (methods, materials,
Attained	interactions . . .)
	Educational Aims or Products (expectations,
	continuities of experience . . .)

MYTHS ABOUT THE FUNCTIONS OF SCHOOLS

Early education was largely private in nature, given in the home or through apprenticeships in crafts, trades, the arts, religious institutions, business, or industries. Thus, the focus was on individual development and certain kinds of practical skills or creative/intellectual abilities. As education was institutionalized and made a public obligation, it tended to assume functions for communities rather than for individual families. One such purpose the schools were expected to serve was the perpetuation of the society itself. Hence, a major myth about education came into existence; namely, that schools are the guardians of the social status quo.

Making the schools—and education—an instrument for maintaining the social system greatly reduced their contribution to diversity. The emphasis became focused on trying to make students alike, rather than different. Curriculums were focused on skills, values, and content that were presumed to be the "common heritage" of people. Instructional procedures, similarly, aimed to produce uniform types of learning for all students. The impact became both anti–individual differences and anti-multicultural.

Another kind of myth about the functions of schooling relates to the behavioral outcomes envisioned for all students. The assumption, for example, that the high school should prepare for "worthy home membership" prescribed training boys and girls for traditional sex roles in the home. Standard English became a paramount objective for all students. Puritanical codes of moral behavior were held before students, presumably as reinforcements for home training.

From Myths to Reality

In institutions such as schools, myths tend to become realities. What begins as a distortion of function ultimately establishes itself as "proven" and "justifiable" practice. Three examples of myths that have become realities in schools in the United States are as follows.

1. *The Common Mold Function.* However people may define the objectives of education, most tend to subscribe to the idea that schools should mold students into reasonably similar products. Thus, colleges and universities speak with pride about the "kinds of graduates" they produce. Secondary and elementary schools give prior attention to "general education," the emphasis in the curriculum that is supposed to make students alike. And teachers develop behavioral objectives to guarantee that learning outcomes will be similar for all students.

2. *The Holding Function.* As technology replaced people with machines in the world of work, the need for child and youth labor virtually disappeared. But urbanization had collected families in cities where idle time, more so than in the rural areas, meant the "devil's work." Compulsory school attendance laws, which had the original purpose of protecting children from factory employment, assumed another function: to keep children under sixteen years of age off the streets. Thus, the school evolved a "holding function" that had little to do with actual learning.

3. *Road to Adulthood.* The school now functions as an almost exclusive road to adulthood for most young people. The work route for growing up is virtually closed. Gang life does represent an alternative for some, but essentially it is an underground passage. Young people must go to school to grow up—to learn how to live, to earn a living, to be citizens, and, most importantly, to attain the credentials required for admission to the world of work.

As myths become realities, they tend to develop constituencies that defend their continuation. Rigidities develop to resist change. Uniformity becomes a function in itself, thwarting efforts to promote responses to multicultural conditions within the society.

Myths about Multicultural Education

Much "multiethnic" and "multicultural" education in the past has, at least implicitly, regarded individuals as if they came to school in solid cultural blocks, such as "plain old American," "the blacks," "Puerto Ricans," and "welfare people." The belief was that individuals should leave the way they came, with perhaps an added understanding of "other points of view." "Subculture" and "ethnic identity" have been similarly regarded. As a consequence, curriculums are isolated from the very dynamics of human relationships without which multicultural education can have little validity and can have no vitality at all.

In such settings, "black history"—or what has often been essentially "white" history—is taught in complete ignorance of how people actually become who they are. The story is presented as a panorama taken from "back when," detached from the many-faceted experiences of the partici- pants and from the complex environing culture, removed from their own real world. So-called cultural history is then a useless and damaging fan- tasy, a process more in tune with the magical practices of advertising than with the realities of everyday life. Following the same pattern, art is presented as mere artifact, not as living experience. Social studies and language arts are wrenched apart—for example, as if the Spanish language and Hispanic culture and Chicano life today had no real relationship to each other or to other aspects of contemporary society. The words *black, Chicano, Polish, native American,* and *WASP* become labels without humane significance. Students assume these labels as truths upon which to base their attitudes and actions.

Four Functions of a School

Though in quite general perspective, John Dewey has shrewdly analyzed the "quality" problem in schooling by distinguishing four spe- cial functions of a school within a complex society.[6] The first function is to provide a simplified environment, one in which the complex life around the student is broken into fairly fundamental and manageable portions. These pieces of experience are presented so as to permit interaction by the individual in a way appropriate to his stage of development. They are progressively ordered to permit movement from the more simple to the more complex. Already at this elementary level, selections are being made so that the individual's learning will not be a haphazard affair. As an implication of Dewey's account, multicultural objectives are called for not just because a given society might be ethnically pluralistic but because the society is complex throughout. Criteria will arise at this level that begin to form a pattern for such objectives by taking social complexity seriously and, at the same time, achieving appropriate simplification.

The second function of a school, for Dewey, is to serve as the chief agency of the society for selecting the best, especially what will make for a better future society. These things are reinforced; what is relatively unde- sirable is excluded, so as to establish a purified social medium for action. We may notice that obvious dangers lurk here, as in any public context where value judgments are being made. The attempt cannot, however, be avoided, because value judgments of this kind will be made in any case. Drawing from this second function in setting multicultural objectives, further criteria must be established that will indicate a range of approaches and experiences within which the more highly valuable cultural elements can be explored and reinforced. Within a more open and democratic society, the list would have to begin with modes of genuinely appreciating diverse ways of experiencing the world through different cultural means.

Dewey's third function of a school within a complex society is to provide some balance among the various elements that exist within the social environment, so that each individual can escape from the limitations of his more narrow inherited environment, can fruitfully mingle with people of other backgrounds, and can unite with them in activity toward common aims. In this respect, appropriate multicultural objectives would not support bland assimilation. They would reject any uniformity by virtue of which people lack respect for differences of belief, custom, and identity and lack knowledge of what to do with those differences. Nor would such objectives support strict separation, in which individuals are encouraged to form factions and to reside there without any regard for alternative ways of life.

A fourth function, for Dewey, is to enable the individual to coordinate the diverse influences of the many social environments he may enter, a "steadying and integrating office" that brings the simplifying, selecting, and balancing functions to fulfillment. In setting multicultural objectives with all these basic functions of schooling in mind, it is important to recall Dewey's depiction of a social environment as consisting of "all the activities of fellow beings that are bound up in the carrying on of the activities of any one of its members."[7] If we superimpose this action-laden picture on my own characterization of culture in terms of human relationships, we shall have to search beyond such broad categories as "black," "middle class," or even "Chicano" in order to find the material toward which multicultural objectives may be appropriately directed.

Summary

Myths about the functions of schooling tend to become realities, thwarting efforts to move toward multicultural curriculums, instructional strategies, and humane relationships. Clearly, the need is to move far away from the timeworn commitment to assimilation that really means bland uniformity and elitism. As Dewey himself well knew, in a more open and democratic society the surprises, the blendings, the new encounters are just as important as the more settled elements. Multicultural education in such a setting must foster these experiences and must provide means for their critical assessment.

The so-called little things often count most, because they are often the best indicators of what is humanely most significant. Therefore to leave them out in the interest of covering only what is most prominent in cultural experience is to imperil the entire effort. Quality, in short, is in no way equivalent to prominence. At this very moment, for example, I am emphasizing the ''little things''—such as the gestures of friendliness, the nuances of dress, and what we carry around in our pockets—through some of the symbols at my disposal and in order to spark a possibility of relationship between myself and the reader. This is a cultural act done within a highly intellectual social setting and with marked feeling. Nonetheless, the point is tucked away in the midst of a longer discourse and must be elevated from that discourse in order to gain the high importance it deserves. It is a ''little thing'' in momentary appearance only.

THE LOCATION OF CULTURAL EXPERIENCE

Culture, in the manner characterized here, is an ongoing interpsychic process that centers on what individuals do with the space between themselves and other people. Culture is not a specific power in human life but utilizes all powers. It is not a context, either of signification or of social habit, but incorporates such contexts and occurs within them. It is not, as such, a formal symbolic system for interpreting or expressing experience but employs symbolic systems for these purposes, some of them quite informal.

Edward Burnett Tylor was so impressed with the interlocking network of social phenomena presented in specific ''cultures'' that in 1871 he defined culture, in a purely enumerative fashion, as ''that complex whole which includes knowledge, belief, art, law, morals, custom, and any other capabilities and habits acquired by man as a member of society.''[8] This most influential of all anthropological definitions includes so much as to permit little discrimination, and it lacks explanatory power. Other definitions tend narrowly to emphasize adaptive powers, ingrained social habits, symbolic systems, or types of social contexts, in each case confusing the process with what it incorporates or utilizes, where it occurs, what its manifest carriers are, or how it is interpreted. Understandably, the same errors have frequently crept into discourse about multicultural education.

Cultural Space

D. W. Winnicott is particularly well known for his long-term work on ways infants and small children experience their relation to personal and nonpersonal objects, especially to transitional objects (such as Linus's blanket in *Peanuts*) and in early play. As an extension of this work, in 1966 he advanced the arresting thesis that cultural experience is located neither in inner psychic reality nor in the actual world but in "the potential space between the individual and the environment," originally that between the infant and the mothering adult.[9] Put in another way, culture takes place in the interplay between union and separation. Its basis in early experience is the baby's trust in the dependability of his social environment, which enables him to venture within it, as Erik Erikson has also argued.[10] In the beginning, Winnicott proposes, nothing is set (as compared with later children's games); everything is creative; everything is "invested with a first-time-ever quality." If a baby has no chance to use actual objects creatively, "then there is no area in which the baby may have play, or may have cultural experience; then there is no link with the cultural inheritance, and there will be no contribution to the cultural pool." And, we may add, there will be no openness to the cultural contributions of those outside his specific cultural inheritance.

Winnicott's observation about the crucial importance of good mothering has been substantiated by numerous independent investigators. What is so startlingly fresh in his thesis is the attempt to explain cultural experience in terms of what human beings do with the space between themselves and other people. It is also striking that the special route which led to his raising the question "Where is cultural experience located?" was his insight some years before that the child is never simply alone but is alone only in the presence of someone, notably the mother present to the child's mind. The insight eventually led him to inquire where the common ground in such a relationship lies.[11]

As an extension of Winnicott's reflections, I now propose that, among other things, qualitatively effective multicultural education enables individuals to be "alone" in the presence of more kinds of people. The higher the quality of their multicultural experience, moreover, the more fruitful are the resources that individuals are able to bring into the silence and the solitude of their own existence. The more successful this process is, in turn, the more richly they are able to *be* (someone) in silence and in solitude as well as in their overt relationships.

Meditative techniques are widely used today in order to transcend the overly separated self. This is, I think, a worthy goal. When meditation is also used to completely renounce the desire for human relationships, I would expect that this action either means that the individual had little capacity for meaningful relationship with others to begin with, or represents an effort to leave cultural concerns behind, possibly because they are on the whole anxious and not joyful concerns. The latter move may have its own temporary value in some instances. On the other hand, meditative states in which regressive-progressive pathways of memory, feeling, and fantasy are left open produce an enrichment of cultural involvement. In the first instance, the space between oneself and other people is emptied. In the second instance, that space is gloriously filled.

More Criteria

Numerous implications can be drawn from these ideas for the purpose of setting multicultural objectives. One whole set of criteria, for example, would have to do with enabling students to fill the space between themselves and others with meaningful objects—objects to view, yes, but especially the softer, more transferable kinds such as shared activities, words, expression of feeling, and ordered ways of looking and listening and thinking.

Another set of criteria would deal with the importance of sharing space with others in the students' immediate environment whose heritage has given them markedly different ways of relating. Of possible equal importance would be efforts to get imagination going, to survey the possibilities of other environments in our present world and in future cultural settings.

Still another set of criteria would relate to the respect for silence and solitude, with the aim of developing ways of understanding, tolerating, and using these experiences culturally. Criteria would also be formed to assure that joy will flourish—as a concomitant of learning and not as a separated experience.

Above all, the means of relationship engendered in the educative process would display our respect for the rhythms of union and separation that arise as human beings grow.

SETTING MULTICULTURAL OBJECTIVES

Among contemporary anthropologists interpreting the American scene, John Greenway has shown special sensitivity to the tenaciousness of cultural processes in his delightful essay, *The Inevitable Americans*. [12] In the light of what he and others have shown, to design a multicultural curriculum for students in America requires being aware of why people hold onto their cultural habits so strongly.

I have only touched on the sociopsychological reasons here, by highlighting the infant's earliest experiences of union and separation. We may be contented, for the moment, to notice that the rhythms of union and separation continue through life, for this is how our personal and cultural identity are both formed and protected at each stage. Once we have formed ways of dealing with the space between ourselves and the "others," we are loath to give these ways up because we depend on them to fulfill our needs.

The Heart of the Program

Especially in a complex society, moreover, these procedures can be expected to form quite variously within a single person, so that one is not a single cultural entity but many, not one totally integrated self but many more or less integrated and more or less renewable sub–self systems. In its mix of conscious and unconscious operations, each subself has its own more or less mature configuration of relationships with other human beings, thus its own way of acting culturally. This is why people present themselves, when we really get to know them, not as totally consistent wholes but as several more or less integrated sets of beliefs, attitudes, and behaviors. Except for those who grew up in an extremely simple, homogeneous, and protected social setting, their corresponding ideological subsystems also tend to shift character, if ever so slightly, according to the specific social domain or type of relationship in question.

In setting multicultural objectives, we can use this awareness of intrapersonal diversity to good advantage, as long as we realize that too much is already there to expect other than gradual and partial change. The greatest services to students occur where the space between them and others can be opened up without severely threatening what is already there, so that each person can grow in his own good time. Abrupt confrontation is sometimes fitting, but I doubt that it can be withstood and utilized if the student has not been helped to develop capacities to explore, to try out, and to evaluate new experiences. This kind of help, then, must be the heart of the program.

Specific objectives must grow out of this situation. The main point for the educator is to be able to think about objectives in an appropriately ordered manner. Our discussion here has highlighted some effective ways of going about this. In shorthand review, then, criteria for setting appropriate multicultural objectives in education are to be derived, in part, from our understanding of:

I. Human Relationship
  A. Characteristics
    1. Relative determinativeness
    2. Distorted images we bring
    3. Our need of the "others"
  B. Capacities
    1. Congenital
    2. Inherited
    3. Acquired
    4. Attained

II. General Features of Schooling
  A. Characteristics
    1. Settings
    2. Processes
    3. Aims or products
  B. Functions
    1. Simplification
    2. Selection
    3. Balance
    4. Integration

III. Multicultural Identity
    A. Some General Features
       1. Mixed backgrounds
       2. Mixed influences
    B. Roots: Cultural Space

IV. Cultural Quality
    A. Socially shared reflective experience
    B. What people most deeply feel
    C. Surprises, blending, new encounters
    D. Significance of "little things"
    E. Meaningful objects
    F. Different heritages
    G. Imaginative surveying
    H. Future possibilities
    I. Silence and solitude
    J. Joy
    K. Rhythms of union and separation

If one adopts this general approach, emphasis will lie on developing process objectives rather than on setting specific performance objectives. This would appear necessary in any case, since the specific cultural uses students will make of the space cultivated are not readily controllable and should not be forced. Getting into genuine cultural processes is the key to multicultural education, although specific *types* of performance can certainly be included among our aims.

A Set of General Program Objectives

In 1973 a School of Education committee of which I was a member developed a set of general program objectives very much in tune with the position developed here.[13] These categories present a scheme for approaching curriculum development that could be useful in other school settings as well.

  I. Knowledge
    A. To expand the participants' knowledge of their own and other cultures
    B. To deepen and to increase the participants' awareness of their own cultural identity
    C. To help participants develop a better understanding of various ways to expand their contacts with other cultural groups, and to become acquainted with their own cultural roles
  II. Philosophy
    A. To develop the participants' capacities for humane, sensitive, and critical inquiry into the nature of cultural issues, particularly as these may relate to education
    B. To study the aesthetic, epistemological, and ethical inter-relationships of cultural life in the United States and else-

where through their psychological, social, economic, and political dimensions
- C. To increase the participants' capacity for examining their own cultural attitudes and values in the light of history and the current situation
- D. To augment the participants' abilities for envisaging future developments and engaging in planning for cultural interchange within an emerging world society

III. Methodology

To help participants develop the ability to plan and conduct multicultural learning experiences by:
- A. Investigating, developing, and testing suitable teaching strategies for a multicultural curriculum
- B. Increasing skills for locating, developing, and using instructional resources for multicultural education
- C. Learning to assess the effectiveness of a multicultural curriculum

Conclusion

Multicultural education presents a great challenge to the educator today. This is true not chiefly as a matter of gaining information but as a matter of broadening one's own capacities for relationship through personal contact and the implements of culture. The challenge comes, moreover, not chiefly as a concern to draw together the culture of the past and present or to do a better job of raising open-minded Americans, but as a concern to learn how to draw from the multiple experiences of culture so as to build a viable world society.

In terms of survival on any humane basis, mankind has already passed the stage of nationalism and ethnocentrism. Likewise, Brotherhood Week is but a pale symbol of what is needed now. In the decades just ahead, we are faced either with the development of a world community in which quality multicultural education has become a prime carrier of progress, especially among the more advantaged nations, or with unprecedented barbarism on a world scale. In this perspective, multicultural education is not simply a way of improving human relations in America. It is a program intended to promote the human survival of mankind.

Part 3

PROGRAMS AND
TEACHING STRATEGIES

9. Modifying Curriculums to Meet Multicultural Needs

Gwendolyn C. Baker, Marshall Browdy,
Clarence Beecher, and Robert P. Ho

If multicultural education is to have any validity at all, it must move from theory to practical application in the classroom. Objectives must be formulated in terms of behavioral outcomes to be achieved. Instructional materials must be designed, or modified, to include appropriate multicultural content and concepts. Last, teachers must learn to use these materials in their classrooms. Before all such professional decisions can be made, however, teachers must have a good understanding of the implications of those alternate theories and approaches to teaching. For many, their need is not so much to achieve a commitment to multicultural education; it is rather to sharpen their perception of the effects of a particular curricular design and instructional strategy.

To show how teachers may become sensitive to a set of instructional materials and strategies designed to meet certain multicultural needs, a case example of one personal experience—that of Gwendolyn C. Baker— is presented below.

A BLACK TEACHER IN A WHITE SUBURBAN SCHOOL

I had just finished a conference with the parents of one of my fourth-grade students when I became aware of the father looking at the bulletin boards in the room. The class and I had spent considerable time preparing what we felt was not only an attractive display but one that reflected what we were studying. I was sure this father was about to pay us a compliment on our Michigan time line. The time line included paper-doll-like figures that represented some of the early explorers of our state. To my surprise,

137

all he said was, "Where are the black faces?" I answered in a confident tone, "There weren't any." He turned to me again and said, "Are you sure?"

After the parents had gone, I sat alone in the classroom thinking about what had just happened. What did he mean, "Where are the black faces?" Who had ever heard or read anything about blacks in Michigan when Etienne Brule, a French explorer, visited the area in 1618? Or when Father Jacques Marquette founded Michigan's first permanent settlement at Sault Ste. Marie? There was absolutely nothing about blacks in any of the resource material I had used. The longer I thought, the more questions I asked myself. I began to wonder, was I really sure? Could I rely on what and how I had been taught or on the resource materials I had recently read as I prepared for my unit? Could I possibly be a victim of what some educators were then saying about the "sins of omission" in our history books? If the answer was yes, then I was guilty of perpetuating a false and inaccurate history. These thoughts forced me to reexamine my role as a classroom teacher: What was I teaching? Whom was I teaching?

I apparently was teaching what had been taught to me. The schools I attended were predominantly white middle-class schools with curriculums reflecting only that culture, a system that encouraged, or rather forced, minority students to ignore their own ethnic identities. They did so without resistance because it was the *modus operandi* of those days. These students had to assimilate as much as was mentally and physically possible if they were to achieve and to survive. No form of deviation from this norm or diversity was tolerated. Most of the teachers and students looked alike, dressed alike, spoke alike, and, except for a very few, even lived alike. How was I to know about black people and their role in the development of this country? My education consisted of persistent exposure to a white world. As a consequence, I have become an instrument for the perpetuation of more of the same.

Whom was I teaching? A class of twenty-five children, 95 percent white and the other 5 percent representing other cultures. What was I to teach? Was it fair to continue the instruction of a curriculum that represented only one culture? Did it matter what I taught to the 95 percent or to the 5 percent? What was I doing to the Jewish, Asian-American, or black children in the class by presenting only the history of a world that was neglecting their cultures? What must I be saying to the 95 percent by this act of omission? By my teaching practices I was encouraging and promoting ethnocentrism. At the same time, I was contributing to the negative self-concepts of the others. There appeared to be only one answer—I had to change the content of my curriculum. The content had to reflect our culturally diverse country and world. I knew I had to change, but where and how would I begin? How could I modify the curriculum in an effort to teach diversity?

I knew I could not teach that which I knew nothing about. My initial step would be to find out as much as I could about as many cultures as possible. Was this going to be practical? What cultures would I study and how many? I immediately became overwhelmed by the task that confronted me. It was at this point that I realized I could not begin to learn about more than one culture at a time. I decided to start with a study of black American history and culture. The decision to begin with this particular culture was prompted not only because of my interest but also because of the availability of resources. The major decisions were now behind me. I was ready to take another step toward modifying my curriculum. I began to establish a knowledge base.

Establishing a Knowledge Base

Some years ago, I learned that children's books could provide a wealth of information. Authors of materials for children have the ability to explain and present much information in a simplistic manner, thus making the acquisition of facts especially accessible to adults. Therefore, I used the school library as well as the public library as a main source for reading materials. After a few hours of reading children's books about black Americans, I began to establish my base of knowledge. As my base began to expand, my interests also grew.

During the sixties, many commercial firms produced audiovisual aids to help satisfy the need for materials that would help with the instruction of black history. Some of these materials were excellent, while others were very poor. Selectivity was essential if I were to modify my curriculum to help dispel myths about black Americans. The sorting process served as a learning experience in which I developed the ability to analyze the objectivity and accuracy of the materials. It did not take long to realize that I could not believe or use all of the information the materials provided. I needed to be accurate.

Not many films were available, but those I was able to preview were helpful. Much of the information presented in the films was inaccurate, and again the art of selectivity proved invaluable. By the time I had exhausted the film supply, I had become an expert (by my definition) in the availability and quality of audiovisual materials for teaching about black Americans.

As I read books, watched filmstrips, and previewed films, I began to get ideas for the kinds of concepts I wanted to teach. I kept a record of major themes, such as transportation and communication, as well as ideas for classroom activities. These ideas often came to me when I least expected them. Sometimes a picture in a book gave me an idea for an art lesson. An interesting phrase or question from a filmstrip or film provided the basis for a language-arts activity. Without too much effort and over a period of a few weeks, I had put together a fantastic resource unit. With my first step completed or reasonably so, I was ready to make my next move.

The next step toward modifying my curriculum was deciding the best way to teach children about black Americans. What teaching strategies would I employ?

Selecting Teaching Strategies

Several points needed to be considered before I could begin. Should I teach about the black American in unit form? Would this do more harm than good? Perhaps I should separate my unit and teach it in short periods throughout the year to give it an integrated approach. Was this really the way, or could I integrate this material throughout the curriculum?

These questions led me to consider my motivations for wanting to teach children about diversity and, more specifically, black Americans. Primarily, I wanted the children to understand and to be aware of the history of black people in the United States. In order to do this effectively I knew that I needed to spend some time on learning and studying about Africa. Further, I felt the children needed to know about the important contributions black people made and are still making in all areas and aspects of life in the United States. Finally, they needed to expose themselves to factual materials about this largest ethnic group in the United States so as to dispel myths and stereotypes and prevent them from further development. These learning experiences would help demonstrate the importance of individual cultural identity. Therefore, it became obvious to me that if I taught about black Americans in unit form, it would be an isolation technique that would further reinforce feelings of separatism in the child. If I were to accomplish my goal of helping children see and understand the role of black Americans in the history and culture of this country, I could not teach about them in isolation. What I taught must reflect the black American's participation and involvement in the growth of our nation. An integrated approach was the realistic answer. This approach would serve as my strategy for the organization and utilization of my instructional materials. I was now ready to teach.

Guiding Learning Experiences

Reading provided me with my first opportunity for trying an integrated approach. We were using a basal reader that at that time included very little multicultural material. However, in this fourth-grade series, there was an introduction to the American Revolution. I saw an excellent opportunity for introducing Crispus Attucks to the class. I chose to do this by including his biography in the room reading collection. This collection also provided material for our interest reading groups. Interest reading groups were units of individualized instruction designed around specific interest areas determined by the children. One of these areas focused on biographies and was an opportune situation for a beginning. I read a portion of a book by Dharothula Milhender, *Crispus Attucks: Boy of Valor* (Bobbs-Merrill), by way of introduction to one of the interest groups. I made sure that this book was also presented to the entire class during one of our book sales. A "book sale" is an activity in which a child who has read a book chooses to share it with the class by convincing other children via a sales talk to also read the book. The "sales talk" provided the introduction of Crispus Attucks to the class. This meant that I could then elaborate on this personality when we studied the events preceding the American Revolution. It also implied a natural kind of inclusion and transition—just what I wanted! This period in history would give me a chance to tie in the literature of that period as an extension of our language-arts activities. I introduced the children to the black poet Phillis Wheatley. The children not only learned about Wheatley and her poetry, but also became involved in writing some poetry of their own. This poetry expressed some of the same kinds of feelings Wheatley was experiencing when she wrote her favorite poem to and about George Washington.

Also presented in this reading series was a section on Washington, D.C., which provided the setting for the children to discover Benjamin Banneker, one of the architects of our capital city. Once discovered, his many accomplishments provided all kinds of possibilities for individual and class investigations. I collected as many books and available reading materials as possible for our room collection. This enabled the children to read and discover, and served as a motivation for several children to explore the use of an almanac, one of Banneker's many achievements.

Reading and language-arts activities continued to present innumerable situations for possible ways to introduce multicultural concepts. The material I wanted to integrate became appropriate once the sensitivity and awareness level in the classroom had been created.

I continued through the rest of that year to use this method of integrating material about black Americans throughout the existing curriculum. I felt I had made a good beginning and looked forward to expanding my knowledge base and teaching techniques to include other concepts and information concerning other cultures in my second-grade curriculum the following year.

Expanding Knowledge of Minority Cultures

Our first unit of study in my second-grade class was in the area of science. Our focus was on "living things," which meant we would spend considerable time learning about plants in the classroom. It seemed natural for the children to learn also about the noted scientist George Washington Carver. Most people assume that everyone knows about Carver's work. Unfortunately, the majority of young white middle-class children have not discovered him. Once again, I relied on a biography and chose to read this to the class while we were involved in our study of living things. The response was more than I had ever hoped for. The children became so interested in George's experiences as a child (George is what the children called him) that they would beg me to continue reading. The book provided situations that led to discussions about inequality of educational opportunity for blacks, discrimination, and the immorality of slavery. It was interesting to see and hear the minds of these youngsters attack the issues and in all honesty express objective conclusions.

The children wanted to grow sweet potato plants and peanuts, "just like George." We experimented with these plants. The children counted the days and waited for the plants to break through the soil. When they did, the joy and excitement was almost uncontainable. They nurtured the plants and charted their growth. They wrote sentences about the plants and about Carver. Later, as we studied paragraph structure, they used this topic to demonstrate their knowledge about the subject as well as about paragraph structure. We used these materials to design an attractive room display under the caption "Our Plant Doctor" for our Open House. We wanted everyone to know what George looked like, so we included a large picture of Carver in the center of our work.

This unit took several weeks, during which time it was apparent to me that while slavery, discrimination, and other topics had been discussed, certain concepts needed further exploration. Therefore, throughout the year we involved ourselves in a continuation of learning about these things. When appropriate, we studied contemporary black Americans, such as Martin Luther King, Jr., examining their work and philosophy. During the study unit on safety we learned that the stoplight was invented by a black American, Garrett Morgan. Our investigation of the discovery of the North Pole led us to the revelation that one of the two men who made that exploration was a black, Matthew Henson. The unit on transportation provided the setting for learning about the underground railroad. This was a very natural outgrowth of our previous work on Carver and what slavery was all about. Because of its involvement in the underground railroad, the town we lived in provided a realistic situation for studying it. The children were introduced to Harriet Tubman through Ann McGovern's book *Run-Away Slave: The Story of Harriet Tubman*. This was an extremely important inclusion, not only because Tubman was black, but also because she was a woman. Women too must be included and presented in the curriculum in an objective way in order to dispel the stereotypes and myths about them that have been learned and taught in our schools.

We could not contain our activity and discoveries within our classroom. We began to involve other classes, and eventually the entire school, as the occasions suggested and permitted. On one such occasion we were able to secure a marvelous set of slides on the underground railroad. We prepared to share these in an assembly with several other classes. I chose several other books on the subject at different reading levels and interest, and encouraged other teachers to read them to their classes in preparation for their participation in our assembly. We were learning together, not only about black Americans but about the world, another culture, and how beautiful and rich our own country is because of its diversity. And so we continued.

The class learned about the heritage of Japanese-Americans through a social studies unit on communication. Through some Japanese visitors to our school, we arranged an art exchange project with Japanese children. This project taught us much about Japanese culture. What we did not learn from the artwork, we discovered through our own research.

Our interest in Japan and Japanese-Americans encouraged us to involve the entire school in this venture. We planned an art display and shared our exchanges with our school. Our student council became involved and sent a gift to our newly acquired friends in Japan.

The children became interested in the language patterns of young people in Japan. This fostered an investigation of the work of a Japanese composer of haiku. We read individually a book by Pearl S. Buck, *Big Wave*. Learning about Japanese culture helped us understand the role of Japanese-Americans in the history of the United States.

Holidays and special occasions provide excellent opportunities for teaching multicultural concepts. Teachers generally do this during the month of December, but we discovered that practically every month of the school year presented us with suitable occasions. September and October found us learning about Jewish holidays. We read Frances F. Sandmel's *All on One Team* (Abingdon). This book describes the development of an interesting friendship between two young boys, one Jewish and the other Christian. The details surrounding the involvement of both boys' families in religious and social activities were enlightening and informative. The class applied many of the concepts presented by this book in the area of language arts. Writing activities such as "My Friend Eli" or "My Friend Terry" (the two characters in the story) gave the children an opportunity to internalize some of the concepts they had learned. Older Jewish children were invited to our class in order to help us understand the traditional Jewish customs. We learned to play with a dreidel, which also gave an opportunity to reinforce arithmetic concepts and skills.

Halloween was the occasion for an investigation of masks and what they mean to other cultures. This activity allowed a brief examination of the significant masks of native American cultures. For example, the children learned that the Iroquois used a certain type of mask to frighten away disease-bearing spirits. The Hopi used masked figures, called kachinas, that represent spirits. In the Mexican Yaqui Indian culture, masks are used to entertain people during festival time. African masks generally represent animals and birds, and they, too, have special meanings. The making of a mask for Halloween, therefore, became a meaningful activity, and it provided a significant learning experience through the area of art.

A study of the first Thanksgiving helped us to reevaluate much of what the children had learned previously about native Americans. We celebrated this holiday through the eyes of the first inhabitants of this land rather than through the eyes of the pilgrims.

Juanita, a book by Leo Politi (Scribner), was the foundation for learning that Easter is celebrated in different ways by different people. The religious figure in the book, the padre, presented another aspect of culture for us to consider and compare. We learned about the role of the padre in Mexican-American culture and compared it to that of the rabbi in *All on One Team.* We extended the discussion to an examination of the roles of priest and minister. The birthday celebration in Leo Politi's book allowed us to compare still another dimension of culture. For some children it is a new experience to discover that in some cultures people do not celebrate their own birthdays.

The second year of implementing a multicultural curriculum was even more interesting than the first. I had discovered a new way to teach and new things to teach about. I was excited about what we were doing and so were the children. We had learned so much. What more was needed? Perhaps more of the same, and there was plenty of that yet to come.

CURRICULUMS FOR MULTICULTURAL SCHOOLS

The foregoing account illustrates how one teacher began to adapt her curriculum to meet multicultural needs. One approach is to plan or redesign the entire curriculum to make it more relevant in the context of a multicultural society. Too often a curriculum is unicultural; it deals with the experiences of only the dominant culture. A curriculum may be ethnically *blind* in that it ignores the minority groups. Whatever the curriculum is, it sets the pattern for teaching and learning.

Purposes of Curriculums

The curriculum system for a state or school provides guidelines for what is to be taught and the instructional strategies employed.[1] It is a written document that lists instructional goals and objectives, as well as suggestions for their implementation and evaluation techniques. Answers to such questions as "What should be taught?" and "How?" typically are found in a school's curriculum guide. Each teacher, in effect, can become indentured to the curriculum guide. If this all-important document reflects insensitivity to multicultural needs, teachers will not be encouraged to move in this direction. A first task, therefore, for the teacher who wants to deal fairly and effectively with cultural diversity, is to make certain the curriculum guide focuses on this objective.

Teachers can and do influence decisions about the design and implementation of a school's curriculum in a variety of ways. They typically serve on committees that make recommendations to boards of education concerning the course requirements and options that should be provided. They sit on departmental committees that formulate the patterns for courses in various subject matter areas. They share responsibilities for setting the format for particular courses. Also, teachers usually have a voice in the selection of textbooks and other kinds of instructional materials. And, individually, teachers implement the curriculum in the classroom.

As influential as teachers are in curriculum planning, some decisions about what should be taught are beyond their control. A state legislature may prescribe by law the inclusion within a school's curriculum of certain subjects, such as health, physical education, and state or national history. In some states, such bodies even approve the learning materials that are to be used. Pressure groups in communities may force boards of education to include courses in the curriculum that professionals do not approve. In recent years, the ways in which teachers implement curricular directives in their classrooms have come under close scrutiny by various interest groups. All such practices suggest that to make the curriculum responsive to multicultural goals teachers must work with citizen groups in their communities and states to further understanding about what needs to be done.

Curriculum Theory: Its Source and Influence

Curriculum theory typically generates from at least three basic sources: *perceptions of social needs; insights into the structure of knowledge;* and *derived knowledge about human growth and development.* In most cases, theories tend to be eclectic, drawing their directives from several possible sources. Whenever one takes precedence over the others, it tends to set the pattern for the guidelines advanced. If the major concern, for example, is for social needs, the curriculum theory will raise basic questions about people—their reason for being, their aspirations, their relationships with each other, and additional types of social manifestations. Such questions, it will be readily recognized, cannot avoid relating to the cultural diversities that prevail or to conditions that promote mutuality among people. A curriculum theory that focuses heavily on the structure of knowledge, on the other hand, may concentrate on cognitive behavior so exclusively that affective needs are ignored. Concern with human growth and development in curriculum theory may direct attention to individual differences and, in so doing, may identify cultural characteristics that all need to understand.

The influence of curriculum theory permeates the total program of the school: the design of the program, the courses offered, instructional strategies, student activities, and criteria for assessing results. Thus, teachers concerned with advancing multiculturalism need to consider the guidelines—or theories—that undergird the school's educational offering.

Curriculum theories may reflect the bias of citizens as well as professionals. At a given time and place, they may reflect local and national concerns and, at times, the mass hysteria that prevails about such controversial issues as sexual, racial, or religious equality. In the past, curriculum theories have tended to reflect the cultural bias of the dominant majority groups. As a consequence, teachers—of all cultures and of all kinds of students—taught the "white curriculum" without reference to other cultural groups. More recently, curriculum theories have acknowledged the existence of cultural diversity by supporting the establishment of separate racially relevant courses. Such *separatism,* which typically makes black studies courses available to students as alternate choices, tends to give each set of biases a chance to compete for the time and endorsements of students. A further weakness of theories that allow for the separation of cultural content into segregated courses is the tendency to propagandize for each cultural heritage—a process that in itself runs counter to the objectives of multicultural education.

Suitable Curricular Designs

The design of a curriculum is a first response to theory. It is reflected by the nature of the objectives, content selection and organization, and the teaching strategies that are recommended. Four types of designs have predominated in elementary and secondary schools in the United States.

Subject Matter Curriculum Design. The most common curriculum design is called *subject matter.* It lists objectives in terms of intellectual skills—for example, the three Rs—and subject matter to be learned. Instructional strategies suggested relate to ways to cause students to master the skills and information. In operation, the subject matter curriculum consists of a collection of discrete courses, some of which may be prescribed as "required" of all students and others elective. It can be readily visualized that the subject matter curriculum can serve multicultural objectives only to the extent that the content of courses deals fairly and objectively with the experiences of all minority groups in the society.

Another question to be raised is whether all students should be required to take the courses. For example, a black studies program designed for black students only may do little to help other students understand the black experience. Similarly, if the goals pursued relate only to the mastery of subject matter, little may be done to promote the kinds of affective behaviors that are essential to living in a culturally diverse society.

Fused and Correlated Curriculum Designs.   Recognition that the subject matter curriculum tends to isolate knowledge into separate categories has led to efforts to relate subjects to each other. When subjects such as biology, earth and space science, physics, and chemistry are combined to form a course called general science, people call it a fused curriculum. Under such arrangements, subjects tend to lose their identity even though they are related to each other, as when English and social studies show the relationship between history, literature, and the communicative arts.

In both fused and correlated courses, opportunities abound for combining information about various cultural traditions. In such arrangements, students can be encouraged to realize that it takes the contributions of all cultures to build a nation or a body of knowledge. The focus on multicultural goals, however, will not be automatic. It has to be specified and nurtured if teachers are to make full use of the flexibility that such curricular arrangements permit.

Persistent Life Situation Curriculum Design

Another type of curriculum design is called the *persistent life situation*. In this format, goals relate to the kinds of tasks that students will meet in life. Learning is focused on skills, concepts, thought processes, and information that will help young people function effectively in life situations. Subject matter knowledge may be drawn from any discipline and applied as needed. Basically, the persistent life situation curriculum is problem-oriented. As such, it takes into account the fact that each generation of learners will face new types of problems. Emphasis is placed, therefore, on learning strategies for problem solving.

Regardless of the design, the teacher plays an important role in selecting and integrating contributions that can bring about an insightful understanding among different groups. For example, in the subject design, if the teacher sets as his goal the appreciation of different cultural contributions, students will have the opportunity to realize this goal. Even though curriculum designs are important and must not be overlooked, the most important factor in facilitating multicultural understanding is the role of the teacher.

Behavioral Goals

In recent years, attention has focused on the value of behavioral objectives in assessing the impact of curriculums as well as individual student development. Those favoring the exclusive use of behavioral outcomes argue that all worthwhile educational results can be observed in the overt responses of learners—and teachers. Their approach is to describe the results sought in very specific terms that permit precise assessments of the desired manifestations. One criterion followed in writing behavioral objectives holds that outcomes must be appropriate for all groups regardless of the ethnic and cultural backgrounds of students.

Criticisms of the exclusive use of behavioral goals suggest that some important outcomes can be stated only in general terms. The point is made that the uniformity of prescribed behavioral changes tends to ignore variations in cultural backgrounds, motivations, and learning styles.

Yet, when the concern is for the affective relationships among human beings, behavioral objectives hold the promise of focusing attention on outcomes that are essential to multicultural situations. Perhaps the need is to formulate descriptions of behavioral responses that are appropriate to multicultural objectives. At any rate, most psychologists and sociologists agree that attitudes and feelings as well as values must become functional in individual responses if they are to make a difference.

Behavioral objectives are not a panacea: they serve as a means for directing and specifying organized learning activities. Such objectives consitute a framework in which teachers can evaluate the goals and objectives of the course as well as the school. In the past, emphasis has been placed on development of cognitive skills to the neglect of the affective component. The following examples of behavioral objectives were designed to combine skill learning with the development of an understanding and appreciation for multicultural differences and similarities within our society.

In a history lesson on the American Revolution, Gwendolyn Baker introduced Crispus Attucks, a black slave who was heroic on the night of the Boston Massacre. A behavioral objective for this activity could be stated as follows: The student should be able to identify and display sensitivity to the cultural backgrounds of at least three minority persons who have made major contributions to the American Revolution. This objective satisfies the cognitive requirement in that it indicates a desired standard of performance (at least three persons). The affective component includes the identification of people from various cultural backgrounds.

In another activity, students observed plant growth. Reference was made to George Washington Carver's experiment with the peanut and his contribution to science. The experiment provided the opportunity for fusing Carver's scientific contribution with the concepts of discrimination, immorality of slavery, and educational inequality for blacks. Another example of a behavioral objective could be stated as follows: The student will be able to identify at least three scientists from different cultural groups and describe their significant contributions to the field of biology. The cognitive component in this case is to identify more than one experimenter and his or her significant contribution to biology. The affective component relates to the different cultural backgrounds of the individual scientists.

The following behavioral objectives have been taken from a high school curriculum guide. Let us try to place them in a framework for a multicultural setting.

Subject Area	*Behavioral Objectives*
1. Economics	Students should investigate the forms of business combinations.
2. Science	Students should be able to identify and name midwestern wild plants.
3. Sociology	Students should identify the way in which various groups arise, develop, and change.
4. History	Students should be able to define and understand foreign-policy and diplomatic terms.

These behavioral objectives all have one thing in common, they are cognitively oriented to the exclusion of the affective component. Most objectives place greater emphasis on subject knowledge.

In order to attain a balance in writing objectives, we must consider both the cognitive and affective components either combined into a single statement or separately described. The following illustrates the two methods of stating objectives.

COMBINED METHOD

Subject Area	*Behavioral Objectives*
1. Economics	Students should investigate the forms of business combinations and also gain an understanding and appreciation of different groups participating in its development.
2. Science	Students should be able to identify and name midwestern wild plants and appreciate the backgrounds of those responsible for their taxonomy.
3. Sociology	Students should be able to identify the way in

	which various groups arise, develop, and change as well as appreciate the ethnic background of these groups.
4. History	Students should be able to define and understand foreign-policy and diplomatic terms as well as appreciate cultural variations in respect to the rationales used by different groups.

SEPARATE METHOD

1. Sociology	*a.* Students should investigate the forms of business combinations.
	b. Students should gain an understanding and appreciation of different groups participating in all capacities of business combinations.

etc.

The sample behavioral objectives have considered the philosophical political and social aspects of multiculturalism.

Implementing the Curriculum

In implementation, the curriculum is used as a point of departure for developing instructional strategies. Research has shown that teachers who participate in curriculum planning will better implement the curriculum. Students and teachers from diversified cultural backgrounds should participate in developing an approach for studying curriculum content. Regardless of cultural heritage, this opportunity will provide equality of participation for teachers as well as students. Teacher-student interaction serves as a medium for facilitating better understanding of likenesses and differences regarding philosophical issues. Classroom discussions will reflect experiential backgrounds and, it is hoped, provide for mutual respect and understanding among the participants.

The curriculum is implemented in the materials—books, pamphlets, films, tapes, audiovisual programs—from which students learn. The choice teachers make will depend upon those approved for use and the goals pursued as well as the characteristics of given groups of learners. No single type of instructional resource can be considered the best for all. Some students learn best by using verbal materials; others are nonverbally oriented. Children and youth from minority cultures often respond better, initially, to firsthand psychomotor activities simply because these are closer to previous experiences in their homes and communities.

When selecting materials for multicultural groups, *variety* must be a guiding criterion. The range in interest and difficulty levels will be extensive if individual differences are to be met. Another guideline is *cultural representativeness*. It is essential that pertinent information about all key cultural groups be included. Instructional materials must be *accurate*, without bias for or against any racial or ethnic group. They must be *relevant*, both to the lives of all students and to the cultural diversity that is being encouraged. Finally, the materials employed must be *compatible* with student interests and learning skills.

In selecting or developing learning materials that promote multiculturalism, the need is for resources that are *culturally honest*, as contrasted with those that are claimed to be *culture-free*. The goal is to focus on cultural characteristics rather than to ignore them. Because cultural backgrounds differ in different sections of the country, schools, and classrooms, inevitably teachers must make adaptations to fit particular groups of learners. Thus, it becomes necessary for professionals to develop and employ their creative ingenuity for the use of inexpensive aids to learning.

Commercial Materials.   The education industry is becoming more sensitive to the importance of dealing with cultural diversity in textbooks, films, and programs for learning. Although many companies are still promoting various kinds of subtle cultural biases in the materials they market, a few are trying to deal with the reality of multiculturalism.

Market demands determine the kinds of commercial materials that commercial companies produce. Unless a product will be purchased by school systems or students, its publication is unlikely. For this reason alone, teachers need to communicate their needs for multicultural materials to the representatives of education industries. As the demand increases, the supply will follow the demand.

Already available are a number of textbook series that focus on the cultural backgrounds of minorities. The black studies movement, despite the isolation it may have generated in some school systems, has done much to promote the development of commercial materials that treat the black experience more fully. Efforts of other cultural minorities to highlight their own cultural traditions have brought about the publication of materials that are more culturally diverse and informative.

Teacher-prepared Materials.   Teachers make and prepare many more materials than they realize. There is seldom a teacher who does not at some time arrange or construct a pictorial display in a classroom. Most teachers, perhaps more elementary than secondary, design games and other teaching aids for their students. These kinds of instructional materials play an important part in multicultural education. Too often commercial companies are blamed for not publishing multiethnic materials while teachers go unchallenged for developing materials that do not promote cultural interaction, involvement, and understanding.

Pictures say a great deal to children about many things. Kindergarten children can be introduced to concepts and generalizations through the use of pictures. To select and display pictures of only one group reinforces the importance of that group at the expense of the exclusion of others. For example, children who see only pictures of white Americans in their school environment cannot help being reinforced with the idea that these are the only people that matter. Pictures of only one type of family group—a mother, father, and two children—cause children to question the validity of other types of families. Pictures that show children representing several ethnic groups, but each child in isolation, convey a negative view of separatism compared with pictures that show a variety of children interacting and participating together. Teachers must be aware that materials as simple as pictures and bulletin boards are teaching aids that can help establish an environment conducive to learning about diversity.

Games designed to strengthen specific skills need to include words, phrases, and pictures that reflect more than one culture. Teachers who take the time to construct such instructional media will be faced with the responsibility for designing the kinds of aids that suggest cultural dialogue and interaction. If pictures and written material are not readily obtainable from magazines, newspapers, and other sources, then teachers must rely on their own ability to create and construct what is needed.

The most widely used materials are those that come under the category of textbooks. Research has shown that textbooks in current use do not reflect the pluralistic values of American society.

Rodriquez, in writing about Mexican-Americans, suggests if any text is going to be meaningful to the truthful representation of minority influence in America, a revision is necessary. However, in addition to placing the responsibility for the revision on the writers and the publishers, he feels educators must serve in a leadership capacity and should be in the forefront demanding revision of textbook content.[2]

Greenlaw's study was designed to ascertain the degree of influence exerted by minority groups on schools and publishers in regard to publishing basal readers. She concludes that publishers do have a responsibility to educators and to minority groups as well. Some progress has been made in basal readers, but minority populations are still not well enough represented. Most of the change occurring in these printed materials has focused on urban black Americans. There is a need for including Indian, Mexican, Oriental, and rural populations as well. Greenlaw found that 84 percent of the sample admitted the lack of minority consideration in their basal readers and gave as their reasons the absence of ethnic groups within their school populations.[3]

The absence of minorities within a school population should not eliminate the use of ethnic materials. Ethnic content is important for all children. Children from the majority culture need to see representation of other cultures in the materials they use. This helps provide them with images and information that will aid the development of positive attitudes toward ethnic groups.

Evaluation of a Multicultural Curriculum

In order for a school to determine whether it is achieving the goals of a multicultural curriculum, the following questions may be considered:

1. Do students behave differently as a result of being exposed to a multicultural curriculum approach?
2. What effect does the curriculum have on students in terms of their group membership?
3. Are minority students selected for major positions within the school?
4. Are teacher attitudes changed as a result of exposure to multicultural behavioral objectives?
5. Are school activities representative of different cultural contributions?
6. Are courses organized to facilitate multicultural values?
7. What effect does student participation have in developing curriculum content and appreciation for affective cultural values?
8. Are instructional materials providing for cultural differences?
9. Are school administrators providing the opportunity for developing a multicultural curriculum?

10. Perceptions of Learning for the Multicultural Classroom

Dolores E. Cross, Gwendolyn C. Baker,
Ralph Hansen, Robert Dixon, and Robert P. Ho

Perceptions of learning tend to relate to goals to be achieved. Early psychologists, concerned mostly with the mastery of skills and knowledge, formulated a theory of learning called Stimulus-Response (S-R). It emphasized, on the one hand, the conditions needed to permit a neutral stimulus to elicit a particular response and, on the other, the conditions needed to learn new responses.

Ivan Pavlov, a pioneer in the S-R field, made significant contributions.[1] He worked on the stimulus side of the model, conducting experiments with stimulus substitution. On the response side, Edward L. Thorndike studied the learning of new responses.[2] Thorndike's work generated a number of "laws of learning" that have influenced the recent research of B. F. Skinner.[3] Skinner has concentrated on reinforcement as the crucial factor in learning. Despite the effectiveness of this approach, Skinner's theory of learning appears to many to be too mechanistic, to pay too little attention to internal mental processes, and to make behavior seem largely beyond voluntary control.

A contrasting major learning theory has been developed recently by scholars who examine behavior with broader perspectives. It is called Cognitive-Field, or Gestalt, theory because it considers *both* an individual's perceptions of a total situation and his overall responses to the perceived situation. This theory, as contrasted to the S-R or behaviorist positions, holds that learning occurs as a person structures and restructures perceptions of the forces and conditions in his environment.

Cognitive-Field theory permits the learner to utilize "insight" in problem solving. Wolfgang Kohler was an early Gestalt psychologist who experimented with chimpanzees to illustrate the concept of insight.[4] Kurt Lewin has been most responsible for many of the concepts of field psychology.[5] It is probably fair to say that this relativistic view with its stress on "meaning" is very attractive to teachers.

Of immediate concern here, however, is the identification of a theory, or cluster of theories, that would have the maximum potential for working in multicultural settings. Such theories can be identified in what is called the Closed Loop Model of Human Learning (CLM) (figure 2).

The developments that led to the CLM occurred largely since World War II. Modern technology during the war years generated many new types of self-regulating devices. These are characterized by two essential features: they all use "feedback," and their various elements are interdependent. A home heating system illustrates this type of interdependent action. It uses self-regulating devices consisting of three main components: a thermometer, a thermostat, and the furnace. These three instruments interact in such manner that the thermometer records the temperature and provides this information to the thermostat, which in turn makes the decision as to whether more heat is needed. If the answer is yes, the information is passed on to the furnace, which then acts accordingly. The new supply of heat effects a change in the temperature, which eventually influences the decision of the thermostat so that the furnace stops burning

FIGURE 2.   Closed Loop Model (CLM) of Human Learning

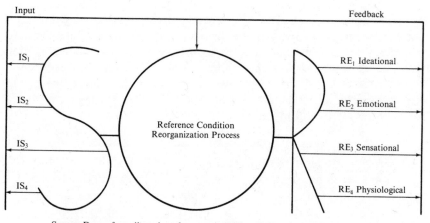

Source: Drawn from discussion of concept in William T. Powers, *Behavior: The Control of Perception* (Chicago: Aldine, 1973).

fuel. The process therefore operates in a continuous circle; hence the concept of the closed loop. Since biologists have long known that the human organism has a built-in drive for this kind of homeostasis, or equilibrium, it was natural to adapt these ideas to give us a better understanding of many aspects of human behavior, including learning.

The large S in figure 2 represents the situation in which the organism or learner is operating. Within this general situation, there can be present any number of independent stimuli (IS). For example, the teacher may be thought of as one IS sending messages to the learner. We can also identify other IS that are perceived by the learner.

On the other side of the CLM is the behavior or responses (R) of the learner, which usually generates four types of response effects (RE). The first type includes a feedback that is *cognitive* or *ideational*. It tells us whether or not the behavior is what we wanted it to be and/or if corrections are needed. The second type is *affective* or *emotional* feedback. Such dichotomies as pleasant-unpleasant, happy-sad, and hope-fear fall in this category. It is clear that such feelings will influence us the next time we are in a similar situation. The third type, *sensational,* refers to the kinesthetic perceptions of movement and position that we acquire as we are trying to learn a perceptual-motor performance. The fourth type is *physiological*. Behavior may alter the organism's physiological state by starting certain biochemical processes. The learner, therefore, is constantly receiving various types of feedback that are used along with incoming perceptual signals to guide behavior.

At the center of the CLM is O, the organism, or the learner. As indicated above, the O picks up incoming perceptual signals from the S and also receives a variety of RE in the form of feedback behaviors. In essence, the organism compares these inputs with the reference condition and take steps to reorganize and redirect behavior as may be necessary.

Why is the CLM better than the S-R or Cognitive-Field theories to explain learning in multicultural situations? Because, basically, it does a much better job of alerting the teacher to the essential aspects of learning. If one accepts the CLM, one needs to become sensitive to a wide range of incoming stimuli that can be perceived by a learner. One also needs to give careful consideration to the feedback as represented by the learner's behaviors. Teaching, therefore, should not be seen as working from the S side of the model alone. Just as important, if not more so, are the RE. Learning, then, must involve the input from S, some action by the learner, feedback as consequence of this action, and reorganization if a reference position has not been achieved or maintained.

Given the CLM as a basic way of conceptualizing the learning process, one may also use it effectively to account for the phenomenon of individual differences in learning. Regardless of the specific learning outcome we seek, we can be certain that our students will demonstrate contrasting variations in both the extent and speed of their learning. In the past such differences have frequently been attributed to the students' abilities and/or motivation. While the CLM does not deny these two variables, it does point up others that need to be considered if we are to do the best job possible of promoting student learning. To illustrate this point let us consider each part of the model in turn.

From the situation(s) the student picks up an almost infinite number of inputs. The teacher has already been mentioned as one source of information. However, the messages coming from the teacher include much more than the facts that may be transmitted. For example, the students pick up signals as to the teacher's feelings about them. If these signals are negative, other messages may never be received. Or they may be perceived as coming from a hostile source and therefore as signals to be disregarded. The curriculum may be thought of as another input. Hence, teachers should be concerned with the way in which the individual student transforms curricular phenomena. What may be meaningful to the teacher may be unacceptable, unclear, or inappropriate to the student.

An examination of the response side of the CLM indicates another source of individual differences. For all intents and purposes the response effects (feedback) are just as important as the information coming from the situation. When one considers the various types of feedback as identified in the CLM, it becomes clear that the nature of a given feedback depends on the student. Feedback that may be profitably used by one may be rejected by another. Moreover, it is important to remember that the teacher represents only one source of feedback; peers, parents, and other adults may be supplying information about the students' learning that can be a help or a hindrance.

The third source of individual differences is the student. It is represented in the CLM by the terms *reference condition* and *reorganization process*. The first is meant to be the perceived nature of some goal condition. It represents a kind of model state with which the learner compares his perception of the actual state of affairs. Behavior and learning take place as an individual tries to maintain and/or approach the reference condition. One of the most difficult tasks teachers face is that of becoming aware of the individual student's own reference condition. Many of the problems encountered by teachers stem from the fact that the reference condition of certain students is failure. Since behavior is always directed at reducing the disturbances in the environment, a student with a "failure reference condition" will do nothing when confronted with those school tasks at which he "knows" he will fail. It is only when the reference condition changes that a teacher will begin to see some positive action on the part of the learner.

The term *reorganization process* refers to a process that commences whenever a person picks up a discrepancy, via feedback, between "perception" and "reference condition." The process will persist as long as the discrepancy exists. Although we know little about the nature of this process, it serves as a construct that can help us think about the way in which learning takes place. The essence of the process is "change"; it is an ongoing process and ceases only when feedback indicates that the reference condition is being approached. The role of the teacher is to facilitate the process by all possible means. The teacher, for example, can accept responsibility for helping students learn cognitive strategies; suggest directions that the reorganization process might take; generate the necessary attitude by which the student can learn from his mistakes; encourage risk taking; and, probably most generally, communicate the idea that to change is to learn.

PROMISING INSTRUCTIONAL STRATEGIES

Responding to multicultural reality focuses attention, foremost and continuously, on teaching behavior. As one traditional wisdom dictates:

> No printed word nor spoken plea
> Can teach young minds what men should be,
> Not all the books on all the shelves,
> But what the teachers are themselves.

The teacher initiates and maintains classroom processes. Whatever takes place as students learn—the goals pursued, the materials used, the attitudes fostered, the ideas considered, the facts defined, the conclusions drawn—the teacher influences. Moreover, interactions between teacher and students reach beyond classroom walls in shaping responses within the community to the cultural diversity that prevails in our society. In a genuine sense, therefore, the role of the teacher—how he feels about and interacts with people, the values he deems important, the relationships he promotes among students—is critical to the promotion of multiculturalism.

Instructional Responses to Multiculturalism

Most teachers who are aware of multicultural conditions in their schools or the larger society, and who believe that such diversity should be nurtured, express their commitments through the instructional tactics they employ. Differences prevail, however, in the quality of these tactics. To understand the variations in the instructional responses that individual teachers may make to multiculturalism, one needs to learn to analyze types of teacher behavior as they relate to their potential within the classroom, school, and community.

The following cases illustrate some differences in instructional responses by teachers who are trying to advance multiculturalism. These samples of teacher behaviors may help us identify those teaching behaviors that are most compatible with a multicultural society.

> Ms. Jones is involved in building a display of ethnic heroes on the class bulletin boards. The students have assisted by mounting pictures, arranging items, and providing captions. One section, which calls attention to reading materials, is clearly labeled "Multicultural Literature." A group of students is planning, as part of the project, to hold an ethnic food fair at Thanksgiving time. They envision providing booths in which the traditional foods of various ethnic groups will be displayed and sold. Each booth will be monitored by students wearing the appropriate ethnic costume.

How well do you feel Ms. Jones is responding to cultural differences within the classroom and the wider community? How would you compare Ms. Jones's professional behavior with the instructional tactics displayed by Mr. Smith in the following case?

> Mr. Smith is involving students in setting up the classroom for individualization of instruction. The pupils are made aware of intraclass grouping and variety of materials. There are differentiated assignments and labels for specific interest areas that suggest traffic patterns in the classroom. Some students work individually; others are studying in groups of varying sizes. The class is multi-aged and ungraded.

What about Mr. Smith's response to cultural differences? Is it more insightful than that of Ms. Jones? How would you compare it with the behavior of Ms. Garcia described in the case below?

> Ms. Garcia is participating in a teacher-pupil discussion to guide the formation of triad study groups to discover accessible cultural resources. The students are also involved in individual projects that focus on what they had discovered about self or others in the class. Periodically, students contribute to a bulletin board that represents cultural-experience building blocks. These blocks illustrate their knowledge of self, others, and the social/political system. The illustration also reflects understanding and facts gathered at different times in the semester as well as materials and personalities used to augment perceptions.

How do you react to Ms. Garcia's efforts to meet cultural differences in her classroom and community?

Here are some analyses by the authors that may help you identify differences in the professional behavior of Ms. Jones, Mr. Smith, and Ms. Garcia. Mr. Smith, for example, differs from Ms. Jones and Ms. Garcia in that he is involved in an interaction process designed to assess the situation, promote development in students, and then reassess results. This process leads to attitudes that view the existence of cultural diversity as a natural condition; a study of the condition is a normal process rather than a "fad of the times." Here the teacher and pupils are assessing all available resources, human and material, of the immediate and wider community. Within this format, the teacher is helping students to understand their relationships to each other and to learn how to use the resources in ways that respect individual integrity. The process teaches all participants to look within self, as well as others, for important cultural characteristics that represent dimensions of the past, present, and future. Moreover, the process conveys the feeling that there is more to be learned, about oneself and others, as one looks beyond the classroom to life in the larger community itself.

The teacher who is responding truly to cultural diversities should provide for pupil participation in (1) assessing human and material resources in the classroom, (2) developing ways to discover and utilize human and material resources, and (3) reassessing at different stages the change or the learning that is taking place.

Characteristics of Instructional Strategies

No particular instructional strategy or pattern of teaching can be singled out as being the best for promoting multiculturalism. It is possible, however, to identify certain characteristics of a given instructional pattern or procedure that is contributing to multiculturalism.

Shared Responsibility within the classroom, between teacher and students and among students, typically characterizes any program of instruction that is sensitive to cultural diversity. When the teacher or a group of dominant or favored students makes all decisions with respect to what happens in the classroom, inevitably some students are treated as minorities rather than as equals. Only when all share cooperatively in the planning and implementation of learning activities is there a chance for individual differences to be respected and utilized.

Mutual Respect is found in the human relationships of any group that prizes cultural uniquenesses. Such attitudes are generated out of the equal partnership that comes from shared responsibility. Equality is a key condition, for without it mutual respect cannot exist. But equality, it must be emphasized, relates to human rights rather than to similarities in talents or defined contributions. It is a value, an agreed-upon relationship, a belief that each individual is important and precious—to self and society. Underscored in such beliefs is the conviction that one has the right to be different.

Participation marks the instructional strategies that can make maximum contributions to multiculturalism. When participation is absent, it is difficult to achieve the necessary understanding and appreciation of the uniquenesses that prevail. Individuals must interact with each other in order to know who everyone is. By working and learning together, students can gain insights into differences that may be vital in any multicultural group.

Access to Knowledge about cultural differences is essential if people with plural life styles and ethnic traditions are to live and learn together harmoniously and beneficially. Ignorance about other cultures is the principal cause of most negative responses to multiculturalism. To understand, to appreciate, to respect all cultural or ethnic groups, one must know about them.

Variety is essential where differences are cherished. Not all students learn in the same way. Not all are motivated by the same goals. Not all use the same language. Not all have identical abilities. Not all bring to school similarities in health, interests, ambitions, work habits, behavioral responses, values, or commitments to formal schooling. Nor are all alike with respect to their interpersonal relationships. If such differences are to be dealt with in a positive and respectful way, variety in teaching techniques must be provided.

Key Steps in Instructional Processes

In addition to being sensitive to the general characteristics of teaching strategies, it helps to be aware of key steps in the instructional process in which the teacher has opportunities to contribute to multiculturalism. Such stages, it will be noted, will not be present in all patterns of teaching. The lecture method, for example, provides a different set of steps altogether. It is also possible for a teacher to move through the steps described below without making much contribution to multicultural goals. Here, again, the important consideration is how a teacher works with a given group of learners.

Assessing Human and Material Resources. A teacher and a group of students explore the human and physical resources of their group and classroom in order to initiate a specific project. In the discussion, students and teacher will share ideas and past experiences in dealing with similar tasks. While observing student reactions, the teacher will make decisions about how best to plan instruction so that members of the group will become involved in the process. Through such interactions students gain knowledge of the task to be accomplished, the accessible resources, and the various contributions that different participants are likely to make. By involving the students in planning and carrying out their own learning activities, the teacher creates an atmosphere of cooperation that underscores the value of the contributions of each. In planning together, students come to see differences as sources of strength rather than impediments to progress.

The assessment process is a systematic activity that may be both personal and interpersonal. On the personal side, it draws from the teacher's knowledge, style, aims, as well as teaching and learning competence. With respect to interpersonal involvement, it depends on data from informal dialogue with students, fellow teachers, parents, and others who know the students, as well as the interpretations the teacher makes of the information assembled.

Developing Learning Activities. In every method of teaching, some provision is made for learning activities. The extent to which such activities are characterized by the conditions that are supportive of multiculturalism might well be a criterion for their selection. Consider, for example, the following description of one way in which learning activities may develop.

> The teacher and students are involved in activities that build upon the knowledge of participants. In completing a specific project, students use accessible resources. Discussion is also directed to awareness of possible activities and exploration in other learning settings. The teacher may also introduce films or stories to show how individuals and groups outside the classroom or local environment might perceive or handle issues involved in cultivating knowledge, valuing, and utilizing resources of a particular setting. Throughout this process, individual students and small groups will plan and carry out a variety of study activities, sharing the results with others in the class. Attention will focus on the perceptions of students as well as those of the teacher. Consideration will be given to alternative attitudes and values without trying to prescribe definitive answers.

Developing learning activities involves deciding on a specific plan. The process can be initiated by the teacher and/or students. Involved is the determination of activities, the sequence to be followed, the personal and material resources required, the anticipated outcomes, and the means of judging results. As the participants "work through" the plan, certain choices will be made: *what to do* (instructional area, content focus, skill involved); *with whom* (independently, small group); *when* (immediately, at another scheduled or to-be-scheduled time); *where* (in the classroom, corridor, library, learning center, at home or in the community); *how* (reading, constructing, experimenting, discussing, dramatizing); and *scope* (extent, length, and intensity of the project). Having a plan for learning expedites the making of choices. The design should be flexible and subject to revision by the teacher and students.

Planning for learning activities can be done on an individual, small-group, or whole-class basis, depending on the tasks and their appropriateness for all or some of the class members. In the interaction that takes place, participation should define the resources of each member as well as the physical resources in the classroom situation. From these, the participants can project the ranges of activities for the learning experience of all.

Reassessing Plans and Progress. A typical example of the way in which reassessment takes place occurs when the teacher and students identify the individual skills and learning processes that will help achieve a given objective. One procedure is for the group to analyze the experience of each of its members. In such sessions, progress toward predefined goals, preliminary results, and possible new directions can be explored.

As with all learning, reassessing is essential. It can involve a series of intermediate evaluations prior to the final evaluation at the end of the project. Such activities usually involve a comparison of judgments by the teacher and members of the student group. How long evaluation sessions will be or how formal they become will depend on the nature and length of the project. The goal is to achieve a spirit of teamwork that focuses on the process, knowledge, and better understanding of self and resources. Assessments may relate to individual contributions as well as to group attainments. Hopefully, students and teacher can observe the progress from one stage of development to another.

The value and power of giving attention to these key steps in the instructional process, in terms of their impact on multicultural goals, are illustrated by the following quotation:

> "First of all," he said, "if you can learn a simple trick, Scout, you'll get along a lot better with all kinds of folks. You never really understand a person until you consider things from his point of view . . ."
> "Sir?"
> ". . . until you climb into his skin and walk around in it."[6]

ORGANIZING INSTRUCTION

The foregoing examples of promising instructional strategies for multicultural classrooms clearly illustrate that the methods a teacher employs do make a difference in learning outcomes. Thus, *how* one teaches must be considered as well as *what* is taught. No matter how well a curriculum is designed, if the individual teacher is insensitive to the goals and opportunities envisioned, learners may fail to develop desired insights and understanding. Furthermore, the teaching strategies employed by a teacher, the classroom climate created, the structural component of any given classroom, as well as the instructional resources selected, will be affected by the students being taught.

It was stressed earlier that there is no single approach or set of strategies that is most appropriate for all situations. The approach a particular teacher employs will depend on the situation, the content and skills to be taught, as well as the individual differences of his students—their learning styles and cultural characteristics.

What the Teacher Can Do

When a teacher assumes the responsibility for teaching a child or group of children specific arithmetic concepts, for example, several generalizations have already been made. It is assumed that the students know little or nothing about what is to be learned, or have learned certain concepts inadequately. Information about the students and where each is in his or her mastery of arithmetic concepts allows the teacher to prepare and design strategies and techniques that will best help to teach what should be learned. Knowing where a student is will help the teacher to begin.

Examples of Teaching Strategies

Once teachers know what must be taught, they can consider the instructional strategies that will best further learning. Byron G. Massialas and Nancy F. Sprague have identified three teaching styles that are useful in promoting multicultural understandings.[7]

The first style is *expository teaching*. In this approach, the teacher explores in advance the issues and concepts to be taught to the students. The students are presented with information and provided guidance as they explore its meaning to assure that predetermined goals are reached. A teacher who uses this method must devote considerable time to researching information and planning lessons. A need is to verify the accuracy and objectivity of the content to be taught. The lessons must be organized in logical fashion and related to the backgrounds and motivations of students. Key questions and activities must be selected that will focus student thinking on important information and desired behaviors.

Expository lessons can be introduced in a variety of ways. Depending on the content selected, the introductory portion may be a lecture, a play, a film or filmstrip, or the reading of material from a selected book. The teacher may choose to involve students in this initial portion of the lesson or may make the presentation alone. The most important consideration is to achieve an effective presentation that will stimulate student interest and participation in the planned learning activities.

Opinion Teaching is the second style suggested. This strategy involves the identification of a problem situation, with both the teacher and students participating in the process. All members of the class can participate in identifying the problem, finding and evaluating pertinent evidence related to its solution, as well as formulating hypotheses about how it should be solved. The interaction that usually transpires in such a cooperative endeavor can promote mutual understanding and acceptance of the ideas, information, and opinions of others. In some cases, in contrast, group deliberations may generate more argumentative responses. Whichever the case, the teacher plays a vital role in guiding students to conclusions that are honest and objective as well as respectful of dissenting views.

Opinion teaching is particularly useful when a teacher is endeavoring to help students to reanalyze causes and reasons for their holding biased points of view regarding multicultural themes. If one group of students finds itself hostile to another, for example, the examination of personal beliefs in relationship to those of others and to objective evidence may lead to revisions of personal responses.

A third teaching style, one that is even more open and promotive of teacher-student cooperation, is called *inquiry teaching*. This approach provides for both advanced planning and spontaneous involvement of students. Even more so, perhaps, than with other methods, the teacher will assume responsibility for making available a wide variety of instructional resources. In reality, this is the method of science in which students are encouraged to identify new dimensions of a problem, formulate hypotheses, gather data, clarify meanings, and draw conclusions. It is particularly useful in helping students to resolve conflicting ideas and attitudes about multicultural concepts. A key goal of inquiry teaching is to develop in students feelings of efficiency and commitments to objectivity. The aim is to help all believe they are able to look critically at problems in their environment, to study and solve them. Thus, feeling able to control their own destiny, they can make their own decisions and influence those of others.

Any one of these three styles may be used in almost any classroom situation. Often teachers will use a combination of the styles. The content to be taught, the backgrounds of the students, as well as the teacher's professional competence and preferences will all influence the choice. The test of validity will come with the results produced. Teaching ethnic content will require a variety of instructional approaches and organization patterns. Such diversity in techniques and organization adds to the excitement and challenge of teaching for multicultural objectives.

Planning Classroom Activities

Planning classroom activities—selection of resources, techniques, student activities, evaluation processes—is the key to successful teaching in any situation. When multicultural goals are considered, it becomes even more important. In addition to deciding *what* to teach and *how,* one must consider *where* and *when* to teach ethnic content.

Certainly to delay instruction about cultural diversity until the secondary school years is a critical mistake. The delayed introduction of ethnic content tends to breed hostility and often produces disruptive behavior between and among various cultural groups. High school students cannot be expected to understand easily multicultural concepts if their previous schooling has been in monocultural situations. Multicultural instruction must begin in preschools and/or kindergartens—and continue throughout all of the years of schooling. Studies by Clark, Goodman, and Lasker[8] have found that children come with negative attitudes already established about people who are different from them. Children bring biases and prejudices to the classroom. Thus, it becomes necessary for teachers to change existing attitudes by replacing them with positive and accurate images of people from other cultural groups.

What the Teacher Can Use

A close relationship exists between instructional materials, methodology, and organization. Instructional materials will be only as effective as the teacher using them. Therefore, it is imperative for educators to evaluate and select materials appropriate for teaching about cultural diversity. The ability to accomplish this task will depend on the awareness and sensitivity of those making the selection as well as the teacher using the materials.

The increasing demand for ethnic materials is stimulating commercial publishing companies to include them in their publication lists. In many classrooms, teachers are still having to adapt materials to suit multicultural objectives. The following is a comment about the selection of such materials.

> Instructional materials, then, are limited tools for the job of attitudinal and behavior change. The only legitimate goals of such content are to prepare materials that correct errors of fact, are free of stereotypes and accurately describe the Negro's role in the American past, and to analyze the meaning of the black American's experience in this country. Academics in curriculum development, supported lustily by commercial publishers, have watered their stock abundantly, promising dividends that will seldom materialize.[9]

What is lacking in most available instructional materials is a cultural dialogue about the pluralistic differences that naturally exist, and need to be cherished and preserved, within our society. Too often materials, whether they are commercially prepared or teacher-made, are monocultural in nature. Finding materials that reflect cultural diversity—books, pamphlets, films, television presentations—is a teacher's first responsibility.

Evaluating Outcomes

An old educational maxim is: *Teachers teach what they test*. While this saying may not be altogether true, it implies that students tend to learn what they know teachers consider important. With respect to multicultural content and concepts, the goals emphasized by the teacher may well shape the outcomes achieved.

Appropriate attitudes and behavior for the multicultural society are *affective* in nature. They concern how individuals feel and act toward each other. Assessment of results, therefore, must give attention to such traits as attitudes, understandings, and interactions of students. Attitudes and understandings can be measured; but interactions must be observed. As a consequence, teachers are forced to focus on the behavioral objectives that are appropriate to multicultural schools and societies, as well as on the expressions of feeling and evidences of knowledge that may be obtained.

11. Language Arts in a Multicultural Society

Ernece B. Kelly

The author's credentials were not impressive. He had failed at everything he had tried. . . . [Then] in 1973 alone, income attributed to his [character's] adventures and the use of his name exceeded $15,000,000. The lifetime total has long since passed $100,000,000.[1]

The author referred to is Edgar Rice Burroughs. The character who made him rich is, of course, Tarzan, whose incredible adventures have been translated into twenty-eight languages. He appears on bookshelves in half the countries of the world and is surely one of America's best-known exports. Besides bringing wealth to the author, the Tarzan books have given millions of readers a wealth of pleasure—and a wealth of misinformation about Africa. According to Burroughs, Tarzan is *king of the jungle,* a part of the continent, incidentally, that Burroughs helped confuse with the whole. (In fact, all of Africa's jungles occupy less area than the Amazon jungle in Brazil.) As king, Tarzan has powers of survival and conquest that most native Africans in the stories apparently lack. Thus, in this popular American fantasy we witness a white man, orphaned in the all-pervasive jungle, beating back its terrors while Africans with generations of experience behind them cower in fear or grin with gratitude.

Yet neither Tarzan nor Burroughs is exceptional in the panorama of popular culture. They are, in fact, representative of one of its dominant themes: the superiority of the white man and the inferiority of dark peoples.

This theme has been around for a long time, and has been expressed in a variety of ways. Around 1902, Bert Williams described the attitude of the entertainment world: "Managers gave little credit to the ability of

168

black people on the stage before the native African element was introduced. All that was expected of a colored performer was singing, dancing, and a little story telling, but as for acting, no one credited a black person with the ability to act."[2] In 1973 the editors of an Asian-American anthology described their collection as lacking in the "snow jobs pushing Asian-Americans as the miracle synthetic white people that America's proprietors of white liberal pop, like Tom Wolfe, ABC television ('If Tomorrow Comes,' 'Kung Fu,' 'Madame Sin'), and such racist henchmen passing from scholars as Gunther Barth and Stuart Miller, make us out to be."[3]

But popular culture is not the only arena in which stereotypes and racial misconceptions abound. In 1937 the poet-critic Sterling Brown published a wide-ranging examination of stereotypes of Afro-Americans in classics of American fiction. Brown isolated several *key* stereotypes recurring in books as early as James Fenimore Cooper's *The Last of the Mohicans* (1826) and as late as Julia Peterkin's *Scarlet Sister Mary* (1928), which won a Pulitzer Prize one hundred years later. In 1963 Cecil Robinson chronicled the rise and perpetuation of stereotypes of Mexican-Americans in his book *With the Ears of Strangers*. Others, in articles and monographs, have noted the racial and ethnic stereotypes that prevail in both popular culture and classroom materials.

Americans continue to be bombarded by the media with racial stereotypes. Even those image brokers who claim to be liberalizing their products are clearly ambivalent in their motivation. Witness *A Man Called Horse*, a highly touted film of the 1960s, which featured the sun dance ceremony associated with many Plains tribes. The principal actor was a white man. With one stroke authenticity is established, with the next it is destroyed. Why?

Answers to that "why" are central to understanding why some multiethnic teaching strategies show promise of eliciting positive responses in English classrooms and why others will, at best, produce only cosmetic changes.

Half a century ago, W. E. B. Du Bois wrote, "The problem of the twentieth century is the problem of the color-line."[4] Evidently few Americans took that as a signal for reflection or behavior modification. And by 1968 their number had not increased, for Tom Wicker was able to write, in his introduction to the *Report of the National Advisory Commission on Civil Disorders*, "This report is a picture of one nation, divided."[5]

There are economic, sociological, and political realities that prove both of these statements to be damningly accurate. Those realities should serve as a backdrop for developing strategies in multiethnic education in English classrooms. The backdrop can help teachers maintain relevance and impact as they make choices in the classroom. Alternatively, the facts of those realities may be incorporated into segments of the language-arts instruction so as to help make sense of the focal materials without distracting from them.

COMPOSITION, SPEECH, AND LANGUAGE STUDY

> Composition and writing receive relatively little attention, accounting for about 15 percent of classroom time. The problem runs deeper, however, for when writing *is* taught, the emphasis is almost wholly on mechanics—spelling, punctuation, grammar, sentence structure, width of the margins, and so on—with little attention to development, organization or style, i.e., to anything larger than the sentence.[6]

Above, an observation; what follows, a recommendation.

> Students who want to write in EAE [Edited American English: the written language of the weekly news magazines, of almost all newspapers, and of most books] will have to learn the forms identified with that dialect as additional options to the forms they already control. We [teachers] should begin our work in composition with them by making them feel confident that their writing, in whatever dialect, makes sense and is important to us, that we read it and are interested in the ideas and person that the writing reveals. Then students will be in a much stronger position to consider the rhetorical choices that lead to statements written in Edited American English.[7]

More than four years separate those two statements. Separating them, too, are vastly different orientations to students and their written expressions. Whether or not one agrees with the linguistic stance assumed in the second quotation, I think it would be difficult to quarrel with its concern for students and their self-concepts.

By way of contrast, the first quotation reflects an indifference to the students' language and implies an indifference to the student. Widespread myths about a prestige dialect permit (and sometimes encourage) teachers to reject alternative systems that students may bring into the classroom. Among the myths are these: that there is a single American "Standard English," which must be taught and so perpetuated; that the future employability of students is directly and significantly affected by the dialect they use; and that a failure to speak/write "Standard English" reflects a limitation in the student's thinking abilities.[8]

Once teachers acknowledge these myths for what they are, they can take steps to translate their new understanding into classroom behavior. One way this may be achieved is by opening the classroom to some use of dialects. The "strangeness" of the sounds and structures may hamper a teacher's full exploitation of the dialects in composition classes. This is a reasonable reaction, given the socioeconomic and racial stratification in America (a stratification that is significantly visible in our teacher-training institutions). However, that's not a good reason for maintaining a linguistic status quo in the classroom. A useful ploy, suggested in *Students' Right to Their Own Language,** is for teachers to listen regularly to tape recordings of alternative dialects so that they become more familiar with them. One way students would benefit from this method is that they, as persons *outside* the teacher's learning experiences, would not be subject to any resentment the teacher might feel, at least not as directly as they would if the teacher were to attempt learning in class from the students themselves.

The same general approaches that have been recommended for writing can be extended to speech classes. Teachers can be more realistic about *why* they teach one dialect and suppress, explicitly or by indirection, others. Too, teachers can become more eclectic in their acceptance of dialects as they are used among students themselves and in student-teacher transactions in the classroom. In other words, teachers both of speech and of the written word are being invited into the process of dealing with language as it *really* works. But then, what does that mean?

SOCIAL CONSTRUCTIONISTS AND THE ENGLISH CLASSROOM

Each of us is able to get through an ordinary day with relative ease, in part because we're able to routinize our responsibilities. One reason we can routinize is because our everyday lives have a core of sameness about them. If we had to think about what to do and how to do each task facing us—from getting up to retiring, and from adolescence to old age—we would get little done. This becomes evident when, after a vacation, we have to reorient ourselves to the daily routine.

In the United States, with its rigidly segregated housing and schooling patterns, most people in educational institutions are involved with people of *similar* racial or ethnic origin as well as similar socioeconomic background. Most personnel, in time, become accustomed to that sort of reality and build a set of expectations around it. And most of the time, the behaviors of their associates confirm their expectations. Hence, the routinization of school activities can and does develop.

But what happens when schools become desegregated (*not* integrated, a goal requiring more, and a different type of, perseverance and sensitivity)? Faced with new clientele, teachers become anxious. How, after all, are they to relate to ethnic and racial minorities and what can they expect from them? Some reports suggest that many teachers and administrators

* See source list at the end of this chapter.

grab hold of stereotypes to quell their own anxieties, using them as a basis for relating to the new student body.

At City University of New York, for example, some vocal professors complained about standards dropping and about academically superior students shying away from the school once open enrollment began in 1970.[9] Four years later, parts of South Boston exploded when youngsters came by bus to attend high school there. Stories of ignorant Americans acting violently and out of fear of and misinformation about minority students emanate from all parts of this country and from all levels of educational institutions.

Sociologists Berger and Luckmann explain these phenomena this way: "The reality of everyday life contains typificatory schemes in terms of which others are apprehended and 'dealt with' in face-to-face encounters. Thus I apprehend the other as 'a man,' 'a European,' 'a buyer,' 'a jovial type' and so on."[10] Beyond the most general of such categories, school personnel may have had only limited experience. If they are encountering racial or ethnic minorities in relatively intimate and ongoing circumstances for the first time, the words "she's a Puerto Rican," for example, may well carry negative behavioral stereotypes and expectations.

What has all this to do with teachers of language arts? Not much if teachers are going to utilize monochromatic materials all their professional lives. But it is terribly relevant if teachers are going to expand the traditional curriculum so that it includes the expression, verbal as well as written, of as many groups as is feasible. And the question of feasibility is relevant to the basic curriculum, not the demographic question of whether or not a teacher's classes are racially or ethnically mixed. That question is irrelevant to the imperative for making language arts less parochial.

A MODEL STRATEGY FOR A MULTICULTURAL APPROACH IN LANGUAGE ARTS

I shall begin this discussion of the objectives underlying the model strategy by referring the reader to the racial and ethnic stereotypes discussed in the first paragraphs of this chapter. I think they constitute an appropriate topic in the classroom. They are varied in character and origins; that variety lends them a flexibility permitting them to be integrated into units on a college level, such as units on logic or, on an elementary school level, units on other people and cultures. If teachers are to be successful, their instruction must have a basis in reality. Part of that reality is stereotypes that *really* do get bandied about in the schoolyard or the college dormitory. And, as Sterling Brown points out, stereotypes do have *some* basis in reality. Working with them openly can given teachers valuable insight into the types of blocks standing between students and their comprehension and/or appreciation of alternative dialects and multiethnic literature.

Too, I think it appropriate to discuss related segments of the distant as well as the current history of each racial or ethnic group whose expressions will be studied.

But before getting into particulars, what are the handful of fundamentals that are central to the course being proposed? They may well be the only things students take away. In the words of Alfred North Whitehead, "The function of a University is to enable you to shed details in favour of principles. When I speak of principles I am hardly even thinking of verbal formulations. A principle which has thoroughly soaked into you is rather a mental habit than a formal statement."[11]

The mental habits we are trying to induce in our students in this model curriculum number three. First is the habit of questioning: Have all likely sources of information been sought out? Have the most discerning questions been raised? Second is the habit of looking for the other viewpoint, or at least anticipating what a counterposition might be: What would a traditionalist say? How would a writer of agitprop react? Does this violate the spirit of Spanglish? Even if questions such as these are raised or answered only part of the time, the fact of their being raised helps to generate a dynamic relationship between the reader and the materials. However, more to the point of our overall objectives, these kinds of questions can habituate the student to looking beyond the conventional corpus of materials in any given unit. And it is by doing so that he or she may tease out the creations of minority artists.

Third is the habit for nonestablishment sources of news, news interpretation, and creative expression. Certainly the *New York Times* and *Drama Magazine* offer news and creative expression. But there are other versions of reality and of fantasy being offered in the *Amsterdam News* and *El Grito*. Students should be savvy about how to locate these lesser-known sources. In short, students who are successful in this type of curriculum would be habituated to raising nontraditional questions and discovering nontraditional sources of information. Their academic and other experiences would thus be expanded.

Much of the thinking of J. S. Bruner, especially as expressed in his book *Toward a Theory of Instruction,*[12] relates to the rationale expressed above. Basic to his thinking are two principles that rest at the heart of my rationale. The first is that education is a process of reorganizing experience. Namely, in multicultural education we are interested in bringing to the fore of consciousness and intelligent understanding the experiences of minorities, experiences that typically are only on the edges of national consciousness. Second, Bruner believes that knowing is a process, not a product, of intellectual activity. It is a process that involves the student as a participant in the discovery process—not so much as a retainer of knowledge. Like Whitehead, Bruner is *not* interested in the accumulation of details. Again, in reference to the rationale, the teacher is working to alert students to less-known sources of information and to foster insight into minority experiences. This is always done with the intention of exciting the student to seek out new sources.

More about the rationale underlying the historical units recommended. I think it is a generally accepted notion that we learn best within a context that makes sense to us, which, of course, also relates to the specific material being studied. In the case of many students, the context for study of multiethnic materials, the one that they bring to class, is a negative one, similar to what Octavio Romano-V describes as a minority status in which the members are "never seen as participants in history, much less as generators of the historical process."[13] Others come to class familiar with a few names of non-Anglo writers of established reputation. This type of knowledge is a very dangerous thing, indeed, for it can lead to the conclusion that those writers are spokesmen. It then follows that their versions of the ethnic experience constitute the Truth. Many students will feel no impulse to go beyond this stage.

The purpose of the history units is to dispel these kinds of notions and to replace them with information that can block the (re)formulation of stereotypes. However, in keeping with my rationale, it is less important that students grasp the historical particulars and more important that they retain a gestalt of a dynamic and multifaceted racial or ethnic group. The historical unit is also designed to act as a framework that informs students about the forces that may have influenced the writer's (or speaker's or artist's) choice of subject, style, or form.

The history is chosen, then, with two main characteristics in mind. It must not be so general as to fail to relate to the specific material being studied. And it must not be so detailed that it becomes an interesting puzzle in itself, distracting from the language-arts materials. It seems to me that introductory chapters to genre collections, such as those written by Darwin Turner and published by Charles E. Merrill, provide one excellent kind of focused history. Each chapter covers one generic type—poetry, essays, drama—and provides information of a literary and historical kind. The prose reads easily. With such a series, teachers could choose the introduction best suited for the genre they wish to study.

Or a more wide-ranging introduction, such as those in books treating the role ethnic groups have played in American history or ones treating the history of only one group, can be profitably read by students. A fine example is *The Negro American: A Documentary History,* edited by Benjamin Quarles and Leslie H. Fishel, Jr.[14] The chronologically arranged introductions examining the economic, educational, and political status of

Afro-Americans at crucial stages of their history in this country offer much to the teacher wishing to give a broad introduction, but one limited to a certain historical period. With this volume, a teacher has much to chose from insofar as period background is concerned.

For teachers who wish to incorporate most of their students' reading in one volume, there are books that combine the multicultural literature with discussions of it from a literary viewpoint. One of the earliest such books is Gerald Haslam's *Forgotten Pages of American Literature*. This type of volume would work best in a course of at least several months' duration.

Here is an example of the succinct manner in which Haslam indicates relationships between Asian-American and Anglo-American languages, preliminary to commentary on the relationship between the two literatures:

> Only in the gradually-disappearing Asian language media in the United States are the literary genres unique to Asian cultures much in evidence in this country. . . . Chinese poetry, based as it is on an analytic language, features . . . rhyming and a complicated pattern of musical tones. Japanese is polysyllabic and among the semantically vaguest, yet most suggestive of tongues; poets take full advantage of its multiplicity of word associations, of its ability to compress many images into very few words. [15]

It is precisely information of this kind that can provide a framework of understanding for the literary pieces to be studied and so bite away at some of the conscious or unconscious biases students may have about multicultural expression in any of its forms.

Perhaps I too casually assume that teachers are persuaded that materials of this kind, organized as suggested, will have an effect on student attitudes. Of course, this isn't universally accepted. However, Thomas Pettigrew advances the hypothesis that racial prejudice can be diminished by attacking the belief that prejudice is the norm of a community. [16] The conforming side of students who perceive that norm reaches out to incorporate those prejudices. If, Pettigrew argues, the visible and vocal elements of the community—and that certainly could include the schools—would make it clear that they do *not* subscribe to prejudices, the pressure on students to do so would be reduced. This, combined with the nonstereotypic image of minorities that the student discovers in classrooms, could help lessen prejudice and the discriminatory behavior that grows from it.

I can't help but wonder what rationale supports the raft of multicultural classroom activities that attempt to introduce students to "other cultures" via taste-tests of their cuisine, bus tours of their neighborhoods, or imitation of their "costumes"—a term that challenges the notion of an *authentic* experience—preparatory to launching an Indian Powwow or a Mexican hat dance.

Such activities generally drag students into the most exotic expressions of culture. They fail to instill comprehension of the historical, cultural, economic, or religious reasons, *why* these activities are part of another culture. In other words, they are swatches from a cultural fabric and, as such, best experienced as mere threads of the whole design.

What, after all, would a foreign student understand about Anglo-American culture by celebrating the Fourth of July in a classroom setting? That Americans like firecrackers? That they are addicted to fried chicken and watermelon? But more to the point, if that student did understand these particular activities on a cognitive level, what has he comprehended about the values that nurture the *things* Americans traditionally do on the Fourth?

I believe that many, if not most, of these "let's pretend" activities are limited to units within a course. As such, the teacher can't reasonably expect to achieve depth of understanding; teachers are really limiting students to superficial acquaintance with external behaviors, for the most part. More harm than good is done. For the culture has been short-changed by what may have been an emphasis on the exotic, the different; and the students, too, have been short-changed if they are left with the impression that they have experienced anything more than a thin slice from a culture other than their own.

Now to the models. The first uses a phase of Mexican-American history for historical background. The booklet used is strictly a history; it has neither literary nor cultural components to speak of. And the literary pieces that rest at the center of the model are all by Chicano writers. I've added descriptions of the works so that teachers can more easily understand both how the historical material illuminates or fleshes out the literary works and how a variety of literary observations can be made by comparing or contrasting—or even treating in absolute ways—a very limited number of works.

The historical resource is *The Mexicans in America* by Carey McWilliams.[17] This is a booklet of only thirty-one pages. If teachers have serious time constraints, I would urge them to use only selected sections. For example, the first chapter, which includes interesting—but not especially germane—information about the sixteenth and seventeenth centuries and related historical background, might well be skipped. Instead, I would read and discuss the next section, which gives a simplified but useful explanation of the waves of immigration from Mexico and the kind of work situations facing Mexicans in this country. This type of background sheds light on the limited kinds of work available to Mexican-Americans in the literary selections that follow (and in so much of the literature) and also provides some background for understanding attitudes expressed by the characters toward Mexico.

The literary selections are from two sources: the short stories from *The*

Chicano[18] and the poem from Haslam's *Forgotten Pages of American Literature.* "Amado Muro," by Cecilia Rosas, is a short story about a love affair between a Mexican-American boy and an older woman who is not interested in his affections. It is an interesting story mostly because we are taken inside the boy's feelings and watch them grow and change in reaction to the woman and in response to his associates and friends who know about the one-sided affair. The story is explicit in its descriptions of what characterizes "Mexican behavior" and about what constitutes assimilation efforts. Also, it includes Spanish expressions.

"Sanchez" by Richard Dokey is another short story about a love affair. This time the characters are older and married; it is a mutual affair. Unlike "Amado Muro," which is set in El Paso, Texas, this story is set largely in the country, and ownership of a parcel of land and its significance to the central character figure importantly in the story. There are explicit references to the prejudice that the husband and wife encounter in the nearby town. Memories of life in Mexico are evoked, acting as a sort of counter to the prejudices of some of the townspeople. Again, Spanish phrases are sprinkled throughout the story.

"To Endure" by Robert Granat is a short story about a personal tragedy. What I find of special interest here is the language, which is a combination of English and Spanish. Here there is no evidence of discrimination or prejudice.

"Turn of a Cycle, off Miami," a poem by David Hernandez, is concerned with the corrosive effects of "progress" on the natural beauty of Miami, Florida. The provocative imagery merits study. Here there is no mention or implication of the writer's ethnic heritage.

Using a model such as this, teachers can involve students in discussion of so many different matters: for example, the literary styles (language, sentence structure, tone, the narrative core, and so on). Because the materials differ so much from each other in terms of setting and character (age, marital status, emotional range, and so on), there is a variety of ethnic experiences suggested by the materials themselves. The teacher need not be explicit about those ethnic dimensions; let the student discover them (or not) for himself.

Because these are *models*, they are shared with the hope that they will trigger in the reader ideas about materials that may be easily fit into the framework. Or, the model may trigger ideas about modification of the framework itself. Obviously, this chapter cannot provide all possible models. However, I do think it worthwhile to show the same model with different kinds of materials having different objectives.

The historical source is *English for a New Generation,* by Hans P. Guth.[19] This book touches on aspects of language arts taught in most schools, and so might be interesting to readers who want a fresh look at traditional subjects. However, for purposes of this model, we are interested only in thirty-four pages in which Guth presents a description of dialects—regional and racial—and their relationship to "Standard English." It would make suitable reading for high school or college students. Upper-grade elementary school students could handle segments of this chapter prior to studying literature in which various dialects appear.

The literary selections that are appropriate include *A Summer Adventure* by Richard W. Lewis, a story suitable for grades three to five. It recounts the adventures of a little boy who enjoys exploring the quarry and woods around a farm. The language is that of EAE, and the main character is an Afro-American. In a very natural way the reader comes to understand that the boy and his father have a very close relationship. There is no racial dimension in the story.

Black Folktales by Julius Lester includes tales of origin, love, heroes, and ordinary people. Two important points that can be made (and that grow organically out of the materials) are that black English communicates effectively, and that black English is sufficiently versatile that it can convey ideas for different purposes and establish different tones.

The collections of poetry for children of June Jordan, Nikki Giovanni, and Ella Jenkins incorporate very informal language, with slang cropping up occasionally in some poems. All are recommended.

All of the materials above are suitable for elementary grades. Certainly it is the teacher who must decide just how explicit to be about the demonstrated versatility and communicative power of the various dialects encountered in the literature. I cannot stress too much the necessity of preceding these reading experiences with some introduction to the nature and history of dialects. Without that, students may tend to dismiss the language as unintelligible or unimportant.

Finally, after all the talk of pedagogy and of rationale for models, there is another way of expressing what our objectives are in multicultural education. It is a poetic way, and Edwin Brock's poem "Five Ways to Kill a Man" says it well:

> There are many cumbersome ways to kill a man:
> you can make him carry a plank of wood
> to the top of a hill and nail him to it. To do this
> properly you require a crowd of people
> wearing sandals, a cock that crows, a cloak
> to dissect, a sponge, some vinegar and one
> man to hammer the nails home.
>
> Or you can take a length of steel,
> shaped and chased in a traditional way,
> and attempt to pierce the metal cage he wears.
> But for this you need white horses,
> English trees, men with bows and arrows,
> at least two flags, a prince and a
> castle to hold your banquet in.

Dispensing with nobility, you may, if the wind
allows, blow gas at him. But then you need
a mile of mud sliced through with ditches,
not to mention black boots, bomb craters,
more mud, a plague of rats, a dozen songs
and some round hats made of steel.

In an age of aeroplanes, you may fly
miles above your victim and dispose of him by
pressing one small switch. All you then
require is an ocean to separate you, two
systems of government, a nation's scientists,
several factories, a psycopath and
land that no one needs for several years.

These are, as I began, cumbersome ways
to kill a man. Simpler, direct, and much more neat
is to see that he is living somewhere in the middle
of the twentieth century, and leave him there.[20]

BIBLIOGRAPHY FOR CLASSROOM USE

Unless the context indicates otherwise, this list can be supplemented
with those books described in the text and cited in the notes. Most are not
repeated here. Appropriate grade level is indicated in the following way:
E = elementary level; **S** = secondary level; **C** = junior college level or
college level.

BROOKS, GWENDOLYN. *Bronzeville Boys and Girls*. New York: Harper & Row,
1956. A collection of poetry with an urban setting and Afro-American
subjects. **E**

CHIN, FRANK, ET AL. *Aiiieeee! An Introduction to Asian-American Writing*.
Washington, D.C.: Howard University Press, 1974. A collection for the general reader. **S/C**

HARRIS, MIDDLETON, ET AL., EDS. *The Black Book*. New York: Random House,
1974. A unique collection of memorabilia of black American life; chronicles
some of the history of average people. Text and photographs. **E/S/C**

HSU, KAI-YU, AND HELEN PALUBINSKAS. *Asian-American Authors*. Boston:
Houghton Mifflin, 1972. A collection of writing from several genres; includes
study questions. **S/C**

LESTER, JULIUS. *Black Folktales*. New York: Richard W. Baron, 1969. Includes
poignant illustrations. **E**

LEWIS, RICHARD W. *A Summer Adventure*. New York: Harper & Row, 1962. An
exciting story of a black boy's exploration of nature. **E**

LOWENFELS, WALTER, ED. *From the Belly of the Shark: Poems by Chicanos, Eskimos, Hawaiians, Indians, Puerto Ricans in the United States with Related Poems by Others.* New York: Random House, Vintage, 1973. S/C

MORI, TOSHIO. *Yokohama, California.* Caldwell, Idaho: Caxton Printers, 1949. A collection of short stories on the lives of Japanese-Americans. E

STEINER, STAN, AND MARIA TERESA BABIN, EDS. *Borinquen: An Anthology of Puerto Rican Literature.* New York: Knopf, 1974. Includes more than 100 literary pieces. S/C

Ting: The Caldron, Chinese Art and Identity in San Francisco. San Francisco: Glide Urban Center Publications, 1970. A collection of poetry, works of art, and various types of writing; includes a bibliography. C

SOURCE MATERIAL FOR TEACHERS

The following materials can provide valuable background for teachers at all levels and, where appropriate, should be read by students.

BRANDON, WILLIAM. *American Heritage Book of Indians.* New York: Dell, 1961. A general history.

BURMA, JOHN H. "The Background of the Current Filipino Situation." *Social Forces* 30 (October 1951): 42–48. Briefly covers important aspects of Filipino life in the United States, including early history and current living conditions.

JACOBS, PAUL, AND SAUL LANDAU WITH EVE PELL. *To Serve the Devil,* vol. 2: *Colonials and Sojourners.* New York: Random House, Vintage, 1971. Features a collection of documents that convey the climate in the early twentieth century from the point of view of selected Chinese- and Japanese-Americans.

KELLY, ERNECE B., ED. *Searching for America.* Urbana: National Council of Teachers of English, 1972. Includes bibliographies and introductory socioliterary essays on four ethnic groups: Afro-Americans, Asian-Americans, Chicanos, and American Indians.

KITANO, HARRY L. *Japanese Americans: The Evolution of a Subculture.* Englewood Cliffs, N.J.: Prentice-Hall, 1969. A psychosociological interpretation of Japanese-Americans from their early migration to the U.S. to the post–World War II period.

MARTINEZ, THOMAS M. "Advertising and Racism: The Case of the Mexican-American." In *Voices,* ed. Octavio I. Romano-V, pp. 521–31. Berkeley: Quinto Sol Publications, 1974.

National Council of Teachers of English, Committee on the 4 C's Language Statement. *Students' Right to Their Own Language.* Special issue of the *Journal of the Conference on College Composition and Communication* 25 (Fall 1974).

ROMANO-V, OCTAVIO I. "The Anthropology and Sociology of the Mexican-American." *El Grito* 2, 1 (1968): 13–26. Reprinted in *Voices,* ed. Octavio I.

Romano-V, pp. 43–55. Good discussion of popular stereotypes, their sources, and contrary historical evidence.

———, ed. *Voices: Readings from "El Grito," 1967–1973.* Berkeley: Quinto Sol Publications, 1974. A collection of articles from a journal of contemporary Mexican-American thought.

STENSLAND, ANNA LEE. *Literature by and about the American Indian.* Urbana: National Council of Teachers of English, 1973. Well-annotated bibliography of literature (including humanities, history, traditional and modern forms of literature) for junior and senior high schools. Useful directories of publishers and resources for classroom materials of a nonbook kind.

SUNG, BETTY LEE. *Mountain of Gold: The Story of the Chinese in America.* New York: Macmillan, 1967. An excellent history of the Chinese experience in the United States since the days of the Gold Rush.

12. Teaching U.S. History for a Multicultural Society

Social History for Schools

Ann D. Gordon

Sudden sensitivity to ethnic groups and subcultures of society reverberates in the history classroom; for through history the nation has defined its special identity and perpetuated common political and social traditions. Each ethnic and racial group has generated research into its past and formulated demands on schools to "cover" the traditions, experience, and heroes of its people in the social studies curriculum. (And now, women and homosexuals of both sexes are pressing for attention.) Whether designed to instill pride and determination in the inheritors of the ethnic tradition or to inform outsiders with appreciation and respect for the lives of ethnic minorities, renewed interest in history challenges the white male Anglo-Saxon hegemony of our history books by demonstrating, in case after case, what has been left out of the dominant story. Faced with demands for reform in historical content from the very people whose past has been ignored, the teacher of history is challenged to revive a dying curriculum by helping all students to learn from their history.

School history, a species very different from the evolving subject historians create, grinds endlessly along on its nineteenth-century rationale. Then it was, proudly, indoctrination into the traditions of a revolution, of a system based on the sanctity of property, and of a classless society. Its values flowed easily from the interests of men in molding cultural homogeneity. Its traditions were those of an illusory "American" who inherited *his* importance from eighteenth-century ancestors. Its methods required little more than rote memory of the substance of that heritage. Neither changes in the expectations for student thinking nor erosions in the acceptance of cultural unity have had much impact on the basic outlines of "American history" (itself a telling phrase about its assumptions) as retained in textbooks. On one hand, the burden of political socialization has passed from history to the social sciences. They have embraced the latest in learning theory and willingly acknowledged diversity in the nation's population. On the other hand, history has lost, or simply not developed, a definition of its distinctive contribution to the lives of students and citizens.

Proponents of ethnic awareness, however, are responding to a popular need for history when they direct people's attention to their historical experience as a subculture of the society and encourage self-conscious ethnicity. Their recommendations speak to a human wish to understand the social circumstances of personal life. Since the basis of those circumstances lies in the nation's history and since public schools assume the burden of defining history, the demands are made on the curriculum. However, if ethnic studies, or multicultural history, proceed in the manner of the "American studies" we now teach, as a dramatic but impersonal paean from the past, they will provide little to satisfy those needs. If, on the other hand, the past is conceived of as a dynamic, human experience, filled with people's choices, successes, and mistakes, the obvious continuity of human life and the demonstrable capacity of individuals to affect its texture can teach the student of history to regard life as a *series of possibilities*. In the words of one historian:

> The method of history is . . . a study of the past so that we can come back into our own time of troubles having shared with the men of the past their dilemmas, having learned from their experiences, having been buoyed up by their courage and creativeness and sobered by their shortsightedness and failures.[1]

The strategies for teachers developed in this chapter speak to the need for students to learn about their lives from history, no matter what the specific backgrounds of their lives might be.

"MELTING POT" REFORMS

Before proceeding on such a general level, let us review two reforms schools have introduced to meet demands from communities, with an eye to their suitability for the social goals this book sets forth. First, schools have created separate studies for different groups, sometimes as special, elective courses, sometimes as "units" within U.S. history syllabuses. By this means students may acquire information about their own or someone else's culture. Second, schools have revised curricular materials to introduce some of the missing people of history by parading individuals before the students while announcing the exceptional contributions to history of each. Ironically, these improvements may *reflect* past relations between cultures in the United States more than they solve problems created by our ignorance.

The first, involving as it does segregated subject matter, perpetuates fragmented knowledge and experience. The preponderance of black students in a course called Afro-American studies raises an unfortunate specter: second period in a school day, a visitor finds Chicano students in one room studying themselves and the Anglos, black students next door reading up on Africa and slavery, Slavic-Americans in yet another room describing the working conditions of their nineteenth-century ancestors, and so on. In each room, the visitor notes, perspective is strictly limited and the "others" involved in an event are, for convenience' sake, stereotyped. Less fantastic is the image of a school without diversity in its student body where no one thought to teach the experience of people from other cultures or groups. In an all-white school, for example, why should anyone take the time and money to introduce black studies? Our visitor replies: simply because in the United States white people and black people have lived within the same social structure and become inextricably linked in their historical development. That shared reality is a critical component of the history of either racial group. Discrete cultural studies obscure tensions that exist in life, recur in the history, and extend into the classroom by segregating the issues and the people.[2]

The second reform, introducing famous people, reinforces the expectation that to make it in this society one must abandon one's origins and take up the values of a more powerful group. Using the example of Elizabeth Blackwell, first woman to enter medical school in the United States, we can examine the problems of learning history by this attention to exceptional individuals. She is remembered not only because she was the first to achieve an important goal for nineteenth-century women but because she gained recognition in a previously masculine sphere. Her success precludes her representativeness. Implicitly we teach students that only when she crossed the threshold of a masculine institution did she make a significant contribution to history. All those women who could not overstep the boundaries of their roles, who could not escape family obligations wherever they lived, are ruled insignificant. Her actions were atypical in her time and remain largely atypical today. Comparable instances could be cited for every group whose lives, through history, were in any way restricted by a more powerful group. By focusing on outstanding people, teachers show students how to place greater value on "them" than on "us"; they set an example of estimating social worth on bases neither their students nor they are likely to attain.[3]

While such reforms mark new awareness by educators that all students do not have an identical heritage, they perpetuate assumptions of a melting-pot ideology and fail as sound responses to the problem of maintaining a society with multiple cultures. Simply by admitting some differences among "minorities" and acknowledging opportunities for excellence for minority group members, the history curriculum cannot transcend its origins as a rationale for dominance. Neither do these reforms address the students' needs within the broad social context of cultural change. The individual lesson that educators intend depends on a precarious, and ahistorical, analogy between a Nat Turner, an Elizabeth Blackwell, or a Chief Joseph and the student, and on an illusive harmony between classroom optimism about minority status and daily life's more practical lessons.[4] Instead of announcing, "It's okay to be black in this society," the curriculum might more realistically ask an enduring question: "What has it been like to be black in this society?" Only if we are all asking such questions of our common and our disparate pasts (in classrooms when we are young and out of them when older) can we expect to achieve the dignified and realistic confrontation with a multicultural past that society needs.

HISTORY AS MEMORY

A good course in history, like a good course in writing, offers students the possibility of exercising their minds in a skilled way on a basic human task: to define one's experience as one lives and feels it, rather than to be defined passively. In our own times, relationships between social movements and historical inquiry are illustrated in the cases of Afro-Americans and of women. Writing the history of themselves has been a cultural concomitant of their search for power, for through that task the group defines itself by its common and varied experiences. History can play the role for a group of people that memory and experience assume in an individual's development of a strategy to solve a problem. Aware that the present does not offer all it could, people survey the past with an eye to enriching their perception of alternatives and strategies. Without memory, or without knowledge of past experience, they might not escape the initial frustration or proceed as thinking beings.[5]

The teacher who is part of the solution finds her role in the need to know the "skilled way" of this human quest. She provides a field of historical inquiry that is wide open to the students' search for everyone's experience, that is available for people to interpret in a number of ways, and that introduces students to the intellectual task of organizing and interpreting clues to people's actions in other times, other situations, and other cultures. She is concerned with a very specific goal for the individual student: the ability to find an identity not simply in the contemporary situation of being a black or a Chicano or a WASP but in the historical condition of any individual whose biography is deeply entangled in a changing social structure. C. Wright Mills defined that goal as "sociological imagination " Of its value he wrote: "Neither the life of an individual nor the history of a society can be understood without understanding both. Yet men do not usually define the troubles they endure in terms of historical change and institutional contradiction."[6]

When we talk about the materials of social studies, we flirt with an individual's ability to relate his or her experience to the social structure. We approach questions on a philosophical level about the human condition, what it has and has not accomplished in world history. On both of these levels we take responsibility for an individual's sense of historical and social self. Careful study of history, study attentive to the demands of historical perspective, must be informed with a strong sense of the present, achieved not only by living in it but by disciplined consideration of continuity and change between the past studied and the present. The two must interact so that both become more accessible as objective phenomena. Human values and individual alternatives are considered in their context.

FOCUS ON SOCIAL PARTICIPATION

The standard fare of secondary school history courses depends on politics, primarily at the national level, in order to structure its events and its criteria for significance. In the nineteenth century, when history became an object of professional attention and a subject in schools, its ends were tied closely to developing a unique sense of national purpose. Historians and educators focused on the structure of U.S. politics emerging out of the American Revolution as the most important phenomenon distinguishing this country from Europe. Political history reveals who holds institutional power at a given time and how competing groups of powerful people resolve their differences, but the swiftest glance at our history turns up groups excluded from power or fighting to gain it. Until they win, until Irishmen become chiefs of police or even presidents, until black men or all women win the right to vote, they are outside the lines of vision employed by the political historian. Participation in society is very narrowly defined. Historians recognized, gradually, what limitations this imposed on their ability to grasp the fullest meaning from the history of society, but textbooks and course outlines have shifted much more slowly. Students, who know from experience that decisions mediated at the level of national political institutions constitute only a portion of their and their families' lives, find the narrative arcane at best.

Themes of participation in other social institutions are more difficult to grasp and measure; they do not have, as yet, the convenient signposts of political history: here a group won the right to vote, here it gained access to jobs in city services, here, finally, it achieved the possibility of national office. Rather, the events are hidden in assessments of cotton's importance to national wealth, of the slave's importance to American history; of unprecedented industrial and technological developments in the nation, wherein its ability to absorb and exploit vast numbers of immigrants can be located; of the character of homes and family life, wherein feeding and breeding took place.[7] This state of the field presents both problems and opportunities to the history teacher. If she abandons the familiar road, she loses the structure of carefully delineated answers. On the other hand, by so doing, she gives students the opportunity to establish their own criteria for historical significance or effective participation in society.

Exploring an Era

One angle from which students could discover the complexities of social participation is called, in Britain, an "era approach."[8] By selecting a particular period of time and opening all questions concerning the era to students' inquiry, the class could begin the task of reconstructing multiple experiences in U.S. history. By way of example, let us look at the 1830s and 1840s. Where are people in those decades? That should be the first question for both teacher and students. What are they doing? If the teacher wants students to explore libraries and other sources to formulate their own program of inquiry into the problem, she might leave the initial questions for the class to answer. If instead she wants them to concentrate on subsequent questions, she can answer the first herself as a guide to selecting materials and tasks for the students. As the class looks through what materials are at hand, information can be organized to answer the next question: How do the work and activity of people in all the situations identified contribute to the maintenance and growth of the whole society?

This approach not only provides an angle for pre- or nonpolitical activity, but it discovers the cultural and ethnic diversity of the times. Students notice and establish the significance of Irish immigrants landing on the East Coast and finding places in the burgeoning industrial machinery of the nation; of Spanish-speaking Mexicans settling in the territory that would soon become Texas and California; of African descendants laboring as slaves on southern plantations stretching from Virginia to Mississippi and as nominally free men and women in the northern states; of women working in textile mills and others adjusting to a new kind of leisure.[9] As students tackle descriptive and analytical problems in each of these and many other categories of experience, they will generate hypotheses, too, about interactions between people in different situations.

The example chosen here to explain the era approach was not selected haphazardly, although the approach itself had no necessary criteria for selection. If one's purpose is to teach about the bases of the multicultural society in which we live today, the antebellum period introduces many themes of nineteenth- and twentieth-century history. Even our current high school textbooks make that point with their slim treatment of industrial development, transportation advances, immigration, westward movement, reform activity, and urban growth. An era might, however, have more significance for one region than another and be chosen on that basis. The 1830s and 1840s illustrate national trends, but also, more specifically, eastern experience. To comprehend the West Coast or the Southwest, the trends might be similar but enter the stage from a different wing and at another time.[10] Teachers can exercise considerable judgment here depending on their goals and the availability of sources.

Exploring a Theme

The balance between an organizational theme or themes and a period of time can be thrown the other way to establish a course around a trend of social development extending across centuries. Such has been the role of "democracy expanding" in many U.S. history courses; the theme governs the selection of significant events and people, while it links the changes over time. That particular theme, however, has appeared as a moral rather than as a heuristic question. Two themes that generate hypotheses for classroom study stand out conspicuously from historians' efforts to explain U.S. history. As they are for the professional, the themes for a student are in need of more accurate definition and refinement on the basis of individual evidence. Immigration and industrialization occurred on such a scale in the U.S. as to shape experiences in widely different times and places and to penetrate most strata of social organization from the circles of government, to the workplace, to the home. After considering each as a social process, students can trace their impact over time through a variety of sources.

The social process of either immigration or industrialization can be isolated from a period of time for the purpose of identifying its parts. In such form both frequently appear in current texts. Each immigrant left her society behind but brought values and experiences into a new setting in North America. She then carved out a new culture from the interaction of those traditions she imported, her new conditions, and her interpretation of values she encountered in the new society.[11] Reactions of different groups have been labeled assimilative, adaptive, or accommodationist in their end result. Labels derive from examining individual instances, however, and in the classroom are no substitute for considering the intense,

personal experience they summarize. The event of immigration of an individual's biography was shared by millions of people. It was not something that the Irish could perform for the Italians or even that the first immigrants from Ireland could complete for the benefit of later Irish arrivals. It repeated itself over and over again. Case studies establish the basic patterns but not the sum total of this phenomenon in the nation's history. Similarly, the impact of industrial production can be abstracted for clarity from, for example, the experience of shoemakers who lost their artisan's autonomy to be submerged in the disciplined and fragmented factory system.[12]

So often did individuals and groups undergo these changes in their own lifetimes that the process ceases to be one of biography and emerges as a basic element of the nation's social structure. Some historians, in fact, conclude that these themes, as much as or more than political institutions, summarize the nation's uniqueness. "Immigrants and the children of immigrants *are* the American people," wrote Caroline Ware. "Their culture is American culture, not merely a contributor to American culture."[13] Her statement suggests a dynamic view of history, particularly of cultural history, from the vantage point of changes immigrants wrought in the total fabric of society. As a guiding hypothesis, her view needs to be challenged by students as a full statement of history and tested for its ability to summarize the experience of different groups at different times. At the same time such a perspective can give unity to the tales of immigration that abound in any nation.

Similarly, the same historian suggests a hypothesis about industrial history as a basis for cultural history. She wrote: "More people have died in industrial accidents than in subduing the wilderness and fighting the Revolution. It is these people rather than the frontiersmen who constitute the real historical background and the heroic tradition of the mass urban Americans."[14] This theme touches only one part of industrialization's enormous impact on national development, that part immediately at the point of production, but nonetheless raises a significant question for students to examine through the changes of history. Again, human experience can be brought to bear on unraveling the validity of this dynamic in U.S. history. Evidence abounds for reconstructing what happened to different groups of people who lived in an industrializing society.

THINKING HISTORICALLY

Neither a course organized by an open-ended look at one era of history nor one developed around hypotheses about significant themes of structural change in history can preserve its value for students learning about their own lives if teachers translate that new structure into the old normative mode. Preaching is preaching. Articles appear in many places to remind teachers of the importance of learning to think in the classroom.[15] Here it seems appropriate only to remind teachers of that body of literature and to emphasize that in the history courses described here, searching is one of the principal values. The territory recommended for students to explore requires a wide-ranging journey on which students can formulate many alternative hypotheses about the meaning of the information they uncover. Historical study is a kind of how-do-you-know study wherein the answer to that question takes precedence over what you know. Revisions take place all the time when one person says to another, "I do not think your way of knowing your conclusions is sufficient or appropriate and I think I can know it differently." As students duplicate that process, they do not simply imitate professionals but imitate themselves in the ways people gather meaning in daily life.

Teachers need to offer guidance in more ways than the initial determination of territory or materials in order for the benefits of historical inquiry to be brought home to the student. Up to this point we have offhandedly referred to developing connections between the historical characters and the individual student, connections between two ways of life, but the ability to carry that off needs cultivation and training. Central to that ability is an awareness that the student's life has "history." An assignment I give to potential teachers is designed to raise just this point. Students first list major events in their lives as an outline for an autobiography and then, with another student, examine the list to identify where those points in their lives were affected by social forces outside of themselves. Some instances stand out: men enrolled in college to avoid serving in Vietnam; women redirected themselves in light of changing expectations about their roles; some black students held scholarships because a civil rights struggle had been fought in their youth. Discussions easily uncover differences and similarities among people of the same generation in the same classroom. The class then moves back in time with interviews of older people who had reached their twenties in the 1920s or 1930s. As a group, the interviews provide data distinguishing young people of one time from those of another. We have "a history."

Students can also discover this in the process of interpreting documents from the past and of distinguishing their own values from those held by historical characters. Frank Keetz described this in an account of his teaching published in *Social Education*.[16] His students could not escape their contemporary sensitivity to racial and sexual attitudes when they read the Declaration of Independence. They immediately labeled the authors hypocrites and thereby dismissed all further inquiry. Keetz recognized that his students could not understand the document unless they appreciated the fact that someone in 1776 had a range of alternatives very different from that each of us has as we adopt values today. If students could begin probing that difference, asking why Thomas Jeffereson tolerated contradictions between his words and his actions, why John Adams didn't take seriously his wife's suggestion that women be enfranchised, then they could begin to appreciate that people make choices within the limits of possibility in their time and that over time those limits frequently change. As Keetz concluded, a student could become more aware of her own life as a series of choices that will, in time, change, too.

What Keetz calls "time perspective" on individuals can also be generalized to a notion of historical sympathy. Students must reserve judgment until they have quite literally "heard" what an individual is saying to them. If students identify with underdogs in an event, as many do, then the teacher's focus might be on sympathy with the powerful person in order that students understand as best they can how and why that person acted as he did. She might have to side with frontiersmen who massacred Indians, or with slaveholders, or with nativists, or with husbands; in another classroom she might push students to see events from the perspective of blacks if they tend only to take sides with whites. Her role, and the skill she is trying to impart, is to see events from the different angles of the participants' experience and to recognize in all of them the internal logic, no matter how damning, of their actions. The skill is fundamental to human communication whether it takes place across classrooms, centuries, or cultures.

A student's ability to grasp the diverse meaning of events to individuals in different situations is controlled in large part by sources. In their selection and use, both teachers and students should be aware of the angle of vision on an event and on society in general presented in a particular source. As native Americans admonish us, westward migration looked one way if a person guarded a pass against invasion by whites and quite another if a person headed up a wagon train. An event's meaning to us and its character for those who took part are discovered in the intentions, actions, and attitudes of all the participants. The habit of teaching political history has weakened our sensitivity to diverse perspectives. Internment of Japanese-Americans during World War II looks very different to students examining Roosevelt's motives or public opinion and fear than to those finding out what people of Japanese extraction thought about the war, what changes they experienced as a result of internment, and what happened to their attitudes about the nation during and after their experience in concentration camps.[17] The story of immigration can be told from the halls of government, the living rooms of nativists, the prows of ships, or the factory workroom.

DISCOVERING THE HUMAN
SCALE OF HISTORY

Sources also permit students to consider history on a human scale, on a scale most like that on which most of us live. The most systematic and thorough records of experience exist for exceptional people. Their families and/or communities preserved personal effects; most were literate and left written accounts of their thoughts and actions; and their opinions appeared in public records that were systematically preserved. To discover information about the "common person" in any period is a more haphazard and fragmentary procedure, but highly rewarding when successful. Teachers and students must come to recognize that the only way into some events will be a song or two, a young man's poem, a photograph, a reconstruction of a house, a diary, and that these sources, when used wisely, are as legitimiate a means to find out about particular individuals as are statemen's papers, Lincoln-Douglas debates, or acts of Congress. Such small and personal records give students direct access to people, to their expressions and feelings, to their day-to-day situation. The human voice in them can speak directly to feelings and experiences already present in students.[18]

Personal, primary sources bring all that the students so far know of life to bear on the problem of knowing about people in other circumstances. I am reminded often of a class that was studying the witch trials in Salem, Massachusetts, in the seventeenth century. After weeks of reading accounts of the trials, family genealogies, and other verbal sources, students examined a map to find where all the characters they now knew lived. Suddenly someone raised a question about distance between the houses and how easily the teenage girls who accused the witches could visit each other. That was a scale of inquiry, too small perhaps to answer grand questions about the meaning of Puritan Massachusetts, but basic to the students' ability to recognize the historical subjects as people who, in fact, walked around the village. The class could then face the more difficult problem of sympathy with the choices people made within the range of alternatives available to them. There but for the acts of time go I.

Reading Sources

Like any sources, personal ones are the raw materials of history and require of the student careful reading, interpretation of meaning in the language and values of a person whose assumptions and alternatives differ from the student's, and creative restatement of that person's existence in relationship to a student's knowledge of the times. The student appropriates useful skills and methods from historians for the purpose of discovering how individuals experience and make history. Take, for example, a poem written by a young Italian immigrant after a few months of studying the English language.

> Nothing job, nothing job,
> I come back to Italy;
> Nothing job, nothing job,
> Adieu, land northerly. . .
>
> Nothing job, nothing job,
> O! sweet sky of my Italy;
> Nothing job, nothing job,
> How cold in this country. . .
>
> Nothing job, nothing job,
> I return to Italy;
> Comrades, laborers, good-bye;
> Adieu, land of "Fourth of July."[19]

His words capture disappointment, nostalgia, humor, and attitudes toward work in a way no textbook narrative of immigrant life at the turn of the century could do. His reaction can be compared to responses of other immigrants who enjoyed their new home, who shared the boy's alienation but decided to stay, or who stayed in order to fight for something better here. The one source is one kind of response and solution; one biography interacts with the social condition of immigration in a particular way.

The source exists because a person had feelings about his life and a need to express the feelings to someone, somehow. That in itself is a historical statement, but the source can carry students much further than that into another person's world. In "Hard Times in the Mill" a cotton mill worker sings not only of the conditions of labor but of the human response to them.

> Every morning at half-past four,
> You hear the cook's hop on the floor.
>   REFRAIN
>   It's hard times in the mill, my love,
>   Hard times in the mill.
>
> Every morning just at five,
> You gotta get up, dead or alive.
>
> Every morning at six o'clock,
> Two cold biscuits, hard as a rock.
>
> Every morning at half-past nine,
> The bosses are cussin' and the spinners are cryin'.

They docked me a nickel, they docked me a dime,
They sent me to the office to get my time.

Cotton mill boys don't make enough,
To buy them tobacco and a box of snuff.

Every night when I get home,
A piece of corn bread and an old jawbone.

Ain't it enough to break your heart?
Hafta work all day until it's dark.*

Like the Italian boy's poem, this song takes students to the crux of the structural and cultural characteristics of its creator's life.

To locate that dimension of something as apparently obvious as a song or a poem takes guidance, initially, until the skills, or questions, are mastered. The students should ask first of "Hard Times in the Mill": Why is this person singing this song? They might reply that the person wants to express feelings, probably very powerful and sad feelings about the conditions of work and life. They might go on to suggest that the singer derives strength from singing, maybe more strength than he feels from work, and that he shares perceptions of his life with the people who listen or sing along. Also, perhaps the song itself is a protest against the life it describes. Discussion could then turn to the specific aspects of work that produce the singer's feelings, for the song is a detailed account of a day's work: mills, bosses, fellow workers, insecure pay, long hours, no daylight, and no time to feel sick or unable to work. Finally, students might consider what things in life the singer values. He has selected details to tell us what he thinks about work: "Ain't it enough to break your heart?" He wants better food, time to relax and sleep late, money for some comforts; he lets people know what would make life right. Students have, at the end of these questions, a remarkably full statement of the situation of a cotton mill worker from someone who was there.

Comparing Sources

The student's direction of thinking, from the individual example out to the world he inhabits, sets up the example of historical thought, its basis for generalizing about an epoch or a group of people, and its "imagination." On one level, the teacher can accentuate the conceptual process by making comparisons within the past. For example, by studying a man's reaction in song to a different job, one with different demands on the

* © John Anthony Scott.

individual, a student can see some of what is constant in human reactions and some of what changes. In the first verse and refrain of "The Girl I Left Behind Me," we can hear a cowboy singing while he rides with a herd.

> I struck the trail in sixty-nine,
> The herd strung out behind me,
> As I jogged along my mind ran back
> To the girl I left behind me.
>
> REFRAIN
> That sweet little gal, that true little gal,
> The gal I left behind me,
> That sweet little gal, that true little gal,
> The gal I left behind me.*

Like the cotton mill worker, the cowboy thinks about more than his work, particularly about the things he can't have while he works, and specifically about his wife or sweetheart who stays behind and perhaps, unwatched, leaves him. His job is lonely because he rides alone, or with male companionship, across great distances with someone's herd. The social structure of his life is radically different from that of the cotton mill, where people work together, the boss is present, and workers can return to their families. In this instance, the contrast is probably not between two different times, as cowboys and cotton mill workers exist(ed) simultaneously in this society. The teacher could, however, make a comparison that illustrated how social structures changed over time. She might contrast a slave's lament, for example, with a freedman's lament to identify the fact that what black people thought about had changed.

Through such documents as these, students repeatedly experience the ways people looked at their own times from the vantage point of a particular set of experiences: of a life. Implicitly and explicitly, teachers can bring this point home to the lives of students. At the simplest level of analogy, students can write songs that express the rhythms of their own lives and describe the fantasies they have of it. Such might be like the countless rock-'n'-roll songs about schools. Substantive parallels can be drawn between the world they know and the world as seen by a historical character. Their comparison of the two worlds leads them into speculation about changes that occurred in social forms between whatever past they consider and their own present. On the scale of individuals, students can duplicate the thinking of historians at its most abstract level in extracting signs of change over long periods of time. They may not be writing history in the sense we have come to expect from professionals and graduate students, but they are appropriating the method of learning from the past in order to cope with the historical dimension in their own lives.

* © Ludlow Music, Inc.

CONCLUSION

In terms of the relationship between the study of multicultural history and the need to equip students with a concept of history, this response on the part of schools to demands for cultural "relevance" implies a shift in the goals of social studies. No more, no less are they based on an analysis of social needs. But unlike the tradition of social studies that carries the burden of Americanization, this method assumes that culture is not created in the schools. People generate culture throughout their lives in myriad forms and transmit it through many institutions. Assuming its appropriate spot within that complex of influences experienced by people, the school teaches the human tasks as best it can because skills, not values, are its specialty. While multicultural history implies a commitment on the teacher's part to specific human values and an intention to encourage historical perspective among citizens, it steers clear of establishing cultural substance in the classroom.

NOTES

Preface

1. Lindley J. Stiles, "The Chosen," *Ideas and Images* (Madison, Wisc.: Dembar Educational Research Services, 1964), p. 63.
2. *The Random House Dictionary of the English Language,* s.v. *culture.*
3. Michel Leiris, *Race and Culture* (New York: UNESCO, 1965), pp. 21–22.
4. *Random House Dictionary,* s.v. *society.*

Chapter 1. Responding to Cultural Diversity

1. Margaret Mead, "Uniqueness and Universality," *Childhood Education* (Nov.-Dec., 1974).
2. Aristotle, "Physiognomonica," trans. T. Loveday and E. S. Foster, in *The Works of Aristotle,* ed. W. D. Ross (Oxford: Clarendon Press, 1913), 6:812a.
3. Abdul A. Said and Luis R. Simmons, "The Ethnic Factors in World Politics," *Society* (Jan.-Feb., 1975), p. 65.
4. Edgar Faure et al., *Learning to Be* (Paris: UNESCO) (London: Harrap, 1972), p. 159.
5. Carl Rogers, *Freedom to Learn* (Columbus, Ohio: Merrill, 1969).
6. Faure et al., *Learning to Be,* p. 157.
7. Adapted from the diary of Dolores E. Cross, written at age fourteen in Newark, New Jersey.
8. Ralph Ellison, *The Invisible Man* (New York: Random House, 1952), pp. 3–12.
9. *New York Times,* May 26, 1974.
10. W. E. B. Du Bois, *The Souls of Black Folk* (London: Constable, 1905).
11. Richard Wright, *Twelve Million Black Voices* (New York: Viking, 1941).

Chapter 2. A Historical Framework for Multicultural Education

1. Frances Welsing, *Washington Post,* September 9, 1973.

2. *Liberator,* March 18, 1842.

3. *Liberator,* August 15, 1862.

4. James M. McPherson, ed., *The Negro's Civil War: How American Negroes Felt and Acted during the War for the Union* (New York: Random House, Vintage, 1967), p. 17.

5. W. E. B. Du Bois, "Reconstruction and Its Benefits," *American Historical Review,* 1909–1910, p. 782.

6. Ellen Tarry, *The Third Door: The Autobiography of an American Woman* (New York: Guild Press, 1966), p. 79.

7. Carter G. Woodson, *The Rural Negro* (Washington, D.C.: Association for the Study of Negro Life and History, 1930), p. 189.

8. *New York Age,* January 10, 1920.

9. Quoted in Celia Lewis Zitron, *The New York City Teachers Union, 1916–1964* (New York: Humanities Press, 1968), p. 90.

10. W. E. B. Du Bois, "The United States and the Negro," *Freedomways,* 1971, p. 16.

11. Kenneth B. Clark, quoted in Bert E. Swanson, *The Struggle for Equality: School Integration Controversy in New York City* (New York: Hobbs, Dorman, 1966), p. 13.

12. Martin Luther King, Jr., "Let Justice Roll Down," *Nation,* March 15, 1965, pp. 271–72.

13. For greater detail on the education of black, Mexican-American, native American, and Puerto Rican children, see Meyer Weinberg, *A Chance to Learn: The History of Race and Education in the United States* (New York: Cambridge University Press, 1976).

14. Adapted from Meyer Weinberg, "Introduction: Race and Educational Opportunity," pp. 1–3 in *Models for Integrated Education,* ed. Daniel U. Levine (Worthington, Ohio: Jones, 1971).

Chapter 3. Our Common Humanity

1. Carl Sandburg, "Prologue," in *The Family of Man,* comp. Edward Steichen (New York: Museum of Modern Art, 1955), p. 2.

2. Lee F. Anderson, "An Examination of Structure and Objectives of International Education," *Social Education,* November 1968.

3. Ruth Benedict, *Patterns of Culture* (New York: New American Library, Mentor, 1946), p. 212.

4. Gunnar Myrdal, "Gunnar Myrdal on America's Dilemma: Present and Future," *World,* August 29, 1972.

5. Juan Comas, *Racial Myths* (Paris: UNESCO, 1953), pp. 20–21.

6. Frank G. Jennings, "Educational Opportunities Geared to Diversity," in *The Educationally Retarded and Disadvantaged,* Sixty-sixth Yearbook of the National Society for the Study of Education, ed. Paul A. Witty (Chicago: University of Chicago Press, 1967), pp. 351–53.

7. Cf. Alvin Toffler, *Future Shock* (New York: Random House, 1970), and Michael A. McDanield, "Tomorrow's Curriculum Today," chap. 6 in *Learning for Tomorrow: The Role of the Future in Education,* ed. Alvin Toffler (New York: Random House, Vintage, 1974).

8. Norman Cousins, "Amchilka and Tribalism," *Saturday Review,* September 25, 1971.

9. Barbara Ward, *Spaceship Earth* (New York: Columbia University Press, 1966), p. 14.

10. Margaret Mead, "A New Look at the Age of Technology," *Prospects* 2, 2 (Summer 1972).

11. Harold Howe II, *World,* August 24, 1974.

12. Sandburg, "Prologue," p. 3.

Chapter 5. You Know the Rules!: Myths about Desegregation

1. U.S., Department of Health, Education and Welfare, *Digest of Educational Statistics* (Washington, D.C.: Government Printing Office, 1973), pp. 153–54.

2. See, for instance, U.S., Civil Rights Commission, *Desegregation in Nine Communities* (Washington, D.C.: Government Printing Office, 1973).

3. See selected passages in Richard Bardolph, *The Civil Rights Record: Black Americans and the Law, 1849–1970* (New York: Crowell, 1970).

4. Numerous examples are provided in Earle West, *The Black American and Education* (Columbus, Ohio: Charles E. Merrill, 1972).

5. U.S., Bureau of Education, "Annual Report of the State of Tennessee," in *Report of the Commissioner of Education* (Washington, D.C.: Government Printing Office, 1870), p. 287.

6. Meyer Weinberg, *Race and Place: A Legal History of the Neighborhood School* (Evanston, Ill.: Integrated Education Associates, 1968).

7. West, *The Black American and Education,* pp. 160–62.

8. *Brown et al.* v. *Board of Education of Topeka, Kansas,* 74 Ct. 686 (May 17, 1954).

9. Although the materials of these school visits are based on observations by the author, the school and teacher names are fictitious. Most of the materials in these school "tours" are selected from various reports of a two-year teacher-training project that contains the data in two publications: James Deslonde and Elizabeth Flach, "The Cadre Approach to Teacher Training: Developing Change Agents for Desegregated Schools," paper presented at the annual meeting of the American Educational Association, April 1942; and *Beyond Desegregation: Problem Solving in Two Elementary Schools,* published as a

monograph by University of California, Riverside. These activities were supported, in part, by a U.S.O.E. contract grant, Contract OEO C-9-70-0037 (037).

10. Elizabeth Hunter, *Encounter in the Classroom: New Ways of Teaching* (New York: Holt, Rinehart & Winston, 1971).

11. Mildred Dickeman, "Teaching Cultural Pluralism," in *Teaching Ethnic Studies*, Forty-third Yearbook of the National Council for the Social Studies, ed. James A. Banks (Washington, D.C., 1973).

12. Charlotte Epstein, *Affective Subjects in the Classroom: Exploring Race, Sex and Drugs* (Scranton: Intext Educational Publishers, 1972).

13. Hunter, *Encounter in the Classroom*, pp. 15–16.

14. R. Rosenthal and L. Jacobson, *Pygmalion in the Classroom* (New York: Holt, Rinehart & Winston, 1968).

15. Ray C. Rist, "Student Social Class and Teacher Expectations: The Self-fulfilling Prophecy in Ghetto Education," *Harvard Educational Review* 40, 3 (August 1970).

16. Jules Henry, "Attitude Organization in Elementary School Classrooms," in George Spindler, *Education and Culture* (New York: Holt, Rinehart & Winston, 1963).

17. G. Rosenfeld, *Shut Those Thick Lips!: A Study of Slum Failure.* (New York: Holt, Rinehart & Winston, 1971).

18. Charles Valentine, "Deficit, Difference and Bicultural Models of Afro-American Behavior," *Harvard Educational Review* 41, 2 (May 1971): 137–57.

19. For more details on instructional problems, see James Deslonde, "Can We Really Integrate the Schools?" *Integrated Education: A Report on Race and Schools* 10, 5 (May-June): 44–51.

20. Mable Purl, "Informal Findings from the Riverside School Study," mimeographed (Riverside, Calif.: Riverside Unified School District.)

21. For more precise, conclusive definitions of the process concept, see James Deslonde, "Toward a Process Component of Multicultural Education," *The Kappan*, forthcoming.

22. See note 21.

Chapter 6. Children's Language and the Multicultural Classroom

1. Kornei Chukovsky, *From Two to Five*, ed. and trans. Miriam Morton (Berkeley and Los Angeles: University of California Press, 1963), p. 10.

2. Ibid., p. 37.

3. Roger Brown, *A First Language: The Early Stages* (Cambridge: Harvard University Press, 1973).

4. William Labov, *Language in the Inner City* (Philadelphia: University of Pennsylvania Press, 1972). William Stewart, "Toward a History of American Negro Dialect," in *Language and Poverty*, ed. Fredrick Williams (Chicago:

Markham, 1971), pp. 351–79. J. L. Dillard, *Black English: Its History and Usage in the United States* (New York: Random House, Vintage, 1972).

5. Martin Joos, *The Five Clocks* (New York: Harcourt, Brace & World, 1967).

6. Ibid., p. 40.

7. Ibid.

8. M. A. K. Halliday, *Explorations in the Functions of Language* (London: Edward Arnold, 1973).

9. Roman Jakobson, "Verbal Communication," *Scientific American* 227, 3 (September 1972).

10. Labov, *Language in the Inner City.* This point is made with particular force in the chapter titled "The Logic of Non-Standard English," which has been widely reprinted.

11. William Labov, "The Place of Linguistic Research in American Society," *Linguistics in the 1970's* (Washington, D.C.: Center for Applied Linguistics, 1970), pp. 64–65. Quoted in Courtney Cazden, "Problems for Education: Language as Curriculum Content and Learning Environment," *Daedalus* 102, 3: 135–48.

12. Halliday, *Explorations,* p. 17.

13. Connie Rosen and Harold Rosen, *The Language of Primary School Children* (Baltimore: Penguin Books, 1973), p. 256.

14. Courtney Cazden, *Child Language and Education* (New York: Holt, Rinehart & Winston, 1972), p. 216.

15. Cazden, "Problems for Education," p. 143. (See note 11.)

16. C. Cazden, J. Baratz, W. Labov, and F. Palmer, "Language Development in Day-care Programs," in *Early Childhood Education Rediscovered,* ed. J. Frost (New York: Holt, Rinehart & Winston, 1968), p. 389.

17. S. Phillips, "Acquisition Roles for Appropriate Speech Usage," in *Language and Cultural Diversity in American Education,* ed. Abrahams and Troike (Englewood Cliffs, N.J.: Prentice-Hall, 1972), pp. 167–83.

18. Cazden et al., "Language Development," p. 390.

19. Courtney Cazden, "Play and Metalinguistic Awareness: One Dimension of Language Experience," *Urban Review* 7, 1 (January 1974): 28–39.

Chapter 7. Intellectual Strengths of Minority Children

1. Gunnar Myrdal, *Asian Drama: An Inquiry into the Poverty of Nations* (New York: Twentieth Century Fund, 1968).

2. Edgar A. Levenson, *The Fallacy of Understanding: An Inquiry into the Changing Structure of Psychoanalysis* (New York: Basic Books, 1972).

3. Robert L. Williams, "Abuses and Misuses in Testing Black Children," in *Black Psychology,* ed. Reginald L. Jones (New York: Harper & Row, 1972), pp. 77–91.

4. A. R. Jensen, "The Race× Sex × Ability Interaction," in *Intelligence: Genetic and Environmental Influences,* ed. Robert Cancro (New York: Grune & Stratton, 1971).

5. Charles Valentine, *Culture and Poverty* (Chicago: University of Chicago Press, 1968), pp. 9–10.

6. Myrdal, *Asian Drama,* vol. 1, pp. *xi* and *xii.*

7. Peter L. Berger and Thomas Luckmann, *The Social Construction of Reality: A Treatise in the Sociology of Knowledge* (New York: Doubleday, 1966). Karl Mannheim, *Ideology and Utopia* (New York: Harcourt, Brace, 1936).

8. R. P. McDermott, "Selective Attention and the Politics of Everyday Life: A Biosocial Inquiry into School Failure and the Persistence of Pariah Minorities across Generations," Ph.D. dissertation, Stanford University, 1974.

9. Lewis Terman, quoted in Alexander Thomas and Samuel Sillen, *Racism and Psychiatry* (New York: Brunner/Mazel, 1972), p. 35.

10. Ibid., p. 42.

11. Daniel Patrick Moynihan, "The Negro Family," in *The Moynihan Report and the Politics of Controversy,* ed. Lee Rainwater (Cambridge: MIT Press, 1967).

12. Nancy Bayley, "Comparisons of Mental and Motor Test Scores for Ages 1–15 Months by Sex, Birth Order, Race, Geographical Location, and Education of Parents," *Child Development* 36 (1965). Anne Anastassi and Rita Y. D'Angelo, "A Comparison of Negro and White Preschool Children in Language Development and Goodenough Draw-a-Man I.Q.," *Journal of Genetic Psychology* 81 (1952): 147–65. Benjamin Pasamanick, "A Comparative Study of the Behavioral Development of Negro Infants," *Journal of Genetic Psychology* 3 (1946): 3–44.

13. Jane Mercer, "Racial Differences in I.Q.: Fact or Artifact?" in *The Fallacy of I.Q.,* ed. Carl Senna (New York: Third Press, 1973), pp. 56–113.

14. J. S. Kleinfeld, "Intellectual Strengths in Culturally Different Groups: An Eskimo Illustration,"*Review of Educational Research* 43 (1973): 341–59.

15. Claude Levi-Strauss, *The Savage Mind* (Chicago: University of Chicago Press, 1962), p. 9.

16. Ibid., p. 43.

17. Ibid., p. 42.

18. J. S. Coleman et al., *Equality of Educational Opportunity* (Washington, D.C.: Government Printing Office, 1966).

19. Christopher Jencks et al., *Inequality: An Assessment of the Affect of Family and Schooling in America* (New York: Basic Books, 1972).

20. James Guthrie, "The New Skeptics Have Gone Too Far," in *Improving School Effectiveness,* ed. Solomon (Princeton: Educational Testing Service, 1973), pp. 15–25. A. Rivlin, "Forensic Social Science," *Harvard Educational Review* 43 (1973): 61–75.

21. Frederick Mosteller and Daniel Patrick Moynihan, eds., *On Equality of Educational Opportunity* (New York: Random House, 1972), p. 25.

22. Stanley Charnofsky, *Educating the Powerless* (Belmont, Calif.: Wadsworth, 1971). Frantz Fanon, *Black Skin, White Masks,* trans. Charles L. Markmann (New York: Grove Press, 1967). Paulo Freire, *Pedagogy of the Oppressed,* trans. Myra B. Ramos (New York: Seabury, 1971). Jane Zahn, "Some Adult Attitudes Affecting Learning, Powerlessness, Conflicting Needs, and Role Transition," *Adult Education Journal* 19 (1969): 91–97.

23. L. Kamin, *South Today: A Digest of Southern Affairs,* Transcripts from the Southern Council's Symposium on Human Intelligence, Social Science, and Social Policy, vol. 4, no. 8 (1973).

24. Bayley, "Comparisons," p. 408. (See note 12.)

25. M. Golden and B. Birns, "Social Class and Cognitive Development in Infancy," *Merrill Palmer Quarterly* 14 (1968): 139–50.

26. Theodora D. Wachs, Ina C. Uzgiris, and J. McV. Hunt, "Cognitive Development in Infants of Different Age Levels and from Different Environmental Backgrounds: An Exploratory Investigation," *Merrill Palmer Quarterly* (1971): 283–317.

27. Francis H. Palmer, "Socio-economic Status and Intellectual Performance among Negro Pre-school Boys," *Developmental Psychology* 3 (1970): 1–9.

28. See note 12.

29. Herbert Ginsburg, *The Myth of the Deprived Child* (Englewood Cliffs, N.J.: Prentice-Hall, 1972).

30. Joan C. Baratz, "Teaching Reading in an Urban Negro School System," in *Language and Poverty,* ed. Frederick Williams (Chicago: Markham, 1970), pp. 14–15.

31. W. Labov, "The Logic of Nonstandard English," in *Language and Poverty,* ed. Williams, pp. 153–89.

32. Jane R. Mercer, *Labeling the Mentally Retarded* (Berkeley and Los Angeles: University of California Press, 1972).

33. Reginald L. Jones, *Black Psychology* (New York: Harper & Row, 1972).

34. G. J. Powell, "Self-concept in White and Black Children," in *Racism and Mental Health,* ed. C. V. Willie (Pittsburgh: University of Pittsburgh Press, 1973), pp. 299–318.

35. N. Trowbridge, "Self Concept and Socio-economic Status in Elementary School Children," *American Educational Research Association Journal* 9 (1972): 525–58.

36. T. O. Hilliard, "Personality Characteristics of Black Student Activists and Non-activists," in *Black Psychology,* ed. Reginald L. Jones (New York: Harper & Row, 1972).

37. Judith Anderson, "Planting a Seed of Hope," *San Francisco Chronicle,* December 27, 1971.

38. See *Newsweek,* "The Common Language," May 4, 1970, for a report on the SEED project.

39. Stephen Strickland, "Can Slum Children Learn?" in *The Fallacy of I.Q.,* ed. Carl Senna (New York: Third Press, 1973).

40. Tom Morganthau, "Ghetto Youngsters Catch On to Math," *San Francisco Examiner,* December 13, 1973, p. 36.

41. Robert Bradfield, Asa Hilliard, et al., "Project B.E.A.M.: An Experiment in Intervention," *Journal of Negro Education,* forthcoming.

42. Michael Cole and John Gay, *The Cultural Context of Learning and Thinking* (New York: Basic Books, 1971).

43. Levi-Strauss, *The Savage Mind.*

44. Robert Rosenthal and Lenore Jacobsen, *Pygmalion in the Classroom* (New York: Holt, Rinehart & Winston, 1968). W. V. Beez, "Influence of Bias, Psychological Reports on Teacher Behavior and Pupil Performance," in *Proceedings, Seventy-sixth Annual Convention of the American Psychological Association* (Washington, D.C.: The Association, 1973), vol. 28, p. 892.

45. James L. Bess, "Integrating Faculty and Student Life Cycles," *Review of Educational Research* 43 (1973): 383.

46. L. R. Aiken, "Ability and Creativity in Mathematics," *Review of Educational Research* 43: 416–17.

47. V. A. Krutetski, "Mathematical Aptitudes," in *Soviet Studies in the Psychology of Learning and Teaching Mathematics,* ed. N. J. Kilpatrick and I. Wirszup, vol. 2, *The Structure of Mathematical Abilities* (Stanford: Stanford University, School of Mathematics Study Group, 1969), 113–28.

48. Charnofsky; Freire; and Zahn. (See note 22.)

49. M. J. Gold, *Education of the Intellectually Gifted* (Columbus, Ohio: Charles E. Merrill, 1965).

50. George B. Leonard, *Education and Ecstasy* (New York: Delacorte, 1968).

Chapter 8. Multicultural Objectives: A Critical Approach

1. Conrad Richter, *The Trees, The Fields, The Town* (New York: Knopf, 1940, 1946, 1950); all subsequently issued in paperback editions by Bantam. William Dean Howells, *The Rise of Silas Lapham* (Boston: Ticknor, 1885); available in several paperback editions.

2. David Madden's edition of original essays entitled *American Dreams, American Nightmares* (Carbondale: Southern Illinois University Press, 1970; paperback, 1972) offers a fascinating pastiche of critical views on this theme.

3. An early influential study by Margaret E. Fries and Paul J. Wolf, "Some Hypotheses on the Role of the Congenital Activity Type in Personality Development," *Psychoanalytic Study of the Child* 8 (1958): 48–62, has been further elaborated by other researchers. The understanding of these earliest interactions is a major interest in current infant studies.

4. R. D. Laing, *The Politics of the Family and Other Essays* (New York: Pantheon, 1969; Random House, Vintage, 1972), pp. 53–57.

5. The distinction of educational settings, processes, and aims or products is part of the conceptual framework presented in my chapter, "Alternatives in Education: A Framework for Inquiry," in *Alternative Education in a Pluralistic*

Society, ed. Charles D. Moody et al. (Ann Arbor: Program for Educational Opportunity, School of Education, University of Michigan, 1973), pp. 1–12.

6. John Dewey, *Democracy and Education* (New York: Macmillan, 1916; Free Press, paperback, 1966), pp. 20–22. In certain respects the entire volume constitutes a development of these themes.

7. Ibid., p. 22.

8. Edward Burnett Tylor, *Primitive Culture* (London: J. Murray, 1871), quoted in John Greenway, *The Inevitable Americans* (New York: Knopf, 1964), p. 16; also see pp. 341–42.

9. D. W. Winnicott, "The Location of Cultural Experience," *International Journal of Psychoanalysis* 48 (1966): 368–72.

10. Erik H. Erikson, *Childhood and Society* (1950), 2d ed. (New York: Norton, 1963). His parallel schedule of "psychological virtues" is contained in a collection of his essays, *Insight and Responsibility* (New York: Norton, 1964). Identity formation is further discussed in his *Identity: Youth and Crisis* (New York: Norton, 1968). All three works are also published in paperback editions.

11. D. W. Winnicott, "The Capacity to Be Alone," *International Journal of Psychoanalysis* 39 (1958): 416–20. This and other related studies are included in his book *The Maturational Processes and the Facilitating Environment: Studies in the Theory of Emotional Development* (New York: International Universities Press, 1965).

12. See note 8.

13. Other members were Gwendolyn Baker (chairperson), Robert Dixon, Jessie Dypka, Herbert Eibler, Lloyd Hughes, Edwin McClendon, Milan Marich, Warren Palmer, Findlay Penix, and students.

Chapter 9. Modifying Curriculums to Meet Multicultural Needs

1. George A. Beauchamp, *Curriculum Theory* (Evanston, Ill.: Kagg Press, 1968), p. 112.

2. Rudy Rodriquez, *Understanding the Mexican-American and His Role in American Culture: A Bibliography* (Flint: Flint, Michigan, Community Schools, 1969), p. 11.

3. Jean Greenlaw, "A Study of the Influence of Minority Groups in the Selection and Development of Basal Reading Programs," in *Teaching the Language Arts to Culturally Different Children,* ed. William W. Joyce and James A. Banks (Boston: Addison-Wesley, 1971), p. 147.

Chapter 10. Perceptions of Learning for the Multicultural Classroom

1. Ivan P. Pavlov, *Conditioned Reflexes* (London: Oxford University Press, 1927).

2. Edward L. Thorndike, *Human Learning* (New York: Century, 1931).

3. B. F. Skinner, *Technology of Teaching*. (New York: Appleton-Century-Crofts, 1968).

4. Wolfgang Kohler, *Gestalt Psychology* (New York: Menton, 1947).

5. Kurt Lewin, "Field Theory and Learning," in *The Psychology of Learning*, Forty-first Yearbook of the National Society for a Study of Education, part 2, ed. Nelson B. Henry (Chicago: University of Chicago Press, 1942).

6. Harper Lee, *To Kill a Mockingbird* (Philadelphia: Lippincott, 1960).

7. Byron G. Massialas and Nancy F. Sprague. "Teaching Social Issues as Inquiry: A Clarification," *Social Education* 38, 1 (January 1974): 10–19.

8. Kenneth B. Clark, *Prejudice and Your Child* (Boston: Beacon, 1955). Mary Ellen Goodman, *Race Awareness in Young Children* (London: Collier Macmillan, 1952). Bruno Lasker, *Race Attitudes in Children* (New York: New American Library, 1970).

9. Jean D. Grambs and John C. Carr, *Black Image: Education Copes with Color* (Dubuque: William C. Brown, 1972), pp. 33–34.

Chapter 11. Language Arts in a Multicultural Society

1. *Mainliner* (United Airlines magazine), September 1974.

2. Ann Charters, *Nobody: The Story of Bert Williams* (New York: Macmillan, 1970), p. 69.

3. Frank Chin et al., eds., *Aiiieeee! An Anthology of Asian-American Writers* (Washington, D.C.: Howard University Press, 1974), p. *xv*.

4. W. E. B. Du Bois, "The Souls of Black Folk," in *Three Negro Classics*, ed. John H. Franklin (New York: Avon, 1965), p. 221.

5. Tom Wicker, introduction to National Advisory Commission on Civil Disorders, *Report of the National Advisory Commission on Civil Disorders* (New York: Bantam, 1968), p. *v*.

6. Charles E. Silberman, *Crisis in the Classroom* (New York: Random House, Vintage, 1970), pp. 176–77.

7. National Council of Teachers of English, Committee on the 4 C's Language Statement, *Students' Right to Their Own Language*, special issue of the *Journal of the Conference on College Composition and Communication* 25 (Fall 1974): 15.

8. Interested readers might look at the study showing the absence of relationship between dialect and students' motivation to achieve in Elizabeth G. French and Gerald S. Lesser, "Some Characteristics of the Achievement Motive in Women," *Journal of Abnormal and Social Psychology* 68, 2 (February 1964): 119–28.

9. See *New York Times*, June 14, 1970, p. 1, for a report of staff member at CUNY indicating that enrollment of students from "academically prestigious" high schools *rose* when open enrollment was introduced.

10. Peter L. Berger and Thomas Luckmann, *The Social Construction of Reality* (New York: Doubleday, 1966), p. 31.

11. Alfred North Whitehead, *The Aims of Education* (New York: New American Library, 1961), p. 37.

12. J. S. Bruner, *Toward a Theory of Instruction* (New York: Norton, 1966).

13. Octavio I. Romano-V, "The Anthropology and Sociology of the Mexican-American: The Distortion of Mexican-American History," *El Grito* 2, 1 (1968): 13–26.

14. Benjamin Quarles and Leslie H. Fishel, Jr., eds. *The Negro American: A Documentary History* (New York: Morrow, 1968).

15. Gerald Haslam, *Forgotten Pages of American Literature* (Boston: Houghton Mifflin, 1970), p. 84.

16. Thomas F. Pettigrew, "Social Psychology and Desegregation Research," *American Psychologist* 16 (1961): 105–12.

17. Carey McWilliams, *The Mexicans in America,* Localized History Series (New York: Teachers College Press, Columbia University, 1968).

18. Edward Simmen, ed., *The Chicano* (New York: New American Library, 1971).

19. Hans P. Guth, *English for a New Generation* (New York: McGraw-Hill, 1973).

20. Edwin Brock, "Five Ways to Kill a Man," in *Invisibility Is the Art of Survival* (New York: New Directions, 1972).

Chapter 12. Teaching U.S. History for a Multicultural Society

1. William Appleman Williams, *The Contours of American History* (Chicago: Quadrangle, 1966), p. 23. All books cited in this chapter are available in paperback editions.

2. Ethnic studies for social studies classes were the theme of James A. Banks, ed., *Teaching Ethnic Studies: Concepts and Strategies,* Forty-third Yearbook of the National Council for the Social Studies (Washington, D.C., 1973). Most essays in this collection discuss the ethnic groups of U.S. society as separate problems and imply separate consideration in the classroom. Despite my difference with that approach, I recommend the essays to teachers in search of themes and materials. For more information, see Kathleen Wright, *The Other Americans: Minorities in American History* (Greenwich, Conn.: Fawcett World, Premier, 1971), a book prepared especially for teachers.

3. Mildred Dickeman, "Teaching Cultural Pluralism," in Banks, *Teaching Ethnic Studies,* p. 19. Carlos E. Cortes, "Teaching the Chicano Experience," in Banks, p. 186.

4. Larry Cuban, "Ethnic Content and 'White' Instruction," in Banks, *Teaching Ethnic Studies,* pp. 108–9.

5. This paragraph is based on an analogy between the uses of history and John Dewey's description of reflective thinking. See John Dewey, *How We Think: A Restatement of the Relation of Reflective Thinking to the Educative Process* (Chicago: Regnery, 1971), chap. 7.

6. C. Wright Mills, *The Sociological Imagination* (London and New York: Oxford University Press, 1959), p. 3.

7. Two articles could introduce teachers to the possibilities of organizing a course around such themes: Herbert G. Gutman, "Work, Culture and Society in Industrializing America, 1815–1919," *American Historical Review* 78 (June 1973): 531–88; Harold M. Baron, "The Demand for Black Labor," *Radical America* 5 (March-April 1971).

8. Peter Carpenter, *History Teaching: The Era Approach* (Cambridge: At the University Press, 1964).

9. For examples of sources, see Frances Ann Kemble, *Journal of a Residence on a Georgian Plantation, 1838–1839,* ed. J. A. Scott (New York: Knopf, 1961); Nancy E. Cott, ed., *Root of Bitterness: Documents of the Social History of American Women* (New York: Dutton, 1972); B. A. Botkin, ed., *Lay My Burden Down: A Folk History of Slavery* (Chicago: University of Chicago Press, 1968).

10. Cortes, "Teaching the Chicano Experience," in Banks, *Teaching Ethnic Studies,* p. 185. One of the "invalid frames of reference" cited in this article is "the idea that U.S. history is an essentially unidirectional east-to-west phenomenon."

11. Caroline Ware, "Cultural Groups in the U.S.," in *The Cultural Approach to History,* ed. Caroline Ware (New York: Columbia University Press, 1940), pp. 62–73.

12. Norman Ware, *The Industrial Worker, 1840–1860: The Reaction of American Industrial Society to the Advance of the Industrial Revolution* (Chicago: Quadrangle, 1964), pp. 38–48. This book provides an excellent, industrial overview of the prewar period.

13. C. Ware, ed., *Cultural Approach to History,* p. 87.

14. Ibid., p. 73. See also Gutman, "Work, Culture, and Society."

15. Cuban, "Ethnic Content and 'White' Instruction," in Banks, *Teaching Ethnic Studies,* pp. 103–3.

16. Frank Keetz, "A Case for Time Perspective," *Social Education* 28 (March 1972): 238–41.

17. Wright, *Other Americans;* Lowell K. Y. Chun-hoon, "Teaching the Asian-American Experience," in Banks, *Teaching Ethnic Studies,* pp. 119–39.

18. The best guidance for teachers in the use of primary sources for secondary school teaching is in John Anthony Scott, *Teaching for a Change* (New York: Bantam, 1972). This book includes many examples of readily available source books for students. Two excellent source collections, aimed directly at the problems of multicultural history are Paul Jacobs and Saul Landau with Eve Pell, *To Serve the Devil: A Documentary Analysis of America's Racial History and Why It Has Been Kept Hidden,* 2 vols. (New York: Random House, Vintage, 1971), and Gerda Lerner, ed., *Black Women in White America: A Documentary History* (New York: Random House, Vintage, 1973).

19. "Song of an Italian Workman," *Rochester* (New York) *Post-Express,* n.d., as quoted in Gutman, "Work, Culture, and Society," p. 554.

INDEX